Through the Eyes of Mary

The Mary Morehouse Diaries 1920-1958

D1568270

Compiled and annotated
by
Sharon Bird

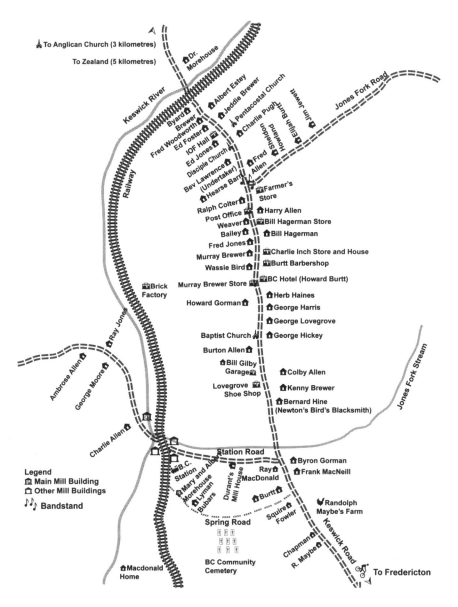

Map of Burtt's Corner circa 1930

Through the Eyes of Mary
The Mary Morehouse Diaries 1920-1958

Compiled and annotated
by
Sharon Bird

Chocolate River Publishing

www.chocolateriver.ca
www.chocolateriverpublishing.com

Library and Archives Canada Cataloguing in Publication

Morehouse, Mary, 1875-1958, author
     Through the eyes of Mary : the Mary Morehouse diaries, 1920-1958
/ compiled and annotated by Sharon Bird.

Includes bibliographical references.
ISBN 978-0-9877470-6-8 (paperback)

     1. Morehouse, Mary, 1875-1958--Diaries. 2. New Brunswick--
Biography. I. Bird, Sharon, 1959-, editor II. Title.

FC2474.1.M67A3 2016   971.5'103092   C2016-905071-8

Chocolate River Publishing
PO Box 7092
Riverview, NB
E1B 4T8

chocolateriverpublishing@gmail.com
www.chocolateriverpublishing.com
www.chocolateriver.ca

Printed and bound in Canada

MIX
Paper from
responsible sources
FSC® C004071

For all of those following and reading my work,
a sincere Thank You.

Special thanks to the Morehouse Family for the use of Mary's Journals,
especially grandson Hugh Hatfield "Buddy" Crouse
(1924-2016)
who trusted me with her journals and numerous photos.

Thanks to my amazing family including Peggy and Dave
for your continued love and support.

D URING MY RESEARCH for two previous books, I was given information, photos, and numerous artifacts. One of the items was the personal journal of Mary Morehouse — a series of notebooks which contained daily entries for the 38 years from 1920 to 1958.

Mary's journals contained entries about the daily weather, regular family tasks at home and at work, community deaths, and miscellaneous other information. These details are interesting to read, but they also serve a more important purpose because they provide readers with an understanding of the way people lived in the early 1900s.

People worked day to day, when and where they could find work. They required little money because they bartered with neighbours and friends for food, labour, and other necessities. There was no such thing as permanent employment, although some who worked for the railway had fairly steady work.

Community residents socialized on a daily basis and always lent a hand when it was needed. The church played a huge role for many families during this time period, and Mary's family was no different. They attended services and events whenever possible, some Sundays attending more than one service at churches of different denominations.

Women obtained the right to vote in a Dominion election on May 24, 1918. By April 17, 1919, they were able to vote in New Brunswick elections. Mary seems to have taken these rights seriously because there are many mentions of political meetings and going to the hall to vote.

Throughout her diary, *Mayme*, as she was known locally, takes readers on a journey of daily life from the 1920s through the Depression and World War II, describing social activities, disease outbreaks, epidemics, events, and new inventions along the way. Of course births and deaths were an important part of the small community, so she makes a note of them as well.

It was impossible to include every journal entry, so this book is a condensed version of Mary's life. Omitted entries included repetitive routines such as Sunday church or going to Women's Aid and various events she attended on a regular basis. Other dates may only have included the weather and daily chores which were captured somewhere else in her diary.

The one thing that stood out about Mary's journals is that they didn't contain any gossip, and I grew to admire and respect her for that omission. There were a few entries intentionally omitted due to privacy reasons, but even those entries were full of compassion and empathy for the families identified.

Places in the diary where Mary's handwriting was not legible are marked with a *[?]*. I have also used the same *[square brackets]* for my comments on Mary's entries. These comments either explain the entry further or point out the significance of a particular entry.

Most of Mary's family perished in the diptheria epidemic. Only Mary, her brother, and her mother survived. Mary is the girl on the far left. Rueben is the boy on the far right. Her mother is holding her baby sister.

MARY'S FAMILY

MARY ELEANOR LECKEY was born to parents Hugh and Debbie *[Hatfield]* Leckey from Chipman, NB. In 1884, her family moved to Devon, a small community on the north side of the Saint John River, which has now been amalgamated into Fredericton.

They arrived just as a diphtheria epidemic was raging. One of the people that helped them during the epidemic was Oscar Morehouse from Upper Keswick who was working on a log boom in the Saint John River near Devon. At the same time, he was studying to become a doctor, so he helped with the diphtheria patients in the area. Oscar liked one of the Leckey girls but when he went to check on the family one afternoon, he learned that she had died from the disease.

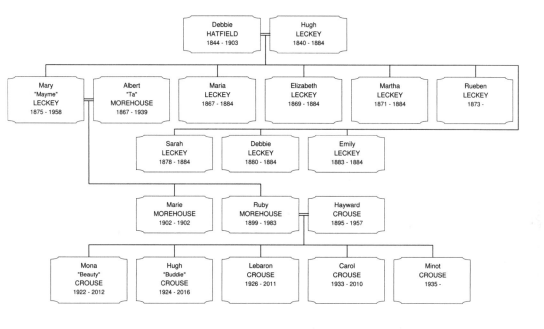

By the time the epidemic was over, most of Mary's ten-member family had perished, and only Mary, her mother, and her brother, Rueben survived.

Oscar's father, Elisha suggested that Oscar bring the remaining family members to their Upper Keswick home. He thought they could give the remaining family a home in exchange for chores and housework. Such arrangements were common at the time.

So Mary, her mother, and Reuben moved in with Elisha Morehouse. Debbie and Elisha later married and built a three storey home for their blended family in Stone Ridge. They had a daughter Grace.

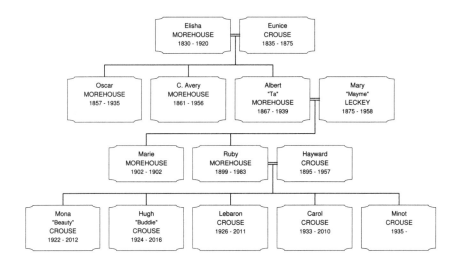

Eventually Mary's brother, Reuben left the family home to find work in Maine. Mary married her stepbrother Albert on April 7, 1897 and the couple moved to their new home in Burtt's Corner next door to the railway station. Mary and Albert had a daughter Ruby plus a child that died at nine months and possibly a third stillborn child. The couple also raised Grace's son Merle as their own.

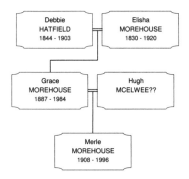

Neighbours

Ethel & Willie Brewer ✦ on the McLean Settlement Road.

Gordon & Gladys McLean ✦ on the McLean Settlement Road

Evie [Evelyn] & Gordon McLean ✦ on the McLean Settlement Road.

Stella & Randolph Maybe ✦ on main road heading towards Fredericton. Their house was on the right side below the cemetery, with their barn and farm on the opposite side of the road.

Mabel & Basil Fowler ✦ Mabel was a trained nurse. Their home sat in front of the community cemetery. Tom Fowler, Basil's father, lived on the first property settled in the area, that of William Boone.

Edith & Harry Bird; daughter Kate ✦ second house before the stone bridge on the right going into the main community.

Lucy & Byron Gorman; daughter Pearl ✦ last house on the right side of the road just before crossing the stone bridge.

Durant (French) family ✦ lived in the mill house between the Morehouse home on the Station Road and the stone bridge.

Gertrude & Lyman Bubar's family ✦ lived on the hill behind the Morehouse property. Their children were Bill, Luke, Ruby, Roy, Ralph, Thomas, Lester, Lyman Jr. and Beth.

Nellie & Robert MacDonald; sons John, Ray ✦ The MacDonald's lived in the former Clayton house between the railway and the Keswick River, east of the station.

Edna & John (Robert's Son) ✦ moved into the Robert MacDonald home to aid with aging parents.

Ethel & Ray MacDonald ✦ lived in the first house on the left on the Station Road by the stone bridge.

Sarah & Newton Bird♦ on west end of stone bridge

Other families in the main community mentioned in the book include:

Edna & George Lovegrove with children Elwin, Fred, Anna and Theora

Kate & William Hagerman, Ruth & Edison Brewer, Inch, Jones, and Burtt along with numerous other families along the road through the main village.

Across the covered bridge from the railway station towards Keswick Ridge, there were Allen, Crouse, Brewer, Staples, Tripp, and Currie families.

All of these families walked miles back and forth to visit each other before cars became popular.

Chapter 1

1920-1924

MARY PORTRAYS LIFE as it was in Burtt's Corner and many rural New Brunswick and Canadian communities during the 1920s. People worked locally for each other or bartered for items they needed. Residents visited friends and neighbours daily, stopping for tea or a meal. Food was plentiful because it was raised or grown at home. These people created their own entertainment through games, musical performances, and dances at private homes. They attended barn raisings, quilting parties, band concerts, and church-related socials. There were many community groups such as the Women's Aid, a young girls' Women's Aid and the Independent Order of Foresters Lodge (Court Bright). The Temperance Movement for the prohibition or ban of alchol had also started.

Most necessities were available at the local stores. People purchased or traded farm products with local merchants to get hardware items, tools, dishes, food, or cloth to make clothing.

Local services included blacksmiths, doctors, undertakers, shoe makers, clock builders, teachers, and wagon-repair people. With necessities close to home, the need to travel outside the settlement was minimal. Transportation was slow with the only means of travel being by foot, horse-power, or train. In the 1920s, cars were affordable for families such as doctors or merchants, but not for the average family until much later. The cars were heavy and did not navigate well in snow, so they were stored for the winter and replaced with the horse and sled. Doctors made house calls to attend sick residents, and everyone helped one another in time of need. Ladies tended to sick neighbours and assisted the local doctor with home care, baby deliveries, and preparing the deceased for burial. Likewise, men helped residents who suffered from illness or injury by helping to plant and harvest their crops or acting as a replacement in their business.

Communication from outside the community came through letter mail and arrived daily on the train. It was then sorted and distributed at the railway station. In later years, the large mail bags were taken to a local store or home where a designated postmaster/mistress sorted and prepared mail for distribution by horse and wagon.

There was plenty of food preparation throughout the year to provide meals for winter. Without modern appliances, most food was canned so it wouldn't spoil.

The school Merle attended was a one-room building like many schools at the time. The teacher taught from grade 1 to grade 8 and all levels in between. The schoolhouse had a blackboard, a piano, and long wooden tables set up in rows with spaces for the children to write. Students learnt to strengthen their memory. They wrote their work on a slate with a slate pencil, and, because their slates were small, they had to remember their work as they erased and started their next task. When the older students finished their work, they helped the younger children. Keener children hurried to finish their work so they could listen to the work for the next grade level. There were no school buses so children walked several miles to school. If the majority of children never arrived due to the long walk in the extreme cold, the teacher cancelled school. School was also closed if the teacher was too sick to teach.

In a railway community like Mary's, everyone made use of the railway bed. It had to be plowed for the trains to travel, so students used it to walk to school if they attended the Pugh's Crossing School east of the community. Everyone used the railway tracks to travel back and forth to visit friends and relatives when the main roadway was too full of snow, but they kept an eye out for the trains scheduled to pass through the area.

There are also discussions of elections. Women obtained the right to vote in Dominion elections on May 24, 1918. By April 17, 1919, they were able to vote in New Brunswick elections. Both Mary and her daughter Mona seem to have taken these rights seriously because there are many mentions of going to the hall to vote, and Mona often functioned as a poll clerk.

1920

Thursday, January 1 ᕆ Mr. Elisha Morehouse, *[Mary's stepfather and Albert's father]* died today about noon. Grace is coming home tonight. Rilla Crouse and Miss Hull were here to dinner and supper. Ruby and Merle went to Zealand to meet Grace on the train. Weather — snow.

Friday, January 2 ᕆ Mr. Morehouse was buried today. Howard Burtt drove us up *[to the funeral on the sleigh]*. Weather cold, clear and windy. Mr. Spencer had charge of the funeral; assisted by Mr. *[Beverly]* Lawrence *[undertaker]*. Beautiful, moonlight evening. Maud's baby *[Rupert]* is five weeks old tonight.

Saturday, January 3 ᕆ Weather very cold; the coldest morning this winter. Grace has gone home this morning. Professor Cadwallader *[?]* was here to tea and tuned the piano. Hayward Crouse was here this evening.

Sunday, January 4 ᕆ Weather still awfully cold. No one has been to church from our family. Ruby has spent evening at Wardlow Bird's. I walked nearly to corner *[Burtt's Corner]* with Merle when he went for milk. *[They got milk from several farmers.]* Beautiful, moonlight night.

Wednesday, January 7 ∽ Weather much warmer; more like spring. I spent the day at D. Jewett's going by train to Zealand and attended W.A. *[Women's Aid]* at Mrs. Henry Burtt's in the afternoon. Seven members attended. Albert has gone to Farmer's Union Meeting at Mouth of Keswick. Ruby's coat cloth came from Eaton's today. *[Mail order parcels came by train.]*

Friday, January 9 ∽ Weather colder again. Fannie Barton just took music lesson *[on the piano from Ruby]*. No more word from Grace. Merle is playing Jack Straws. Ruby is embroidering a towel. Merle started to go to scout meeting but couldn't find any boys to go with. Patched my blankets today, a job I've been dreading.

Sunday, January 11 ∽ Merle and Ruby have gone to Sunday school and church. Weather is warm and snowing. Ruby has gone to church this evening again. Mr. Spencer gave her five dollars this morning; a gift from the W.A. for faithful services as organist.

Monday, January 12 ∽ We washed. It's snowing some. I have been up to Mr. Lovegrove's. He has been sick for two weeks. Mr. Spencer was there this morning to administer the sacrament. Mr. and Mrs. Spencer called here about dinner time. Ella Christie came after dinner to make Ruby's coat. Wind blowing this evening, drifting some. Merle spent evening at Howard Burtt's playing games.

Wednesday, January 14 ∽ Cold and clear. Ella finished Ruby's coat tonight. Albert, Ruby and Merle have gone to a social. Randolph *[Maybe]* came for Ella. I drove up to the social with them *[in the sleigh]*. We had quite a gathering; made about nine dollars *[for Woman's Aid]*. The night is very cold and windy. So glad to get home.

Friday, January 16 ∽ Weather warmer. Not much snow fell; about half an inch. Our Eaton order has arrived. Willie Crouse had dinner here today. Nas *[?]* Palmer was here for a kettle to steep tea in. Today is Marie's birthday. She would have been eighteen years old. *[Marie was Mary's daughter who only lived six months.]*

Monday, January 19 ⌒ Awfully cold, wind blowing and snow drifting. Didn't wash. I made Ruby an apron dress and most *[almost]* made another. Flour has taken another advance. It is now 17 dollars *[a barrel]* but two dollars cheaper in Farmers Union. We bought a bag of sugar tonight paying fourteen dollars *[50 lbs]*. Some price for sugar; expect it will advance again. Merle is studying and fretting. *[One of the local stores was called the Farmer's Store so they may have been getting a store discount or their membership in the United Farmer's Union, a political party that was growing across Canada at the time, may have entitled them to a discount.]*

Tuesday, January 20 ⌒ Very cold. Burton Allen froze his hands driving from his home out to the station *[on sleigh]*. We washed today. The lumber is about all loaded. *[The railway siding and mill were next to the Morehouse home on the south side.]* Willie Gilby was hurt very badly today — kicked by a horse. Ruby had a card letter from Reuben. The Gleaner *[newspaper]* states today that flu is raging in Chicago. Hope it won't sweep the country again. *[She was referring to the Spanish flu epidemic that occurred after the soldiers returned from WWI in Europe.]* We have heard that one of Theora's children was run over by a team *[of horses]*. I supposed it is Arnold.

Wednesday, January 21 ⌒ Snowing and blowing but warmer. Yesterday was a day of accidents. The Doctor's gas machine blowed up and burned him very badly. *[This would be a type of laughing gas that was used for operations and dental procedures because the local doctor performed both types of service at his home office.]* One of Theora's children got his leg broken. We haven't heard which one. I have done quite a lot of sewing today. Had a letter from Reuben.

Thursday, January 22 〜 Weather, very cold this morning but a beautiful afternoon. Albert was up to Doctor's. Things certainly were tossed about by the gas machine exploding. It was only a flying story *[gossip]* about one of Theora's children being hurt. Willie Gilby is hurt very badly alright. Rilla Crouse was here for a music lesson and brought some cucumber pickles, which is a treat. Pearl Tomilson was here for a lesson also.

Sunday, January 25 〜 Mr. Spencer was at the station to meet the Bishop. It's been a very cold day. We had two lovely services in the evening. The Bishop spoke on the *Forward Movement. [This was a group from the Episcopal Church whose mission it was to energize the life of the church.]* I drove home with Ruby and Hayward. Merle came home before the service. Albert was up in the morning.

Wednesday, January 28 〜 Fine and cold. Albert is staying with Willie Gilby again today *[because he had been kicked by the horse and hadn't recovered. Albert may have helped in Willy's Blacksmith shop.]* I was down to Mrs. Squire Fowlers this afternoon. Took the cost of Forward Movement literature down. Ruby has gone to a Forward Movement Meeting at the church.

Thursday, January 29 〜 Very cold and windy. No one from our house attended the Methodist church it being so cold. It's some warmer since sun has gone down. Rilla was here for a lesson; also Pearl Tomilson. Our Eaton order arrived today and everything satisfactory. Ruby is pleased with the puff she sent for, and the towels. Have cut out a work dress for myself, did some sewing on it, and have made nearly a quarter yard of lace, plus knit a mitten wrist.

Friday, January 30 〜 Snowed last night and blowed all day. Is blowing and drifting just fierce tonight. Very cold. I have nearly finished my dress. Must put more wood in stove and go to bed. Albert has worked today shovelling the switch *[for the railway next door]* and tallying *[lumber]* for loading car. They began hauling lumber from the new mill at Cardigan yesterday.

Saturday, January 31 ∾ The very coldest yet. All night was terrible and wind blew all night. I was so cold I couldn`t sleep. *[At the time, there was no electricity for heating or furnaces, so their only source of heat was a wood stove.]* It`s warmer tonight. Train was two hours late this morning. Hayward Crouse was here to dinner. He was walking to look over their section *[railway]*. He waited here to warm while the noon train went down. Started to use a new bag of flour today. Want to time it to see how long it will last. Albert has gone to *[Foresters]* Lodge. *[This was a Meeting House just west of the edge of the village. The Foresters was originally an organization that helped those in need; later it became a financial investment organization]*

Tuesday, February 3 ∾ Warmer. Lovely sunshine; quite windy. Have finished my house dress; cut out another. Mr. and Mrs. Spencer have left their horse here and took train to Fredericton. I am going to quilting bee this afternoon. Have been to Edna`s quilting and had such a nice pleasant time. We quilted one quilt and bound it, put another on frames and quilted one side. Five quilters were there. This is a lovely moonlight night; and not very cold.

Friday, February 6 ∾ An awful storm on. Snowed and blew all night and all day. Awful drifts. Albert has worked shovelling for CPR today. This is Merle's Birthday. He is 12. He got two books, a dollar and seven chocolate bars. I have finished Merle's mittens.

Saturday, February 7 ∾ Stormed all night with rain and sleet. The roads are drifted and a hard crust frozen. The road plow has been on the road. *[A large team of six to eight horses hauled the road plow.]* It snowed all day. Albert has been on the railway shovelling all day. Awfully hard work. Hayward Crouse has been in twice. Merle has done some shovelling and got very tired and cross. *[At 12 years, he also shovelled for the railway to earn money and help his family.]* It's blowing tonight again. Merle is just taking his bath. *[Saturday was bath night for most* *people, so they were clean for church on Sunday.]*

Monday, February 9 ◠ Warmer and snowing some. We washed. I collected some for Forward Movement. Called at three houses. Ruby has been up to the Doctor's *[her uncle]* this evening. I started but was afraid of meeting the train as the track is banked with snow. *[And she wouldn't have been able to step off the track to let the train pass. They travelled the railway tracks on foot because it was a shorter route than going around on the roadway through the village.]*

Thursday, February 12 ◠ Sat up all night with Janie *[Jennie]*. *[She]* has slept all day yesterday and all night. A heavy sleep. Can't seem to hear, see or understand anything. Revived around 4 o'clock this morning. Knew us all but can't talk. Her tongue is thick, you can't understand her. Avery has given up all hope. I'm afraid Avery is taking the same disease. His tongue is coated and he is feeling poorly. I came down on the train this morning. The day has been very pleasant. I am going to bed as I am sleepy.

Friday, February 12 ◠ A raw wind blowing today. Snow and blowing tonight. A carload of flour for the Farmer's Union has arrived today so it's been a busy day. *[Men were unloading the rail car.]* All sorts of men have been hauling. Have sold $1600 worth today. We got two barrels of it. Willy Brewer brought us a barrel of potatoes today.

Saturday, February 13 ◠ Both Albert and I were sick. Sent Merle up to doctor's for powders.

Tuesday, February 16 ◠ We all put in a very bad night. The night was so terribly cold. Merle and I suffered a lot. Merle is worse. We sent for Doctor. *[The local doctor made house calls and provided patients with required medication. There was no pharmacy in rural areas.]* Hayward is carrying some wood for us. Hope Ruby doesn't take this disease. We would certainly be in a bad fix.

Monday, February 23 ◠ A beautiful warm day. Mrs. Bubar called and kindly brought some lovely cream, fresh eggs, and apples. *[The apples would have been stored from last fall.]* Ruby has been to give Oscar a lesson. There is a storm on tonight.

Tuesday, February 24 ◠ Snow all day. Ruby washed this afternoon. Albert and I made mincemeat *[She would have used the apples from the day before and some canned meat from fall.]* Had a letter from Reuben and one from Annie Staples.

Wednesday, February 25 ◠ Snowed all day. Have made hop yeast and minced pies. Ironed. *[The iron would have been a "sad iron" made with a thick slab of delta-shaped cast iron with a wooden handle. It was heated on top of the wood stove. When it was hot, it was used like a regular iron to remove wrinkles. They also had miniature ones to iron dainty clothing or fine linens.]*

Thursday, February 26 ◠ Wind blowing; snow drifting. Worse storm of season. Reuben's birthday. He's 47 years old. A big storm on and everything is blockaded. No trains today at all. I started my quilts today. We started using our 40lb jar of butter today, our last jar.

Friday, February 27 ◠ Very cold. The train hasn't arrived yet. The engine and plow just passed now, twenty five after ten in the evening. We have had no mail since Wednesday. *[Mail came daily by train.]*

Saturday, February 28 ◠ Trains got thru today. Willy Brewer has been here waiting for train to meet Mr. Gorman coming from woods; he's sick. Train never arrived until after 11 o'clock tonight.

Saturday, March 6 ◠ Began to storm about noon, a big snow storm tonight. Has been soft *[mild]* 2 days. Flu is at Zealand Sta. *[station]*. Herb Staple's daughter died last night.

Tuesday, March 9 ◠ A beautiful morning. No trains yet half after ten in the morning. I have been to the corner this afternoon. Got something *[material]* to set the quilts together. Also 2 remnants *[left over pieces of material]*. Ruby has been to the Doctor's. Theora is there today.

Monday, March 15 ∽ Still snowing and drifting. Train is tied up again. Morning train didn't get here until about three this afternoon, the other train is off track on the Pinder line, and plow is off track somewhere between here and Woodstock. The cookhouse *[for the mill]* opened today. *[It would have been shut down over the winter while the men cut in the woods.]* We washed today, baked bread and did a number of other things.

Saturday, March 20 ∽ Janie *[Jennie]* died this morning about half after four. I have been up there all day. The funeral is tomorrow at 1 o'clock. There is a bad snow storm tonight again. I don't expect we will be able to get to funeral. Began using a new barrel of flour this morning.

Friday, March 26 ∽ Another warm day; raining tonight. Albert has been up creek scaling *[logs]* today. Had a hard snowshoe *[to get to work]*. We finished our fourth quilt today [for Women's Aid]. Merle has been to scout meeting and got 2 badges today.

Monday, March 29 ∽ Ruby washed, I cleaned my bedroom, cleaned the ceiling, had mattress out on the snow and glad I did. *[Her mattress was likely a feather tick and she would have put it outside to air out.]*

Tuesday, March 30 ∽ A lovely clear morning, rained almost all night. Very high water. Merle has some trees tapped; expect big crop of honey. Mr. Spencer has service 3 times this week. Monday, Wednesday, and Good Friday.

Monday, April 5 ∽ A cold raw wind. Annie Staples and I called on Lovegrove's and gave them some of the Easter flowers from church. Ruby and Annie called on Mrs. Wesley Jones this afternoon and gave her some flowers. We attended the band concert in the hall this evening. It was good; both the play and music. A terrible rain storm to come home in. *[She would have walked.]* Annie went home on evening train. Rilla Crouse and Edith Burtt stayed all night.

Wednesday, April 7 ∽ A nice day. We all have nasty colds. Water so high, mill can't start. *[The mill sat at the junction of two streams.]* Am going to bed very early. I am feeling so mean with cold. We were married 23 years today.

Thursday, April 8 ∾ A beautiful day. Rilla Crouse was here for a piano lesson. She tried to learn me to tat *[teach her to make lace]*. Don't know if I can ever learn or not. Had a letter from Grace.

Tuesday, April 13 ∾ A cold raw day, snowing and raining. We expected a few in to spend evening to have some music but it was raining hard. *[They would have all been walking.]* Ruby took tea at Wesley Jones, Reuben and Merle was over to McKeen's sugar camp yesterday. Got both honey and candy. Having some treats while Reuben is home. I am making my voile dress. Hayward, Rilla and Rankine came after all; Rankine with his fiddle. We had some great music with the fiddle and piano. It rained so hard, Rilla stayed all night.

Wednesday, April 14 ∾ Still raining, very high water. The mill is down. Mud and water everywhere. Mrs. W. Kelly from Keswick was in waiting for the noon train. I have been to Mr. Estey's today. Reuben's talking about going back to Houlton.

Thursday, April 15 ∾ Cold, sunshine at times. Rena, and her baby, Edna and the boys have been here. Also Rilla C. for a lesson. Albert shingled the end of the shed today. Reuben has gone to Houlton again. He's going to stream drive somewhere in Maine.

Monday, April 19 ∾ Merle has been on his wheel *[bicycle]* for the first time this year. Mr. and Mrs. Spencer have gone to Fredericton *[by train]*. They left their horse here. Had a letter from Reuben, he's going to stream drive for Bryson.

Tuesday, April 20 ∾ Most beautiful day like summer. Ruby and I drove *[horse and wagon]* down to Mr. Estey's for potatoes. Then Ruby cleaned the door yard this afternoon. Albert has fixed the wood shed and window screens, and many other things which makes such improvements

— among them a page wire fence around the yard. *[Page wire came in rolls and looked like pages of a book or squares. This type of fencing was about four feet high and was used before electric fencing allowed a single strand of wire to contain farm animals.]* I have cleaned the clothes press this afternoon.

Thursday, April 22 ∽ Ruby and I drove out and called on the bride, Mrs. Horace Gorman. Called on Mrs. Willy Brewer and also Mrs. Byron Gorman. The mill has begun work again. They are paying $4 a day. Sugar is 25 cents per pound.

Friday, April 23 ∽ Lovely morning; colder by noon. A cold rain by 2 o'clock. Been cleaning out boxes and trunks, and scrubbed the shed. Had a letter from Reuben. He has hired on the Ashland drive.

Sunday, May 2 ∽ Very cold like winter. Snowing and awful wind. Merle and I have been to church. He went on his wheel and I went up with Maude. Rupert is a dear. Ruby and Hayward took tea with Mr. and Mrs. Wardlow Bird.

Tuesday, May 4 ∽ A cold day again. We've done a hard day's work. Cleaning shed, ironing and moving stove. *[Each spring and fall, they moved the wood cook stove from the summer kitchen to the main kitchen. Using a summer kitchen kept the heat from the stove out of the main house so it was cooler for sleeping during hot summer weather.]*

Thursday, May 6 ∽ A warm day. Papered the clothes press off the dining room, cleaned the door yard, made vinegar, sent teeth to the dentist, can hardly do without them. Aching back tonight. Rilla C. was here for a lesson.

Monday, May 10 ∽ Nice morning, grew colder. Rain and wind this afternoon. Thunder and lightning tonight. A cold heavy rain has set in. Water is very high; over the road between the Doctor's and the school house. Ruby has been sick this afternoon. Merle has a sore nose. He and little Jack Wilcox have been tearing down his playhouse. We have done a big wash today.

Tuesday, May 11 ∿ A cold windy day. Have done the hall and sitting room ceiling with green wall tinting *[paint]* Took me so long. Heard of a terrible accident at Marysville; 3 men killed. A wash out the cause *[could be road or railway]*.

Wednesday, May 12 ∿ Cleaned the sitting room, cleaned the hall and finished the kitchen, Byard Brewer's little boy was run over by a loaded wagon.

Thursday, May 13 ∿ There's a napkin social at Dunk Brewer's for the W.A. Ruby and Merle have gone.

Thursday, May 14 ∿ Warm; cooler toward night. We have cleaned the dining room, varnished the chairs and dining room floor. This is Arbour day. Merle, Jack and Flavis have been getting trees. The Scouts have been setting out trees for Mr. Lawson. Have each taken cake for the evening. They had a nice time. We made over $16 at our *[napkin]* social. Ruby won a pair of bedroom slippers at the bean guess.

Monday, May 17 ∿ Mr. Harvey Jones is dead. He was brought here for burial on the evening train. *[People originally from the community were brought back on the train for their funeral and burial.]* Merle has had a headache all day.

Wednesday, May 19 ∿ A very warm day, hot. I have varnished mine and Merle's floor. *[Bedroom floors were often softwood boards and either varnished or painted.]* Ruby done the chairs. We have been to W.A. Mrs. Spencer has started a girl's club tonight.

Friday, May 21 ∿ Painted the steps this morning and varnished hall floor. They have sent for me to go to Wesley Jones. Mrs. Jones is sick again. Stayed all day. Mrs. Jones very low. The Doctor has been down three times. Don't think she'll live the night.

Saturday, May 22 ∿ I stayed up all night with Mrs. Jones. The Doctor has come. She passed away about seven this evening. Iona Wilson, G. Christie and I laid her out. *[Burtt's Corner had no funeral home, so services were held at home or the church. These women cleaned and prepared her for the funeral. The undertaker lived within the community. The funeral was usually the day following the death. Regardless of the time of year, men dug the graves for immediate burial.]*

Monday, May 24 ∽ I did no wash today because Mrs. Jones was laid to rest. *[It was a sign of respect for the deceased and their family not to have clothes out on the clothesline.]*

Wednesday, May 28 ∽ A lovely fine morning, rain needed badly. Forest fires in many places. There is a play in the hall tonight; "*Plum Valley*". The play was great.

Monday, May 31 ∽ A lovely fine day. We washed and oiled kitchen floor. *[Kitchens and main rooms had hardwood flooring.]* Finished my voile *[dress]* today. Merle has gone to a show in the hall. Some dark-ie *[Although not appropriate today, this was the term was used for a black person at this time]* had a show. Ruby has been up to give Oscar a lesson. Albert has been to Dell Pugh's to pay the taxes. *[Dell would have been a trustee who collected taxes for the county. Albert was the Collector of Rates and Taxes for the Parish of Bright. Men also performed road-work such as grading with their horse teams or plowing in winter to help pay their tax bill.]*

Tuesday, June 15 ∽ We went to Fredericton and ordered a new fence *[page wire]*; cost $19.85. Came up on the afternoon train.

Wednesday, June 16 ∽ A nice shower this morning. Canned 5 qts of rhubarb, and dyed my silk waist. Cut my finger and so forth put me back with my work. I am tired and lame from yesterday's trip.

Saturday, June 19 ∽ My wallpaper has arrived. We have been to the band concert. Edith Burtt, G. Morash and H. Crouse have been here. Opened a new barrel of flour. *[She opened the last one March*

20 — about two months per barrel.]

Monday, June 21 〜 A lovely morning; raining by noon. We washed and got covering ready for hall floor. *[Perhaps oil cloth flooring]* Albert has gone to a men's club meeting in Methodist church.

Tuesday, June 22 〜 Still cloudy and unsettled. I have the roofing all down on floor. Ruby and I picked about a quart of strawberries for tea. Ruby has been to the girls club at George Pugh's.

Thursday, June 24 〜 A lovely day. Mrs. Bubar and I have been put on the committee for temperance work. *[People involved in the Temperance Movement favoured a non-alcohol society. Some believed that alcohol was the root of evil while others just saw it as a menace to society. The Temperance Act of 1878 gave individual counties or municipalities the right to ban alcohol. During the war, restraint from alcohol was seen as a patriotic duty.]* Ruby is up to Choir practice.

Friday, June 25 〜 A lovely morning. I am having bad luck with my canned rhubarb. Had to boil it over. We had such a lovely shower tonight. Merle has stayed playing so late tonight he had to have a scolding, so I'll have to keep him from the water *[swimming in the creek]* for a while to punish him.

Thursday, July 8 〜 Very close and sultry all day. Thunder showers tonight. Ruby was up to give Kathleen Bird a lesson. Got soaking wet. Have finished Ruby's skirt and made myself a waist.

Saturday, July 10 〜 Lovely; real July morning. Ruby has gone up to be polling clerk at the election. Mr. Sylvester Jones was here to dinner and supper. Hattie and Winslow brought 4 lbs of butter. H. Crouse is here tonight. 22Y votes for prohibition and 76 for votes at this polling place *[The Dunkin Act of 1864 gave counties and municipalities permission to forbid the sale of alcohol. Building on that, the Canada Temperance Act was approved in 1878 to cover the whole Dominion. According to sources at the Provincial Archives of New Brunswick, NB enacted prohibition in*

1917 and repealed it in 1927.]

Monday, July 12 ∾ The bands men had their picnic. We have all been there. It's rained but a big crowd. Albert got bad fall last night coming home in the dark.

Tuesday, July 13 ∾ Very warm, dull morning. Showery. We all feel tired. Albert hurt his hand very badly in his fall. Pained all night and all day. They made about nine hundred dollars at the picnic. Big expenses to come out of that.

Thursday, July 15 ∾ Another dull day. Cooler than yesterday. Have finished my waist with the tatting. *[A waist was a corset that covered the waist area from the bottom of the ribs to just above the hips. It was also called a waist cincher.]* Ruby was up to Kathleen Birds. Hattie and Winslow brought a 20 lb jar of butter. Albert's hand is improving.

Monday, July 19 ∾ Terrible rainy day; has beat our corn all down. We washed and I finished Merle's pants. Made a roller towel, and cut out a nightdress and another pair of pants.

Sunday, August 8 ∾ Very, very hot; a lovely breeze this afternoon. We didn't go to church tonight of course. I wanted to go but Ruby seemed to think it was too hot. I know we should have gone. Hayward took us around the block in his new car. *[This may have been the first ride in a car for Mary, Albert, Hayward or Ruby.]*

Wednesday, August 11 ∾ Very warm, muggy. Very warm last night. *[News]*paper states Monday the hottest day since 1912. *[34 °C at UNB]* Miss Wilcox was here for tea. Ethel Bird and Ferne called.

Thursday, August 19 ∾ My birthday 45 today. It's been a beautiful day. Gave my hall floor the second coat of paint. Ruby gave me a pair of gloves, and Merle money for a gold cross and chain. Bless his heart it was so thoughtful of him.

Friday, August 20 ∾ A lovely day. Ruby, Merle and Jack were in swimming. Ruby and I have been to Randolph Maybe's for the milk. Merle and Jack are out riding with the pony and wheel. *[One with the pony, one with the bicycle.]*

Saturday, August 21 ∽ A lovely day. Mr. and Mrs. Spencer called. Also Ella Christie and Clara Ferris have done Merle's sore eye up in tea leaves and bound up two sore toes. *[A cold teabag was used to reduce eye swelling and irritation.]*

Monday, August 23 ∽ Cloudy all day but cleared toward night. It's a perfect evening. We have washed and made two loafs of cake and some tarts for our Sunday school picnic tomorrow. Flossie Lawrence was in tonight.

Tuesday, August 24 ∽ A perfect day for our picnic. Hayward came after us and brought us home. Merle and Jack went with the pony. We had a nice time.

Wednesday, August 25 ∽ A lovely day. Ella Christie and Clara Ferris were here to tea. We have all been up to Chivaree *[a noisy party for newlyweds to keep them from sleeping or anything else they might have planned. It would also wake them from their first night's sleep if they were lucky enough to get to sleep.]*

Thursday, August 26 ∽ A lovely day. My little gold cross came from Simpsons today *[Simpsons was a mail-order catalogue company like Eaton's.]* It's a sweet thing. We have all been up to an ice cream social at the corner. The band has just stopped playing. We came home in the Wilcox's car. It's a beautiful evening.

Sunday, August 29 ∽ A very hot day; foggy this morning. Cleared toward noon. We have been twice to church. We walked up this morning. Hayward came for us tonight. It's a lovely evening. Albert's eye is better tonight. He had a bad day with it.

Tuesday, August 31 ∽ Cloudy. Warm some times. Rain and thunder this evening; a heavy thunder storm this morning about four o'clock.

We are to have a social Thursday evening at Sam Crouse's. The band will play. We have finished some of the club things to sell at the social.

Saturday, September 4 ∿ A lovely day; fine for our social. Ethel Bird made the guess cake. I put up a basket of green gage plums today. Made pumpkin pies, a loaf of cake, baked bread and cooked a roast of lamb. We are all ready for the social. Our social was quite a success. Made $73.20.

Sunday, September 5 ∿ A lovely day. Have been twice to church. Stayed to Darius Jewett's all day. He had us for a little car ride. Hayward brought us home tonight.

Wednesday, September 8 ∿ Still raining very, very hard. I was going to F'ton to have the fence finished around our lot. Hope it's fine tomorrow. We bought half barrel of apples from Mr. Coy, Gilbert. Had a letter from Grace.

Monday, September 13 ∿ Raining hard; has rained all last night. Water all over the flats. Have done some colouring today, put tomatoes in brine and other jobs.

Tuesday, September 14 ∿ Still raining and very cold. Have done three 3 gals. of pickles and a peck and half of chow *[For an explanation of Imperial measurements — see glossary].* Did two qts. of beet, put away five dozen eggs, did some colouring *[dying clothing],* made bread, fixed cucumbers in brine for mustard pickles. Am tired. Had a letter from Reuben. The club met here tonight.

Wednesday, September15 ∿ Still cloudy. We washed. I did ten qts. of mustard pickles. Wardlow Bird, Ethel and Fern were here this evening.

Thursday, September 16 ∿ Cloudy morning; cleared at noon and lovely afternoon. Clouded up about 4 o'clock. Raining again tonight. Merle wheeled to the mouth of Keswick to the Farmer's Picnic. *[This would have been the Keswick Fair.]* He, Bill Bubar, Paul Tomilson and Luke Bubar. Albert, Ruby and I went down this evening in Wilcox's car. A big crowd there.

Saturday, September 18 ∽ Still raining; has rained all day at times. I have fixed my cask of vinegar for the winter. I'm glad that's done. I always dread it. Hayward brought us a lot of hazel nuts tonight. *[Hazel nuts are native to this part of the province.]*

Monday, September 20 ∽ Very cold. We washed. Maud came after me this afternoon to can corn. We canned sixteen qts. Just came home. A lovely cold moonlight night. Winslow Jones brought a 30 lb jar of butter tonight.

Friday, September 24 ∽ Another hot day like July. We bought a barrel of apples today. Have steamed pumpkin for pies and done several other things.

Saturday September 25 ∽ Another lovely day; like summer. I have made pumpkin pies, dressed chickens, made cake. Ruby has gone up to stay with Rilla. Her father and mother are away.

Wednesday, September 29 ∽ Raining hard all day. I have finished Merle's bedroom. *[She had finished wall papering it.]* It looks fine. Ruby and Hayward have gone to chivaree. Howard Bird and Annie Burtt were married today. We, Albert and I were up to see Hall Brewer. I don't think he will live through the night. Poor Maggie, I feel so badly for her.

Saturday, October 9 ∽ A most beautiful day. This is election day. Ruby has been poll clerk and Albert has been working also. I was up and voted for the Farmer's. Hayward is here. *[This was the 35th New Brunswick Parliament. There were no official parties yet, but candidates had started to organize along party lines. The United Farmers elected 9 candidates, the Conservatives 13, and the Liberals 24. It may have been Mary's first time voting other than the prohibition referendum because women got the vote in New Brunswick on the 17th of April 1919. Women were able to vote in Federal elections May 1918.]*

Wednesday, October 13 ∽ Cold and clear. We have been to the Dr's to the W.A. Have started a white quilt with blue clover leafs. We moved our stove in the hall today. Ruby and Merle have been at confirmation class.

Friday, October 15 ᴄᴡᴜ Cold and clear yet. Ruby had a letter from Reuben. Hall Brewer passed away about four o'clock. Poor fellow has had a long hard sickness. I have made some pumpkin preserves. It's lovely. Another nice night. No rain for two weeks.

Saturday, October 16 ᴄᴡᴜ Beautiful weather. Mr. Lovegrove died last night. Mrs. Wellington Brewer's dead also. Was brought home from Fairville yesterday, where she has been since last of June or first of July. Merle's been working for Randolph Maybe this afternoon. He's a dear smart boy.

Sunday, October 17 ᴄᴡᴜ A nice day, but cloudy; looks like rain. Albert, Ruby and Merle was to church this morning. We were all there this evening. Mrs. Wellington Brewer was buried this afternoon. Hall Brewer is to be buried tomorrow. Mr. Lovegrove buried Tuesday.

Tuesday, October 26 ᴄᴡᴜ It's been a lovely day. Ruby and Merle were confirmed tonight. 24 confirmed here and at Brewer's Mills.

Friday, October 29 ᴄᴡᴜ Still raining; warm and muggy. We have moved the kitchen stove today *[into the main house from the summer kitchen]*. Such a lot of work we have been all day straightening things up.

Saturday, October 30 ᴄᴡᴜ Colder. There have been a number of people in tonight. Tomorrow is Halloween so the young folk are playing tricks tonight for tomorrow is Sunday.

Saturday, November 13 ᴄᴡᴜ A real winter day snowing and blowing. We have had a very musical evening. Mr. Angus McDonald, Johnnie, Ray, Ethel and Hayward have been here. Merle's new Mackinaw *[heavy waterproof winter coat made from woolen plaid]* has arrived today.

Sunday, November 14 ᴄᴡᴜ A nice warm day. Was two immersions *[Bap-*

tisms] at the bridge. Mr. Cook had one this morning and the Baptist Minister this afternoon.

Tuesday, November 16 ∽ A lovely day. We, Albert and I has been to town to have our eyes tested. Went down in Mr. Wilcox's car.

Thursday, Nov 18 ∽ Got the call to Birds last night alright. They have another girl. They are disappointed. They expected a boy. All are smart *[well]. [Pregnancies were not discussed. People only spoke of someone having a new son or daughter once the baby arrived.]*

Saturday, November 20 ∽ We all had a good night's rest. Ethel isn't so well today. They only have seven more days to name the baby. Doris Andrews is working here. She is a good little girl. I am making bread today; been down home awhile. Lovely evening. Albert hurt the other leg today.

Sunday, November 21 ∽ A perfect day Albert was up to tea. Mrs. Bubar and Beth called *[at Bird's to see the new baby].*

Monday, November 22 ∽ a lovely day. Ethel and baby are doing nicely. We have been down home this evening Doris, Fern and I.

Thursday, November 25 ∽ Warmer didn't get much sleep with the baby last night. They have named the baby Geraldine Mary. We have been down home awhile this evening. *[Mary had been at the Bird's home for a week helping out with the baby and household while Mrs. Bird recovered from the birth.]*

Sunday, November 28 ∽ Have Dr. *[tending]* to Albert's legs all day. Think they are some better. Rupert's birthday.

Monday, November 29 ∽ Have stayed all night with Ethel. Think she is better. I came home about ten o'clock am. Albert's legs are no better. Was a very cold night last night. Mr. and Mrs. Spencer have called and others.

Wednesday, December 8 ∽ A lovely day. Ruby has gone to Hattie

Jones. Mr. and Mrs. Spencer called. Elwood Burtt, Sandie Jones, Mrs. Merrithew has been here. And Mr. Whitfield Estey and George to see about the insurance. Our Eaton order came for xmas. Hattie sent us a bottle of cream. Albert's leg is some better.

Thursday, December 9 ᗧ A lovely day. Albert is improving fine. Has been as far as the mill on his crutches. Ruby has been to practice. Hayward has had the car out today.

Saturday, December 18 ᗧ A lovely warm day again. Merle has been up to Clarence Jones today. I had a letter from Reuben. He is coming home the 24th. Albert's leg is gaining nicely. He has been to the Foresters Hall to a meeting tonight.

Monday, December 20 ᗧ A lovely day; colder. Albert has worked today. Is at the Farmer's annual meeting tonight. We received our first xmas presents this morning.

Tuesday, December 21 ᗧ Colder. I have been helping Edna Jones dress chickens today— fourteen. I had a letter from Grace. She has sent our *[Christmas]* box. We have sent hers.

Wednesday, December 22 ᗧ A lovely day. I have made fancy cookies for xmas, doughnuts and bread.

Saturday, Xmas day ᗧ Very, very, cold. We have all got such lovely presents. Santa Claus has certainly been good. Hayward is here. He brought presents from Ida Morehouse and Hattie Jewett.

Sunday, December 26 ᗧ Bitter cold weather. We are all dining. Couldn't get to xmas service last night. Hayward is cold stormed here. Mrs. Gilbert Coy and Elsie have called.

Wednesday, December 29 ᗧ A very nice day. Reuben has gone away again. We all had such a nice xmas again. I have been out with the envelopes for the minister's salary. *[The minister's salary seems to have been paid for with donations.]*

1921

Monday, January 3 ∾ Nice mild day. We have washed. The clothes have dried lovely *[outside]*. I have been far as John Brewer's with church envelopes. Albert has been to Mr. Whitfield Estey's this evening.

Tuesday, January 4 ∾ A lovely warm day. We have been to Mrs. Spencer's to W.A. Ruby went up on train this morning to Zealand. Gilbert Coy has been in this evening. Our new school teacher arrived this morning. A Mrs. Spence I believe.

Wednesday, January 5 ∾ Warm again. Has snowed quite hard this morning. Ruby, Merle and I have been over to Mrs. Coy's and spent the evening. Mrs. Coy gave us a kettle of apples. Ruby has 42 tickets; sold 7 on our W.A quilt today.

Thursday, January 6 ∾ A lovely day. I called on Mrs. Lyman Bubar this afternoon. She's going to Boston for a visit for her health. We sold 5 more tickets today. Ruby has been up to Harry Bird's and the Drs.

Sunday, January 16 ◠ Marie's birthday; would have been 19 years old today. This is a lovely day like April. Ida and Oliver Morehouse were here to tea. Merle was to Sunday School and church this morning. Ruby was there tonight.

Tuesday, January 18 ◠ Cold; awfully cold. Wind blowing at an awful rate. Hayward was here to dinner. Ethel Bird and Fern were here this afternoon. Mrs. Harry Bird wants me to nurse her *[in her own home]*. I wish I could.

Saturday, January 22 ◠ Most beautiful day; the evening is lovely. So moonlight and warm. I have been over and spent the evening with Edna MacDonald. Albert has just returned from Lodge. Merle has been up at the corner playing. Had such a good time, he didn't want to come home.

Tuesday, January 25 ◠ Colder still. Have made lots of mincemeat and finished a night dress. Mrs. Eldrick Staples was in on her way to F'ton to see Reggie Staples.

Wednesday, Jan 26 ◠ Cold; very cold. I have been to Sam Crouse's to W.A. Quite a number for such a cold day. Albert came up on afternoon train to tea. We came back on train tonight.

Friday, January 28 ◠ A lovely day. I was over to Edna Jones. She was away. I called on Mrs. Coy. I sold 5 quilt tickets. We all spent evening at Wilcox's. Ruby gave Hazel Estey a music lesson. Pearl Tomilson was here for a lesson today.

Sunday, January 30 ◠ A most beautiful day, Ruby, Merle and I have been to morning church. Albert and I have been to Baptist church this afternoon. The walking is something lovely, but a storm is blowing up.

Tuesday, February 1 ◠ A very fine cold day. Last night the coldest this winter. We have had many callers today. Albert has worked this afternoon. Have sold one ticket today. Ruby and I have spent evening at Johnny MacDonald's. Gordon Mclean had his hand taken off today at a mill in Cardigan. Poor fellow.

Wednesday, February 2 ᕊ Another cold fine day. Ruby was to W.A. I thought it too cold to start. We have had hazels and butternuts and tomato soup tonight. Quite a combination.

Wednesday, February 9 ᕊ A lovely day. I walked a way out on the lumber road. I called on Mrs. Squire Fowler. Poor old lady; should have called on her before. She bought a ticket on our quilt and gave me $2 for Mr. Spencer *[Anglican Minister]*. This is Ash Wednesday.

Thursday, February 10 ᕊ Another lovely day. I called on George Lovegrove. I bought a pound of yarn from Edna. Ethel Bird called today.

Monday, February 14 ᕊ Johnny MacDonald came after me early. They have a new girl baby. I am staying here for a while.

Wednesday, February 16 ᕊ A nice day; kind of a cold wind. The Doctor called today. The baby cried all night. The Doctor said to give no milk but catnip. *[Catnip tea was used to calm muscle spasms and relieve colic in babies.]*

Thursday, February 17 ᕊ The baby slept just fine last night. We are giving her olive oil and it's working wonders with her. Mrs. Bird and Ethel called this afternoon. I been over home a while.

Monday, February 21 ᕊ Most lovely day. We didn't put in too bad a night last night. The baby is sure whooping her up now.

Tuesday, February 22 ᕊ Another lovely day; very cold this morning. Baby was very good last night but has the cold now. Have started her on milk today. She has been fed on olive oil for a week.

Wednesday, February 23 ᕊ A storm on. I am home. Edna is up today; fairly well. Only has cold making her feel miserable. I am going over every morning for the next few days to wash and dress the baby. Had a letter from Grace; $5 for Merle. Her knee is getting better, under a new treatment.

Monday, March 7 ∾ Lovely afternoon. I was in to see Edna MacDonald; she was a little better. Ethel Bird's baby is very sick. I took my boots to Mr. Bird to have the heels fixed. *[Harry Bird was the community shoe maker.]* Was in to see the baby. Ruby and I called on Mrs. Inch and Mrs. Spencer this evening.

Thursday, March 17 ∾ Very nice. Didn't go to W.A. Thought wind was going to blow *[and she would have had to walk]*. Ruby was there. I was in to Wardlow Bird's to see baby. It's better. Was in to see old Mrs. Burtt also. She has been very miserable all winter. We have heard Avery married a widow, a Mrs. Quartermine.

Monday, March 21 ∾ Rainy all morning; cold tonight. We washed, had our clothes dried and in. Mrs. Willie Gilby was operated on today. Olga Pugh was operated on for appendicitis. So many cases. Albert has hired with a new concern *[employer]* to tally for a while loading. He hasn't been working since the 26th of February So we are very glad to hear of some *[work]*.

Tuesday, March 22 ∾ A nice day, cold wind, snow is going fast. Have made Ruby a night dress, all but the trimming. Was over to Edna's to see baby. She, Edna is so poorly, I feel so sorry for her. Wardlow and Ethel were in tonight.

Wednesday, March 23 ∾ A most beautiful day; the evening is something lovely. I would have gone to church if had thought of it in time. Albert has worked today. I have almost made Ruby a bungalow apron. *[A bungalow apron looks like a dress and was used to cover a good dress while cooking.]*

Sunday, Easter Day ∾ Lovely. Hayward came down with the motor *[motorized railway trolley]* and took us to church. We were to Crouse's to dinner. He brought us back in afternoon. Rilla came down to tea. They all went back to evening service. I got such a pretty tatted handkerchief, an Easter present. We spent evening at Wardlow Bird's.

Monday, April 4 ᦓ Very cold. Albert was out to Elwood Allan's to a farm sale. We washed and put another quilt on frames.

Friday, April 9 ᦓ Cold; raw. Albert has fixed the sink drains today. I was down to see Mrs. MacDonald. She is sick, very sick with her heart. I do hope she gets better. Ruby was up to give Hazel Estey a lesson and Oscar.

Wednesday, April 13 ᦓ Fine; the warmest day yet. We finished the quilt about five o'clock; is lovely. I was awful tired. I was out for a walk, in to Wardlow's and up and asked after Cobie Allen's wife. She is very sick. Johnnie MacDonald moved down home today. Ray has moved in new house.

Friday, April 15 ᦓ Not so warm today; been an awful wind. I was up to the corner this morning picked such pretty paper for my bedroom. Ruby's new hat came this morning. It's raining tonight. Mrs. Jeddie Brewer was in a few minutes waiting for the train.

Wednesday, April 20 ᦓ A lovely warm day. I have the dining room almost finished. The frogs are singing tonight and it's nice moonlight. *[Weather lore said that for each warm day that the frogs croaked in April, they laid back or hid for that many cold days in May.]*

Friday, April 22 ᦓ Lovely day; cold wind. Winslow brought 4 lbs of butter, the first this year. I did the dining room curtains today. Merle caught another muskrat; two this spring. *[He would have sold the hides.]*

Monday, April 25 ᦓ Ruby's birthday. Nasty and cold. We washed. Mary Jones was in a while poor old thing. Ruby's suit arrived today. Its nice.

Tuesday, April 26 ᦓ Dull all morning. Fine this afternoon. We have cleaned Ruby's bedroom and painted around the border of oilcloth. *[As people started to upgrade, they placed an oil cloth in the center of the* *room like a carpet, leaving an outside border of the softwood flooring showing.]*

Wednesday, April 27 ∾ A real summer day. We have cleaned Merle's bedroom; turned and painted the oilcloth, made hop yeast. I had a letter from Reuben first since he has gone back four weeks ago. Said he had been on a *[log]* drive the other side of the lake. Albert is at a Farmer's Meeting at the corner. Mrs. Wilcox was over tonight. Hayward is here.

Saturday, April 30 ∾ Cold again; such a change. Last night so warm we could sleep with bed clothes; tonight a big fire in the house and quilts piled on.

Thursday, May 5 ∾ Cold wind. I have painted my bedroom floor. I called on Mrs. Cobie Allen. She is very sick. Mr. Winslow Jones brought about ten lbs of butter.

Friday, May 6 ∾ Some warmer; cold wind. Have finished the bedrooms and changed *[curtains and bedding]* for the summer. Had a letter from Grace. She has had the Grippe. She is sick a lot lately. We have had the first fiddlehead greens today. I planted some sweet peas tonight.

Saturday, May 7 ∾ Warmer; lovely. Ruby cleaned the upstairs hall. We have been to F'ton *[Fredricton]* with Wilcox's in the car. It's very cold tonight. We got out in the ditch and had to have a horse pull us out. *[The roads would have been muddy and the cars were heavy.]*

Tuesday, May 10 ∾ We have cleaned the hall, the sitting room and kitchen. Ruby has varnished the sitting room floor. Maud and Dorothy was in a while on their way to F'ton to a play.

Wednesday, May 11 ∾ Cold but sunshiney. I painted stair steps and hall woodwork, a screen door and scrubbed dining room to varnish. Ruby ironed and varnished chairs.

Thursday, May 12 ∾ Fine but an awful gale blowing this afternoon.

We have painted the floor in the hall upstairs, and varnished the hall floor down stairs, and the dining room floor. Ruby has gone up to give Kathleen Bird a lesson. I have wrote to Reuben.

Friday, May 13 ∿ We have varnished floor, chairs, doors. Painted the front screen door, cleaned the hall stove and oiled the kitchen floor, put up curtains, made cookies.

Saturday, May 14 ∿ Dull; looked like rain all day. We did some ironing, cooking and put up kitchen curtains and finished house cleaning. Merle, Jack, and some boy from town have been fishing. Went in Roy's car. Merle caught two dozen.

Thursday, May 19 ∿ A nice day, cold wind. We have been to the W.A. Ruby is to be married the first day of June. I wish girls never got married to leave home. What a lovely world it would be.

Friday, May 20 ∿ A windy, cold disagreeable day. Mr. and Mrs. Spencer were here this evening. We have an old man here tonight, some old agent *[railway]*. I'm afraid I'll have some washing by the odour that's coming out of the bedroom.

Saturday, May 21 ∿ Nice, warm. Our old man started on the road real early. I expected to find lice but I didn't. We had a heavy thunder storm tonight. Very heavy for this first. Ruby, Merle and Hayward have gone to a band concert and ice cream social.

Monday, May 23 ∿ Empire Day. Cold, very cold and windy. Such a change from yesterday. We did our wash and I have made two fruit cakes and a big nut cake. *[Before the introduction of processed flours, both the wedding and groom's cake were fruit cakes. It's possible that Mary made these cakes for Ruby's wedding. However the wedding was eight days away and they had no freezer storage in the 1920s.]* Ella Christie is here and has started my dress *[for Ruby's wedding]*. Albert has gone to F'ton to hear the Prime Minister *[Arthur Meighen]* speak in the Opera House.

Wednesday, May 25 ⌒ A lovely day. Ella has finished my dress and gone over to sew for Edna Jones until Ruby's silk comes; have been expecting it for two days. We had a letter from Reuben. He can't come; he sent Ruby Twenty Dollars for a present. Grace don't think she can come either.

Friday, May 27 ⌒ A lovely warm day. Hot this afternoon, getting nice and cool this evening. We have all had such nice baths. The silk for Ruby's dress hasn't come yet. Ruby has such a cold and also a blistered heel, hope they all get well by Wednesday, Mrs. G. Lovegrove has a young son, Elwin.

Saturday, May 28 ⌒ A very warm day. It's election day. Ruby is poll clerk again. *[This was the York-Sunbury by-election of the 13th Canadian Parliament. The incumbent died in office January 7, 1921. Mary wouldn't have been able to vote in the last election because most women didn't get the vote until May 1918. She would have voted before her peers because of this by-election in her riding.]* Merle and Ervine has been fishing all day. We got uneasy and started cooking *[looking?]* for them.

Tuesday, May 31 ⌒ Some cooler. Ella will finish Ruby's dress today. Grace has come tonight she brought Ruby such a handsome present. The people have had such a beautiful shower for her. Must have been 75 people here.

Wednesday, June 1 ⌒ Ruby's wedding day. She was beautiful. At eight this evening. The church was beautifully trimmed, everything was fine. We had about 27 in for light luncheon. She got some more nice presents tonight; a lovely blue and white quilt from Hayward's mother and eight dollars more and other things. Hope her life will be happy. Very cold today.

Thursday, June 2 ⌒ A lovely day. Ruby and Hayward started for Chipman about eight o'clock this morning. They have a lovely day. I hope they reach there, safely. Grace went home this morning.

Friday, June 3 ∾ Cloudy; raining this afternoon and evening cold. I was in to see the new Lovegrove baby. Also Mrs. Cobie *[Allen]*.

Saturday, June 4 ∾ A lovely day pretty cool. Merle and Bill was out Duck Lake. Merle caught a big trout 15 ½ inches. We have all been up to the band concert. Some women spoke on red cross work. Ruby and Hayward haven't arrived yet. Hope they are enjoying themselves.

Monday, June 6 ∾ A lovely day. I washed and scrubbed. Maud and Rupert were here to tea. Avery and his wife called soon as they left. Hattie and Winslow come soon as they left. It was near ten o'clock when I got the dishes washed and clothes in *[from clothesline]*.

Tuesday, June 7 ∾ Another fine day. A nice shower this afternoon. Ruby and Hayward arrived at noon.

Sunday, June 12 ∾ Very warm this morning. Merle and I was up to see Mrs. Cobie Allen. Merle took the little cripple boy some pants. He was so pleased, poor child. We were in to see Mrs. Burtt too. She is worse again. Something killed our little black kitten last night. Merle felt so badly. We have all been to church. Ruby and Hayward appeared out tonight. *[This was their first time in church as a married couple.]*

Wednesday, June 15 ∾ Nice cool. raining some tonight. I finished ironing and called on Mrs. Cobie *[Allen]*. Took her some pie. Hayward and Ruby came down tonight. Had a letter from Reuben.

Friday, June 24 ∾ A lovely cool day. I made a lemon pie, cookies, and bread this morning. Annie Estey and Hazel were here this afternoon. This is a lovely night.

Monday, June 27 ∾ Is very warm; no rain. I called on poor Mrs. Cobie Allen. Poor thing is failing fast, suffers terrible at times. I feel so sorry for her. We were out for a car ride. Maude, Dorothy and Rupert were down.

Tuesday, June 28 ∾ Cloudy. Looked so much like rain all day but no rain yet. Tomorrow night we are to have a social in the hall for to raise money for an organ for the church.

Wednesday, June 29 ∾ A lovely shower, We; Ruby, Hayward and I were to town this afternoon. We have our social tonight; made about 75 dollars. Pearl Kantnor got the lucky quilt ticket. Ida and Arnold are here tonight.

Friday, July 1, 1921 ∾ Warm. We have been to the *[Burtt's Corner]* Hotel to Florence Crouse's shower. Not many there. Newton Bird's little boy buried today.

Tuesday, July 12 ∾ Hot but not sultry. We have been to the 12th celebration *[annual Orangemen Parade]*. A terrible thing happened. Randolph Maybe lost control of a car and it ran into the crowd hurting so many people. It was a terrible sight.

Friday, July 15 ∾ Such a beautiful rain this morning. Last night was so close and oppressive. Rena Estey and children were here today. Mrs. Wilcox has just gone home. Such a beautiful cool night. We feel like a different people. The wounded people are recovering *[from the Orangemen Parade car accident]*.

Sunday, July 17 ∾ A lovely day. Coughed all night and we didn't get up until barely nine. Albert Merle, Ruby and Hayward were to church tonight. I didn't feel like walking up. There were seven baptized here in the Forks *[stream]*.

Thursday, July 21 ∾ A lovely day; I have been down to see Mrs. MacDonald. She is a little better. We have heard that Mrs. William Jewett has diphtheria.

Friday, July 22 ∾ A lovely day; quite hot. I've been feeling sick all this afternoon. Merle is having his wheel *[bicycle]* cleaned and painted.

Monday, July 25 ∾ Hot; very hot. I was up at four o'clock this morning. Started my wash at five to get it out of the way before the day got too hot. The band is playing tonight.

Wednesday, July 27 ◯ Hot; very hot and no rain. Oh how I hope rain will be sent. We, Albert and I have been for such a nice car ride with Mr. and Mrs. Wilcox down as far as Charlie Jewett's and up as far as Hailey Crouse's. The band stand is started. *[It sat in the intersection of the Jones Forks Road and the Keswick Road, with enough space for horse teams to go around on either side.]*

Saturday, July 30 ◯ Not so hot but very, very dry. The mill is closed for the men tonight. Fire up the crick *[Keswick River]* on Elwood's *[Burtt]* ground and I guess fire is bad. They will have to go tomorrow unless it rains. Oh how I hope it will.

Sunday, July 31 ◯ Cooler. We had a little rain about four o'clock this morning. Merle and I were to church this morning. We were all there this evening. It turned cold and is raining some. I do hope it will rain all night.

Monday, Aug 1 ◯ It's cool; cold tonight. Rained most all night last night. We got our first raspberries of the season today. Ruby and I picked about three qts. So cold tonight I have a fire built in the stove. We have started to shingle the house. I can't say how glad I am.

Friday, August 5 ◯ Lovely all day; tonight big wind has risen and it's blowing a dense smoke from somewhere. I hope it rains hard before morning. I picked about five qts. of chokecherries this afternoon to make jellie. Merle has a sore hand. I hope it isn't a felon *[A felon was an abscess on the underside of the finger tip that often become infected. It was caused by a puncture or splinter.]*

Saturday, August 6 ◯ Warm again; still no rain. Last night's smoke was from Lake George. We have all been to the band concert. The new band stand is fine.

Sunday, August 7 ◯ Looks so much like rain. I went up with Merle to the Dr. I guess it is a felon on his hand. He said he could lance it in twenty four hours. It's been very painful but have kept him easy for about four hours with aspirin. It's rained a little this afternoon. Nothing to speak of. Westfield was burned yesterday; a summer resort above St. John. *[It is now a year-round community and has been renamed Grand Bay-Westfield.]*

Monday, August 8 ᔆ Such a beautiful rain that we have had. It began raining about one o'clock this morning and it's certainly poured until noon. The water is away up; our well a lot more water in. Such a blessing. Ruby had Merle up to the Dr. this afternoon and had his hand lanced. I hope it will be all right now. Ruby and I were over to Mrs. Coys this evening. Gladys is home.

Tuesday, August 9 ᔆ A lovely day; we washed. Verna Staples came up. She and Ruby were to Willie Crouse's to tea. I have been up to see Mrs. Cobie Allen. She is sinking fast. I was in to see Mrs. Newton Bird also; she is miserable *[just lost her young son]*.

Wednesday, August 10 ᔆ A lovely day. Ruby, Verna and I picked 3qts. of raspberries. I preserved some. We had a raspberry pudding and new potatoes for dinner.

Thursday, August 11 ᔆ Very hot again. Merle's hand began to pain this morning. I took him to the Dr. He took the core out and it's better. Minnie Burtt was here to dinner. We were up to Mrs. Jones funeral. Mrs. Jewett and Cora were in awhile this evening. Albert has the front of the house shingled.

Sunday, August 14 ᔆ Rainy all day. Merle was at Sunday School this morning. Mr. Spencer had service at Crossroads this morning [*Crock's Point Anglican*]. We didn't get to church tonight; it looked like rain. We were down to Randolph's awhile. Milt Burtt had an open air meeting in the band stand.

Thursday, August 18 ᔆ It's rained all day; poured. Ruby has gone up to Crouse's to stay a week while Mrs. and Mrs. Crouse is away. We feel lonesome. I have been crocheting on a mat all day. Have the rags all used up.

Tuesday, August 23 ∾ A lovely day. Merle has wheeled to Nashwaaksis and Jack *[Wilcox]* has gone with the pony and wagon. Mr. Estey went home this morning; finished sawing today. I guess or hope Albert will have work loading but a big cut in wages.

Thursday, August 25 ∾ We have been to Marysville today and in the Cotton Mill. We had dinner with Mrs. Brogan. There is a big time in Marysville with Mill Days. A guides festival. Mrs. Brogan wanted us to stay up for the evening and come down on the 9 o'clock train but we had no way so we came down at five.

Saturday, August 27 ∾ We came home this morning. Merle wheeled up *[from Fredericton. It would be about 17.5 miles or 28 kilometres]*. I met Miss Wood on the train. She is to teach at Bristol. We have had a nice band concert.

Monday, August 29 ∾ A hot day. We have washed. School opened to-day. Miss Sparks is the teacher. I hope Merle gets along alright with her. I had a letter from Grace.

Tuesday, August 30 ∾ Warm and dry. Water very low again. Had no rain since a week Saturday Albert has the side of house next to the rail all shingled.

Thursday, September 1 ∾ Another lovely day. Ruby and I have been to Willie Brewers. He brought us home tonight; gave me a basket of tomatoes. A kettle milk. Ruby bought a calaflower *[cauliflower]* and 1 box of yarn. There is a chicken supper at the hall for Mr. Cook. *[Mr. Cook was the Methodist Minister, so this may have been a fundraiser for his wages.]*

Saturday, September 3 ∾ Hot and dry still. Ruby and I pickled our tomatoes; had seven bottles each. Albert has started the new paint *[on the house shingles]*. I believe it will be alright.

Wednesday, September 7 ∿ A lovely day. Very warm this morning. The Farmer's Picnic was today. This is Hazel Estey's wedding day also. Ruby and Hayward have gone to the church.

Friday, September 9 ∿ A lovely day. Have done a peck of crab apples, also a peck of plums and apples together.

Monday, September 12 ∿ Raining hard; a lovely rain. I got my cranberries all stewed. Ready for jellie. Ruby has done some apples. Reuben surprised us all by coming home tonight. Dear good hearted boy; he gave me twenty dollars.

Tuesday, September 13 ∿ We had a thunder shower last night and such heavy rain. I guess it was terrible heavy at Keswick; burned a barn. Ruby, Hayward, Reuben and Merle have all gone to Dunk Brewer's to a little W.A. social. Albert and I both have headaches and didn't go.

Wednesday, September 14 ∿ A lovely day. We have been down to Mr. Elias Estey's awhile. Have also been up to the pictures this evening *[in the Forester Hall]*. They were good. It's a very cold night.

Friday, September 16 ∿ A beautiful day; cold and windy. Reuben has gone again. We miss him. Ruby was to town with Maud this afternoon to try the new organ for the church and will be up in the morning for the Harvest Thanksgiving. 19 years today Marie was buried.

Saturday, September 17 ∿ Very nice all day. The opening F'ton exhibition. *[It had been operating in Fredericton since 1827.]* It's raining some tonight. Albert's been very miserable *[not feeling well]* all the week. I have cut out two pairs of sleepers *[night clothes similar to pajamas]* for Merle today.

Sunday, September 18 ∿ Raining this morning. No one got to church, but we were all there this evening; our thanksgiving service. We have much to be thankful for, a new organ included.

Monday, September 19 ∿ Cold this morning; warmer as the day wears on. We have washed, cut up two pecks of tomatoes and seven lbs. of onions, folded the clothes and stitched four sheets, mixed sponge and I am ready for bed. It's a lovely moonlight, cold night. *[They made their own flat sheets from large pieces of fabric. Mixing sponge was the process of mixing flour, water, and some yeast and letting it ferment so that the yeast worked better. Their home-made yeast wasn't fast acting like the processed yeast we use today.]*

Monday, September 26 ∽ Cold and a little rain. We washed. Maud and Mrs. McKeil were here this afternoon. Rupert and Evelyn and we have been up to the hall to a mass meeting for the monument for our fallen soldiers. The band was in attendance. *[They discussed fund raising for a community Cenotaph to honour those that never returned from World War I.]*

Tuesday, October 4 ∽ Raining; has rained all night. Albert has moved the drain and sink to the other side of the shed again *[They did most of their home repairs themselves. Sometimes the repairs were crude, but they worked.]*

Saturday, October 8 ∽ Very windy and rain this afternoon. Merle's been gathering apples on Stone Ridge with the Bubar boys. Hayward has brought five partridge tonight. We also have some deer steak.

Sunday, October 9 ∽ A very cold day; cold as winter. I was up to see Mrs. Cobie Allen this morning. Took her some partridge soup. Merle started for Sunday School on his wheel. Was so cold he turned back. We were all to church tonight.

Monday, October 10 ∽ Wind and rain. It's election day. *[for Prohibition and New Brunswick voted against importing liquor for personal use.]* Ruby has been up working all day, pole clerk. I've washed. Didn't finish until after two. Winslow brought our butter 88 ½ lbs. I started using tonight; 3 gal. jar. There's a big storm on tonight; rain and wind.

Saturday, October 15 ∽ A beautiful day again. Angus Macdonald,

Johnny, Edna Maud and the McKeils were here and had music.

Sunday, October 23 ∾ Cold and heavy wind. We were up to Baptist church to their unveiling of the new bell *[for the bell tower added in 1920]*.

Tuesday, October 25 ∾ Cold; a little snow this morning. I went away over on pine hill with Merle to see if we could gather some princess pine. There is a man here from Nova Scotia gathering it for decorating. *[Princess pine is a feathery club moss that was used to make ornamental wreaths for Christmas and other occasions It's relatives date back to the dinosaur era.]*

Tuesday, November 1 ∾ Five months tonight since Ruby was married. I'm glad to say she is better today. *[Maybe morning sickness? There were no contraceptives in the 1920s.]* She came down stairs about four o'clock.

Wednesday, November 2 ∾ Snow; our first. Albert wasn't working this morning so he put the new windows in the shed and fixed storm door. I have scrubbed our old table for Ruby; a kitchen table. Mrs. Coy and I were up to see Mrs. Cobie Allen. She is sinking fast, what a blessing if that she passed out of it all.

Sunday, November 6 ∾ Cold like winter; lots of snow. Merle was to church and Sunday School this morning. Hayward brought the car down this afternoon for us to go to church tonight but roads are bad and we didn't go. Albert is laid up with a stitch in his back. *[A stitch in this case meant a kink or ache.]*

Friday, November 11 ∾ Armistice Day. Warm. Albert is some better. He had shingled quite a lot today. We have made sausage meat tonight.

Monday, November 14 ∾ Another big snow storm. I cleaned my sideboard dresser this morning. We washed after dinner; it cleared up after dinner. It's warm tonight. Albert's been shingling today.

Tuesday, November 15 ∾ Another awful snow storm. Snowed all day;

blowing tonight. Merle has got dandy nice pair of shoe packs today. *[A heavy, warm lace-up boot usually made of animal hide.]*

Friday, November 18 ∾ Warm seems like rain. Albert is home shingling. He has the other side finished. I have cleaned the sitting room today. Mrs. Cobie Allen died today poor soul. What a happy exchange. *[She meant that the woman was no longer suffering.]* Harry Elliot's little girl died last night.

Saturday, November 19 ∾ Foggy; snow wasting away. Mrs. Cobie Allen was buried today. Funeral at the house. I was up. Ruby was up working in her house today.

Monday, November 21 ∾ Dark; looks so much like a storm. We washed. Albert finished shingling the house and has the side of shed most done. Hayward was down and moved Ruby's dishes, bedding and preserves, pickles and things. We all feel so badly about her going. Oh if we could always all live together. If there was no partings.

Wednesday, November 23 ∾ A lovely bright day but cold. Ruby has gone up to the house today. I went with her. We got things straightened around and some cooking done. I stayed all night. In evening we went down to Mrs. Spencer's to a meeting to see about the xmas tree *[for the Church]*.

Thursday, November 24 ∾ Cold, storming tonight; snow. I came home this morning. I don't know which felt the bluest, Ruby or I. I've cried until I'm nearly sick. If she was well I wouldn't feel so badly. I've kept it all from her and have been so cheerful before her. It makes it hard for me.

Saturday, November 26 ∾ Cold day; coldest yet. Ruby and Hayward are here tonight. Ruby seems so much better. Hayward got her a lovely new pair of nine dollar boots yesterday. I feel so contented tonight. I made doughnuts, pumpkin pies, and brown bread.

Friday, December 2 ∾ A nice warm day. We had Herb Staples come and take the piano up to Ruby's. We have made mince meat tonight and going to *[bed at]* eleven o'clock. I'm dead tired.

Sunday, December 4 ⌒ I went up on the motor with Ruby and Hayward to Church and I stayed all night for Maud wasn't there *[at church to bring her home as she usually did]*.

Monday, December 5 ⌒ I came down on the motor this morning. It's been a lovely day. I washed the clothes already but left them out. Ruby came down tonight to be ready to work at the election tomorrow. I sent my xmas Eaton order today.

Tuesday, December 6 ⌒ Nasty and cold. Ethel Brewer was here awhile waiting for Willie to come from Election. Osborne led here and at most county poles, but Hanson led in F'ton and Devon. Ruby and Hayward have gone back home tonight. *[This was the 14th Canadian Parliament and the first federal election where women could vote. Mackenzie King got in nationally. The Progressive Party which included the United Farmers that the Morehouse family seem to have supported dominated out west, but only captured one seat east of Ontario. It was Thomas Wakem Caldwell for Victoria-Carleton. Richard Hanson, the Conservative Candidate took York-Sunbury. The Progressives actually captured enough seats to form the official opposition, but they declined to form it, so the Liberals did.]*

Thursday, December 8 ⌒ A nice day but cold. The W.A. met at Ruby's today to quilt a puff for Mrs. Spencer; a xmas present *[for the Minister's wife]*. I found Ruby sick. We had sixteen there in all counting Ruby and Hayward. We got the quilt done and another one bound.

Monday, December 12 ⌒ A most beautiful day. Had my washing all done by ten o'clock; clothes brought in tonight. Ruby came down on train this morning. Albert went up on train tonight for to attend a meeting in the church. We got our first eggs for this winter today *[from their own chickens]*.

Wednesday, December 14 ∼ A lovely warm day. Merle and I were up to the store this evening to get a few things for xmas presents.

Friday, December 16 ∼ Cold; nice and bright. Merle went up to Ruby's to stay until tomorrow night. Albert is at a farmer's meeting; it's near eleven o'clock. I was up to the store tonight. We heard from Reuben on the phone this morning from Houlton. [*Doctors and merchants in the Keswick area had phones as early as 1907. This is first time the phone is mentioned for the Morehouse family and they likely received an earlier message by mail or from the Doctor's home that he was to call them at that particular time.*]

Wednesday, December 21 ∼ A lovely day; colder tonight. The furs came today. They are lovely. I received a little apron and two cards also. We sent Grace a box tonight. [*It would be interesting to know if these furs were from pelts that Merle took somewhere for curing, or whether they ordered them specifically.*]

Thursday, December 22 ∼ Such a terrible cold day. We have been to the school concert in the hall. Ruby came down to stay over xmas. Albert came home from the mill tonight.

Friday, December 23 ∼ Cold looks like snow all day. Snowing some tonight. Getting much warmer. I've done a lot of cooking today. Mince pies, doughnuts, two kinds of cookies and made sausage meat and prepared fowl.

Saturday, December 24 ∼ Cold; a little snow. We have been so busy. Merle went to the band concert. Hayward came this afternoon. Reuben came tonight. He was married last Wednesday, He says her name is Marie Parade. I don't know, I hope it's for the best.

Christmas Day ∼ A lovely day. Santa Claus was good indeed. We haven't been to church today, I'm sorry. We were up on the motor to Ruby's.

1922

Saturday, January 7 ∿ A lovely day and beautiful moonlight evening. Ruby did not come tonight for Hayward has the water tank fire to look after morning and night. *[The water tank sat near the railway for the steam trains. When a train stopped, the water had to be hot so the train's hot boiler wouldn't crack from cold water. Hayward kept a wood fire going under the tank all night.]*

Wednesday, January 11 ∿ Been quite nice until afternoon, and tonight there is a wild old fashioned storm and sure blowing, snowing and drifting. Rilla Crouse was down today.

Thursday, January 12 ∿ Such a wild night last night. Blowed one of Bubar's big pines down. Rained all this morning. Colder tonight. Lots of drifts. Albert awfully miserable again today. I do wonder what ails his stomach. He won't see a doctor. *[His brother was the local doctor.]*

Monday, January 16 ∿ A fine but cold day. I washed. This is Marie's birthday. She would have been 20 years today.

Wednesday, January 18 ∿ Blows like a storm again. I've ironed, washed yarn, been to the mail, sent a small order to Eatons. Called to see Mrs. Fred Jones new baby. Have written to Reuben tonight.

Friday, January 20 ᖴ Very blustery today. I have all my cakes baked for Sunday. I am expecting Ruby down tomorrow if nothing happens. Jack Bird died this afternoon; had pneumonia.

Monday, January 23 ᖴ Very cold last night. Was a terrible wild night. Tonight is coldest yet; 21° below *[Fahrenheit or - 30° Celsius]* before we came upstairs. Ruby went home this morning. I feel lonesome after she stays a couple of days and goes back. I know she does too. Mr. Tom Fowler and Willie Gilby were here to audit the Forester books tonight. It's two months today since Ruby moved up *[to the Crouse home]*.

Tuesday, January 24 ᖴ Very, very cold yet. Been a bitter day. Didn't send Merle to school. *[The school would be a one or two mile walk from their home.]* Very cold still tonight. I washed. Grace Jones was in waiting for the train this evening.

Saturday, January 28 ᖴ It's been a lovely day. I was to the corner this afternoon, and got cotton and came home and made three pair of pillow cases. Merle went up to Ruby's on train to stay all night. Albert has been to lodge *[Foresters meeting]*.

Tuesday, January 31 ᖴ A lovely day. I have ironed and put pockets in a pair of pants for Merle. Wrote Grace tonight. Ethel Bird and baby were here this afternoon.

Monday, February 6 ᖴ A big storm on tonight. Merle is fourteen yrs. today. Don't seem possible. Ruby came down today. Stayed all day. So glad to see her.

Friday, February 17 ᖴ A bitter cold day the coldest yet. Such a terrible wind. I felt so uneasy about Merle for he wasn't dressed for such a cold day. Didn't realize it was so cold when he started for school. I haven't felt well all day. Those numb prickly feeling*[s]*. I wonder what causes it. Had a note from Ruby wanting me to go up tomorrow night if all is well.

Saturday, February 18 ∾ Last night was a terrible cold night; the coldest this year. Snowing this afternoon. I did not go up to Ruby's. Was afraid of a big blow *[wind]*. Didn't feel very well anyway. Will Burtt's crew has finished in the woods today. Are moving out of the cook house tonight. *[They would be moving back to community of Burtt's Corner soon for the spring log drive. The men cut in the woods all winter, came out for log drive on the streams in the spring, then worked in the sawmills all summer.]*

Monday, February 20 ∾ It's been a most beautiful day; warm and thawing. I've washed, made bread cleaned hall stove, scrubbed hall kitchen, some of the shed. Cleaned water closet. Mr. Israel Burtt died yesterday morning. *[The water closet was a compartment or tiny room that was set aside for a toilet. It was usually located in an inside corner of the shed attached to the house. It was a step up from the cold of an outside toilet before the introduction of indoor plumbing allowed for a flush toilet.]*

Tuesday, February 21 ∾ A lovely day. Hayward brought Albert such a nice rocking chair. Mr. I. Burtt was buried today. A large funeral. Saw so many friends.

Saturday, February 25 ∾ A lovely day; very cold last night. Albert is so lame; makes me so uneasy. Merle was out to the Mill at the Ridge today. Ruby and Hayward are here tonight; our family complete. Mrs. Willie Hawkins is not expected to live poor woman, and such a family of little children. One only a few days old. *[She was likely failing due to complications from childbirth. Women delivered their babies at home with assistance from the local doctor and midwives.]*

Sunday, February 26 ∾ A most beautiful day. Willie Brewer came and drove us all out there today. We had a lovely day. Ruby and Hayward went too. They have gone back on the pede *[This was a later name for* *the motor car.]* Ruben is 49 yrs today.

Monday, February 27 ∾ A warm snow storm. I haven't been feeling very well. I was up tonight to see on Mrs. Willie Hawkins. She, poor thing. I don't think will live till morning. Oh such a family to leave. Six pretty little pictures, the oldest only nine. *[Many families were large with children close in age.]*

Tuesday, February 28 ∾ Very nice this morning; blustering later in the day. Wind blowing hard tonight. Mrs. Inch and I have been to Ruby's all day. Poor Mrs. Hawkins died about six o'clock this morning.

Saturday, March 4 ∾ Lovely and warm. I've got an awful cold. Ruby was expecting me up; didn't feel like it. Had a visit from Trilby *[local hobo lady]*.

Wednesday, March 8 ∾ Such a rain last night and wind. I've felt kind of used up after being out so late last night.

Friday, March 17 ∾ Cold, but not so cold as yesterday. We had a nice pleasant day yesterday. We had the Holy Communion in the morning and finished with our Business meeting. Had dinner at Mrs. Burtt's. Quilted all the afternoon, had tea at Mrs. Burtt's, service in the church in the evening. Mr. Nichols address was lovely. I stayed at Ruby's all night. Merle and I came home on the motor this morning.

Friday, March 24 ∾ Quite a nice day, but windy. I was down to Mrs. MacDonald's awhile. They sent for me to go up to Clarence Burtt's. Ruby had another bad spell. I was there until nearly 12 o'clock.

Tuesday, March 28 ∾ Raining. Mr. George Christie was buried today. Reggie Staples wife died this morning very suddenly. Poor thing has been very miserable since a baby was born four weeks ago but they thought yesterday she was much better. Passed away in the night or early morning. She leaves two tiny babies; one a year and one four weeks.

Thursday, March 30 ∾ Still cold and windy. I went up on train to

Ruby's. We were all to W.A. I came back with Maud. Mrs. Reggie Staples was buried today. Willie Hawkins baby died yesterday. *[The child's mother had died a few weeks ago.]*

Friday, March 31 ∾ A lovely day. We, Merle and I; we done quite a lot of cleaning in the yard. I was up to see Mr. Hawkins this morning. Their little baby was buried this afternoon.

Monday, April 3 ∾ Quite nice but wind still blowing. Warmer tonight. I have ironed, made cookies and patty pans *[cupcakes]*, cooked meat and cleaned the range *[wood cook stove]*, mixed sponge and I'm tired. Expecting Ruby tomorrow to stay the rest of week.

Wednesday, April 5 ∾ Very nice. Mrs. Macdonald and Ethel called. Ruby and I were at the corner tonight to Wardlow's. Mrs. Harry Allan is sick. I had a letter from Reuben. He is working at Dyer Brook. His wife is in the hospital. *[May be complications from pregnancy as she had a child born a few weeks later on April 29th.]*

Sunday, April 16 ∾ Easter Sunday. A lovely day. We have been to church twice and enjoyed the day. I came down with Dorothy and Muriel as far as their place *[and walked rest of way home]*.

Tuesday, April 18 ∾ Raining all day. I cleaned the clothespress *[storage space for clothing]* today. The wind is blowing awfully hard tonight.

Wednesday, April 19 ∾ A very nice day but cold. I have cleaned the three bedrooms. *[During their spring cleaning, they washed walls, windows, curtains, and floors.]* I'm so tired and lame I can hardly walk.

Monday, April 24 ∾ Cold wind, but a bright Sunday, Merle and I cleaned the shed and Ruby did the house work, but we have had one busy day. Merle worked like a beaver. Maud and Rupert was here awhile.

Tuesday, April 25 ∾ Ruby's birthday; 23 years. It's been a nice day, only such a cold wind. I have been to the city to get my teeth reset.

Friday, April 28 ∿ A terrible cold, windy day like winter. Our Eaton order came. Also my teeth. They fit so much better than the old plate.

Thursday, May 4 ∿ A lovely day. I have things more settled. Ruby came down today. She cleaned all my silver and tidied my rooms for me and helped me great. Ethel Bird was in awhile.

Friday, May 5 ∿ Nice but a cold wind. I washed the woodwork in the kitchen, ironed and baked bread. Merle is still miserable. I don't know what ails him. There was a big forest fire at Zealand today. I expect Ruby was scared nearly sick. I've been uneasy about her. Reuben has a young son born the 29th of April.

Thursday, May 11 ∿ Cold as winter. I have scrubbed my hall floor 7 or 8 times trying to lighten it before I varnish it. I almost tired myself sick. I varnished it this afternoon and painted Ruby's bedroom floor. We are getting our years wood — 3 loads yesterday and three today.

Friday, May 12 ∿ Cold but warmer than yesterday. I have varnished the chairs, the hall floor again. Hanged the curtains, ironed, made cake and several other things. Mary Jones called this morning. Ethel MacDonald this afternoon. 3 more loads of wood today. *[They varnished every spring as part of their annual cleaning. The varnish was not water based like today, so it had strong fumes.]*

Saturday, May 13 ∿ Cold; rainy. I've made cake and pumpkin pies and roasted meat, made curtains and done a lot of fixings. Ruby and Hayward are here tonight.

Tuesday, May 16 ∿ A lovely day. I've done a lot more painting, varnishing and washed outside windows and ironed. Albert is at a Farmer's Meeting Three more loads of wood today.

Wednesday, May 17 ∿ Very nice. I have done a lot more painting and varnishing and I haven't felt a bit well *[maybe due to the fumes from the varnish]*. I made bread also. Merle picked the first fiddleheads tonight.

Monday, May 22 ∾ A lovely day. I've washed scrubbed and painted three chairs, sink and a door. I got awfully tired. Edna McDonald was in awhile tonight.

Tuesday, May 23 ∾ A lovely day. I have finished painting and oiled kitchen floor. Was over to Ethel MacDonald's for a while. We have all our wood — 20 loads.

Thursday, May 25 ∾ Ascension day. It's been showery today. Great growing weather. I have felt all used up from a long walk yesterday. There was service tonight; we was not up.

Saturday, May 27 ∾ Nice but cold. Awfully cold tonight. Ruby and Hayward are here tonight. I made brown bread, four loaves of cake, cooked beans, made dressing and prepared the rooster.

Wednesday, May 31 ∾ Very nice, warm. I went up on the train to Zealand. Ruby and I did what we could to the graves *[spring cleanup of weeds etc.]*. We all cleaned the church; 8 or 9 of us. Ruby has come down to stay awhile. It's a year tonight since her shower.

Thursday, June 1 ∾ Ruby's wedding anniversary. Warm; an awful wind. A bad fire at Bird Settlement. All the mill crew have been there fighting it today and it's now under control.

Saturday, June 3 ∾ Raining hard all the afternoon. Hayward fishing away up the creek; Merle out the forks. Hayward got 65 and Merle 34 trout. We had ice cream tonight.

Friday, June 16 ∾ I should feel much older for I am grandma. Ruby has a daughter. Maud has been here all day. I am feeling some better of grip. Rilla is here helping me. Mrs. Rankin Brewer has a daughter also born this morning. *[There was no previous mention of the pregnancy because it wasn't discussed until the baby arrived. Even though Mary's private journal has mentioned Ruby had been sick a few times, she hasn't used any terms like pregnant or expecting.]*

Saturday, June 17 ∿ Day is warm. Ruby is pretty well. Baby awfully good. I am feeling awfully miserable today. So lame, I can hardly cripple around.

Monday, June 19 ∿ Rained all day again. Roads are like early spring. Ruby is doing nicely. Baby doing nicely and I am feeling better each day. The baby's name will be Mona Mary. Mrs. MacDonald and Ethel were in tonight.

Thursday, June 22 ∿ Raining; and still raining down river and up. I guess is floods. Ruby and baby are doing nicely. Baby is a dear. I'm getting her crib fixed up today.

Friday, June 23 ∿ Cleared off about noon; been a lovely afternoon. We have had 10 callers tonight. Ruby and baby are doing nicely.

Sunday, June 25 ∿ Is very warm. Baby cried most all night last night. Has slept all day. Have had 12 callers today. Merle was to Sunday School and church this morning. Mona got her first present today. A pair of cute boots; quilted silk.

Monday, June 26 ∿ A lovely day. The baby cried all last night again. Mary Jones, Mrs. Jewett and Mrs. Harold Jones called tonight. I hope we get some sleep tonight.

Tuesday, June 27 ∿ Is fine day. Ruby set up an hour; not feeling very well. Baby had a 6 hour cry from 4 until ten. Mr. and Mrs. Willie Brewer and Vera [?] were in this evening.

Wednesday, June 28 ∿ Very nice day. Baby slept good last night, I preserved a quart and half of strawberries. Ruby set up nearly two hours. Baby had her 5 ½ hour cry. Rilla and Merle were to the corner to a pie social. Edna Lovegrove and Theora called tonight.

Friday, June 30 ∿ Very nice; warm. School ended today. We picked 3 qts. more berries. Ruby is not so well. Hayward had to go to the Dr. Baby awfully fretful tonight.

Sunday, July 2 ∾ Raining hard this morning; cleared away and been hot all day. Had quite a heavy earthquake shock this afternoon. Baby's been awfully troublesome this afternoon. Ruby is still in bed. Merle has had a headache all day. We had all Horace's family to call this afternoon and Drs. family.

Tuesday, July 11 ∾ A most lovely day. Baby has been better today. I have begin to feed her oatmeal gruel and I believe it will be better. *[This baby was only a month old, but some babies were given solid foods earlier than others because milk wasn't enough to satisfy their hunger.]* I have ironed and done some preserves.

Thursday, July 13 ∾ Very dull. Merle went down to F'ton this morning to spend a few days with Jack Wilcox. Verna went up to Willie Crouse's this afternoon intended coming back tonight hasn't come yet. The baby is getting good.

Monday, July 17 ∾ Very warm. I washed and done quite a lot of other jobs. We have began to use Melliam's *[Mellin's]* food for baby. *[Mellin's baby food was one of the first processed food products for infants.]* Mrs. Ray McDonald was in to call this afternoon.

Monday, July 24 ∾ Cool wind all day; turned awfully cold tonight. Merle has picked about six qts. of raspberries today. I canned them. I also did a big wash and made bread. Baby hasn't cried so much today.

Thursday, July 27 ∾ Very nice day. I have been to the W.A. at Mrs. Spencer's; a quilt on. Had such a pleasant afternoon. About 21 in all. Had a nice car ride. Baby has been better this afternoon. Mr. Coy and little Myrtle was here tonight.

Friday, July 28 ∾ Cloudy all day; looks like a heavy rain. Baby's been terrible troublesome all day. Edith McKeil was here for tea. Rilla was in on her way to singing school, We are expecting her to stay all night.

Saturday, July 29 ∾ Very nice; day lovely. Ruby has been up home all day. I had the baby; she has been good. We have been up to a band concert.

Tuesday, August 1 ∿ A very fine day. Just 19 years tonight since poor mamma passed away. Ruby moved back *[home]* tonight. She got a terrible fall down their cellar steps. We had such a fright. I was so afraid her limbs were broken. Oh, I am so thankful. She got some bruises but I hope that's all. Mrs. Staples came up there tonight. She went on to Zealand with us. Hayward and Jimmy brought us home in the car. Ruby and baby came too.

Tuesday, August 8 ∿ A lovely day. I did a big wash this morning. Merle and I went raspberrying this afternoon. We picked about 7 quarts. This evening I made jellie, jam, pie and biscuit. May, Annie and Maud called. It's a beautiful evening. Merle and I are planning to go blueberrying to the mouth of branch if nothing happens and all is well.

Wednesday, August 9 ∿ A perfect day. We have all been blueberrying up upper Keswick; 22 of us. We have some walk to find them and we were certainly tired out. Merle and I picked ten qts.

Friday, August 11 ∿ Very nice day. I have been very busy all day. Made three pies, bread, and stringed half a peck of beans, made bean salad, ironed. By that time it was five o'clock. Got Merle ready to go camping at upper Keswick. He and Luke *[Bubar]* went on morning train. Expect to be back tomorrow night. *[Stringing beans was a method of drying and keeping them for winter use.]*

Saturday, August 12 ∿ A lovely day. Merle came home tonight with two pails of blueberries. They have a new baby girl at the French home. *[The Durant's lived next door.]* I was over to see it. It looks to be 5 months old. Ruby, Hayward and baby came down late after I had given up all hope of them.

Tuesday, August 15 ∿ Very hot. I ironed, made bean salad, oiled the sewing machine, made four roller towels *[Roller towels hung on a rod and were moved along as each section became wet.]* and cut out and nearly made the baby a petticoat *[similar to a slip, and worn under a baby's or lady's skirt]*.

Saturday, August 19 ᐰ Very hot. It's my 47th birthday today. I got a nice book, a brush, comb and mirror and $3.00 for birthday gifts. Went up to Ruby's on train. Stayed all night for she and Hayward to go to Church in morning.

Wednesday, August 23 ᐰ A lovely day; very warm. I cooked for picnic; bread, beans, two loaves of cake, dressing and will have a potato salad. Have the salad made now.

Thursday, August 24 ᐰ The day of unveiling of the monument. *[A cenotaph to commemorate those who had died in WWI sat just east of the village until 1965 or 1966. During construction of the Mactaquac dam, the community-funded monument was moved to Mactaquac Provincial Park to make room for a large electrical substation at its former site.]* It's looked like rain any minute but has not yet. A large gathering at the picnic. Must have been over a thousand there. There is a concert tonight.

Friday, August 25 ᐰ Awfully windy. I was down to MacDonald's and picked some good cherries. I finished Mona's little slip and skirt. Mary Jones was in awhile.

Saturday, August 26 ᐰ Heavy rain; began about two o'clock this morning. Has rained all day; thunder and lightning. We have all been to the corner. There was a food sale left from picnic. Must have made 12 dollars *[for cenotaph expenses or other community events]*. Albert was to the city today.

Monday, August 28 ᐰ Still raining. Rained hard all night and all day. I washed and about half made a house dress for Ruby. School started today. Merle thinks he will like the new teacher; Miss Parker. I do hope he will.

Thursday, August 31 ᐰ A most beautiful day. Ruby and I took Mona and we stopped to Ida's to W.A. Albert has got the job in Farmer's store. Edna MacDonald was operated on.

Friday, September 1 ∾ Very warm; raining a little tonight. Albert thinks he will like his new job. I hope so.

Saturday, September 2 ∾ A very warm day. It's a beautiful moonlight night. Ruby and Hayward and baby are here. We had baby to the Farmer's store to have it weighed. It weighed 9 lbs, but she is gaining so. Ruby weighs 149; I, 164. *[There were two scales in the store. One was a table-top one for weighing small bulk items like candy and babies. The second was a floor scale for weighing large bulk items like flour, grains, etc. and people]*

Tuesday, September 5 ∾ A most beautiful day. I ironed and picked over a peck of cranberries. The evening is perfect.

Wednesday, September 6 ∾ A lovely cool day. I preserved about eleven qts. of damson plums, strained the cranberries for jellie. Cut out a house dress, the evening is perfect but very cold.

Thursday, September 7 ∾ A lovely but cold day; heavy frost last night. Ruby and I have spent day at Mrs. Wardlow Birds. We called on Mrs. Laird, Theora and Mrs. Dunk Brewer. Called at Wardlow's this evening. Hayward brought us home in car tonight. Ethel, Wardlow and children coming for a drive. It's a beautiful cold night.

Saturday, September 16 ∾ Cold, rainy. Mona is 3 months old today. Merle has been out butternutting *[picking wild butternuts which were similar to walnuts and used for cooking]*. 20 yrs today since little Marie was buried.

Sunday, September 17 ∾ A nice day cold tonight. We were all up to the Orange Sermon. The band was in attendance. We have all been to church. Maud brought us home. *[Orangemen were Protestant supporters of King William III of Orange. At one time the order discouraged any association with Catholics. For example, a Protestant who married a*

Catholic could not become a member of the Orange Order.]

Tuesday, September 19 ～ Nice day, but cold. I finished Ruby's house dress. About all I did do. I have a cold, don't feel extra good. There are detectives around trying to find the thieves who broke into the station Saturday Night. Had a letter from Grace today.

Thursday, September 21 ～ A lovely day. It's Albert's Birthday (55). Ruby and little Mona were down. Mary Jones was here to dinner. Ruby and I were over to see the French baby.

Friday, September 22 ～ A lovely day. I started to make mustard pickles and Albert came. Said we were invited down to the experimental farm with Mr. and Mrs. Will Hagerman. We left everything and went. Didn't even have breakfast dishes washed. Had a lovely trip. *[The Experimental Farm was an Agriculture Canada farm for testing new food crops, farming methods, and breeds of livestock.]*

Saturday, September 23 ～ A lovely day like summer. I have had to do two days work today to pay for yesterday. I'm tired. Mary Jones was here for dinner. Merle has been butternutting. He got over a bag full.

Tuesday, September 26 ～ Cold. I have been sewing at my silk waist all day. Have made about 3 qts of lovely clear crab-apple jellie, and made bread.

Thursday, October 5 ～ A lovely day, but cooler than yesterday. I've stitched two pairs of curtains. Am going to crochet an edge on them.

Friday, October 6 ～ Today Bennie Swim was hanged in Woodstock for double murder he committed last spring. I was in to call on Mrs. George Harris today. Also Mrs. G. Pugh. Our first snow today. *[She likely read about the hanging in the newspaper; because this is not a Burtt's Corner name. Bennie Swim murdered his ex-love and her new lover in a very grisly murder. He actually had to be hung twice because they cut him down early, and he survived the first attempt.]*

Sunday, October 15 〜 Looks so much like rain this morning, but cleared away. We have all been to church morning and evening. We were at Ruby's all day. Mona is getting so fat. Maud brought us home tonight. It is children's day as well as Harvest Thanksgiving.

Wednesday, October 18 〜 Cold, snowing some tonight. Awfully cold and windy now. We have all been to the coon show in the Farmer's Hall. *[In this time period 'coon' referred to black people. It is now considered a rude reference.]*

Saturday, October 21 〜 Still very cold. Have been busy all day bringing things out of the cold. Have one pair of my factory cotton curtains finished and up. Just read of a terrible accident on Saint John River down Kings County. Steamer dreans 4 lives lost. *[The steamship Dream sunk in about a minute near Gorham's Bluff on October 20. Five passengers died.]*

Monday, October 30 〜 Windy and rainy. Hayward said Mona seems better. Merle is at the hotel to a Halloween party for the Methodist church. I have washed and done a number of things today.

Tuesday, October 31 〜 Very nice but windy. I was up to confirmation. Such a lovely sermon by the Bishop. I was to Ruby's to dinner. The teacher has had a Halloween Party for children and parents. Merle didn't get home until nearly six.

Monday, November 6 〜 Thanksgiving day *[was first celebrated in Canada in 1879]*. Quite a wind. Little Mona has had cramps all afternoon. Ruby and she went home tonight. Hayward came after them. I see the little nest in pillow where *"Beauty's" [Mona]* head was and it made me lonesome.

Saturday, November 11 Armistice 〜 Four years today. Been quite warm today; raining tonight. I got windows washed outside today. Haven't been feeling well.

Sunday, November 12 〜 Squallie all day. Bad roads. Merle was at Sunday school this morning. We didn't get to church tonight. It's well we didn't, for its turned terrible cold and snowing. Mr. and Mrs. Coy spent the evening. So glad to have them.

Wednesday, November 22 ∞ Quite cold; squallie. I made Mona a dress today. Ruby gave me a nice pitcher. Mona a lovely girl. I expect she will be going home tomorrow.

Thursday, November 23 ∞ Nice and pleasant, but cold. Ruby and the Beauty went home tonight. Feel so lonesome without them. We made mince meat tonight. The Edgecombe block was burned today in F'ton.

Tuesday, November 28 ∞ Cold; looks like snow. I finished Mona's dress and made her two bibs. Was over to the French peoples. Murray Bird is here with Merle tonight.

Friday, December 1 ∞ Warm like summer. Feels like a big rain. I ironed and did some patching and fixing Merle's drawers *[long underwear]*.

Monday, December 11 ∞ a lovely day cold this morning. I washed, washed woodwork in kitchen and hall. Finished the ends for Graces scarf and some other things. My glasses haven't come yet.

Wednesday, December 13 ∞ Awfully cold and windy. My glasses came tonight. They annoy me awfully; the double visions. Have done quite a lot of xmas work today.

Thursday, December 14 ∞ A very nice day. Was so sure Ruby and baby would be down. I want to see Beauty so much. I was in to Mrs. Birds this afternoon. I finished a baby jacket tonight.

Friday, December 15 ∞ Cold; snowing all day. I made my fruit cake and a big loaf of ribbon cake and five mince pies. Merle is up to Bubar's. It's Bill's 14th birthday.

Wednesday, December 20 ∞ Very cold. We killed and I dressed four chickens. Last night was a very cold night.

Thursday, December 21 ∼ Warmer; snowed some little this morning. Ruby and Mona came down this morning for xmas. Mona has a lovely fifteen dollar sleigh. We sent Grace's parcels today. Ruby, Hayward and Merle are to the school concert. Murray Bird was here for tea.

Friday, December 22 ∼ A lovely warm day. We had the baby to corner in her new sleigh. She is so good, the darling. The concert was good last night. Didn't get home until quarter of 12.

Monday, December 25 ∼ Christmas Day. We have had another nice Christmas. We have all been well remembered. Mona and all been spared to meet another Christmas. The day has been perfect. Ruby, Mona and I were up to the Drs. this afternoon. Merle has been up to the Sunday school tree at church.

Friday, December 29 ∼ A terrible old time snow storm and drifts; wind gone down some tonight. I shortened Ruby's skirt, cut out two pair of sleepers for Merle, and started to make another pair.

Saturday, December 30 ∼ Very nice; but cold. I'm awfully tired and sleepy. It's after eleven. I've just bathed. Lucy Gorman was here for dinner.

Sunday, December 31 ∼ Very nice day; lovely moonlight night. We were down to see Mr. MacDonald. Don't think he will ever be much better. Will say good bye to the old year with all my mistakes and missteps. Mr. Bailey was laid to rest today.

1923

Wednesday, January 3 ᘓ A lovely day. I have been to Ruby's. Mona lovely. We were down to see Oliver. I got new oil cloth for my table. *[Some people used thin oil cloth floor covering on their kitchen table. It was strong and could handle a lot of wear. Those lucky enough to have a fine dining room table only used it for special occasions with a good tablecloth.]*

Monday, January 8 ᘓ A big snowstorm on tonight. I washed today. Don't know where my clothes will be by morning. *[She had hung them outside to dry.]*

Tuesday, January 9 ᘓ A terrible snowstorm. The clothes line broke. Albert was out at half after five this morning getting the clothes in. I've been all day getting them dry. I cleaned clothes room today. My Eaton order came; got a new copper wash boiler. *[There were no washing machines yet so she would have used the wash boiler to heat water on top of the stoves. She would have washed the clothes by stirring them around with a fork-like piece of wood or scrubbing them on a washboard.]* Very warm tonight. Lots of drifts everywhere.

Monday, January 15 ∿ Nice today, but a big snow storm on tonight again. Albert was helping shovel snow *[for the railway]* all the morning, drifts everywhere. Ruby and baby came down tonight. Baby had an awful crying spell; gas on her stomach. She is such a lovely big girl. I washed today. Hope the lines won't break.

Tuesday, January 16 ∿ Snowing again. Mr. Robert MacDonald died this Morning. Found him dead. Must have passed very peacefully in his sleep. I have been down there all day. Albert was to town today to have his eyes fitted. Twenty one year's today since little Marie was born. Mona is eleven months today.

Monday, January 22 ∿ Nice day. I washed; clothes are dry. Mrs. Durant was over this afternoon. She wants to talk English so much. Mrs. MacDonald has come up to Ray's *[her son's place]*.

Thursday, January 25 ∿ Worst snowstorm of the season. I fixed a mackinaw *[heavy coat]* for Merle and some other jobs. Jimmy Crouse ate his dinner in here. He said Dorothy and Rupert spent the day with Ruby yesterday.

Tuesday, January 30 ∿ Terrible cold; the wind is wild. Drifting. Blowed all night terrible. A *[railway]* car caught on fire tonight in the switch. Albert and Cobie saw it first. They kept it down with snow until a crowd come. It looked for awhile as if all the cars in the switch would go; station. A terrible night for a fire. *[The railway cars during this time period were wooden with steel corners.]* Mr. Will Allen was buried today.

Saturday, February 3 ∿ Snowed all day; wind started tonight. I done quite a lot of sewing today. Merle got a lovely box of chocolates today and a book from Grace. *[His birthday would be in a few days.]*

Monday, February 12 ∿ Very cold. I didn't wash. Thought I'd give my cold a chance to get better. There hasn't been any school today. Teacher sick. Edna MacDonald has the grip *[grippe]*.

Tuesday, February 13 ∿ Snowed all day. My cold is most well. I made a underwaist *[a slip]* and done several other jobs. Put clothes to soak *[in wash boiler]*.

Thursday, February 15 ∾ nice day. I have a very lame neck. I'm going to bed early. No school today; teacher is sick again. Merle is such a good boy; so thoughtful. Washed the dishes for me this morning without asking him.

Friday, February 23 ∾ Very nice day, but very cold wind. Mary Jones was here for dinner. Had a letter from Reuben. He says five foot of snow over there *[in Maine]*.

Monday, March 5 ∾ A big storm; the worst of the season. The heaviest. I have sewed all day made two nightdresses and pair of pillow cases.

Thursday, March 8 ∾ A terrible storm. Was blockaded up to Maud's. Couldn't get home until this morning. No train last night. The worst storm of the season. Elsie is still at Ruby's. The train got through from Otis this morning. Dr. and Maud went down to the opening of the house *[Provincial Legislature]*. No Woodstock train yet, and it's half after nine.

Wednesday, March 14 ∾ Snowing all day. My clothes [from Monday's wash] are still on the line loaded with snow. The snow is piled so high along the railroad, we can't see over them *[the snow banks]*. I have done quite a lot of sewing today. Albert is feeling miserable.

Thursday, March 15 ∾ Very cold this morning. 22 below zero Fahrenheit *[- 30° Celsius]*. Been pleasant today but cold wind. Was to the *[church]* annual. *[The Church annual was their directors meeting and was held in different parts of the province each year. Mary spoke about going to Miramichi one year for the event.]* Went up on train. Mrs. Spencer entertained us. Wasn't many there; roads are so bad. Ruby is suffering with toothache. She must go to town and have it extracted.

Wednesday, March 28 ∾ Awfully cold, the wind just howling. I made a housedress, all but pocket and snaps; scrubbed kitchen. Ethel MacDonald was over this evening. I had a letter from Annie Staples today and Easter cards from Grace.

Thursday, March 29 ∽ A terrible cold day. Everyone says last night coldest yet. I have been up to Ruby's. Albert is suffering terrible with a pain in ankle. Took him so suddenly. I have been bathing it in hot mustard water. *[This was a home remedy.]*

Friday, March 30, Good Friday ∽ Very nice; much warmer. Albert's ankle is better. Stella Maybe was in awhile this morning waiting for the train.

Saturday, March 31 ∽ A terrible snowstorm blowing and drifting like January instead of last of March. We intended to go up to Ruby's for Easter and go to church, but couldn't. I am disappointed for I thought I could get to church Easter.

Sunday, April 1 ∽ Easter Sunday. Cold and windy; nicer this afternoon. I was up to Baptist meeting and I enjoyed it. The singing was something beautiful. I was over to Mrs. Coy's this evening. Gladys and family are up. Was in to see Mrs. Jewett. She is very sick.

Wednesday, April 18 ∽ A lovely day. I scrubbed and ironed and went out for a little airing.

Friday, April 20 ∽ A lovely day; more like spring. I have been up to Ruby's all day. She is house cleaning. Mona and I had a great time.

Saturday, April 21 ∽ A lovely day. Snow going fast. The Tay Creek Mill crew came today.

Sunday, April 22 ∽ Not a very bright day. Merle was to church. The roads are very bad. We were over to see Mrs. Wesley Jones this afternoon. Merle has trapped two muskrats.

Friday, April 27 ∽ A lovely day. Ruby and the Beauty went home this morning. Miss the lovely thing so. I cleaned my bedroom. Haven't felt well. Frank Estey and Rena were in waiting for the train. Mr. Wesley

Jones died last night.

Sunday, April 29 ∿ Rained all night. A big freshet today. Water every-place and still rising. The French people has to move out to the cook house. *[They lived in the field next door but the ground was lower and more likely to flood than the Morehouse home.]* I was in bed until three o'clock this afternoon. A bad aching back. Tilley Bird's house burned.

Monday, April 30 ∿ It poured again all night and nearly all day. It is a perfect flood here. I guess the worst ever remembered. It's just flowed around our house all day and I thought maybe we would have to move upstairs but water has fallen a lot tonight. Looks like more rain. The *[railway]* track is simply torn to pieces. Have no idea when we will ever have a train.

Tuesday, May 1 ∿ Very nice day. Water has all gone down, but the wreck is sometimes unbelievable. Don't look as if things could be nor-mal this summer. It's terrible all over the country. I had 5 railroad men to supper. *[When additional railway men were brought from outside the community, they were housed in the railway work train that came during the summer for routine maintenance. Since these were unplanned repairs, they were fed by local people. The Morehouse home was closest to the railway, so they often served food to the railway workers as well as travellers waiting for the train.]*

Wednesday, May 2 ∿ A lovely day. I did a big wash. The train came as far as here. The damage every place is something awful. The Dr. *[who lived next to the river]* says it will take a thousand dollars to fix his place as it was before. *[$1,000 would be equivalent to $14,000 in 2016.]*

Friday, May 4 ∿ Cold, windy; feels like snow. I cleaned Ruby's bed-room and painted the floor. The mail came up today.

Saturday, May 5 ∿ Cold; windy and rain. The train has only got far as Stone Ridge. They will have to build a piece of new railroad above Stone Ridge.

☙ *1923* ❧

Wednesday, May 9 ∽ Very nice. Heavy wind this afternoon. Looks like a big rain. Merle and I moved the stove and cleaned the shed. We have had one hard day. I'm some tired. The train has made regular trips today for the first since the freshet.

Sunday, May 20 ∽ A lovely day; the warmest of season. I went to Ruby's last night. We were to church tonight. Walked home. A hard walk. I got a drive with Mr. and Mrs. Harry Brewer far as Drs. The Dr. folk have a new car.

Tuesday, May 22 ∽ Raining all day, but the trees and everything are looking lovely; *[rain]* bringing them right along. I cleaned upstairs hall and ironed quite a lot this evening, and put up four pairs of curtains. Mrs. Horace Gorman was in awhile waiting for the train.

Wednesday, May 23 ∽ Cold rainy. I started to clean down stairs hall. Am having a bad time with it trying to get the green *[paint]* off. I washed it and whited *[whitened]* it and it's a terrible sight. I tired myself sick over it. Mary Jones was in to dinner. Mrs. Inch was in this evening waiting for the train.

Thursday, May 24 ∽ Cold and windy. I finished hall. Had a terrible time with it. Gave ceiling another coat of green after all. Merle has picked sacks worth of greens *[fiddleheads]* today. He has gone to the concert or play tonight.

Friday, May 25 ∽ Awfully windy, quite pleasant. Very much like rain tonight. I've finished the house cleaning; lots of finishing to do yet. Merle got $14 dollars for his seven muskrats, two dollars apiece.

Saturday, May 26 ∽ Cold and showery. I went up to Ruby's on the train and back on next one. Mona is so cute. Jeddie Brewer was burned out last night. All the buildings, but a little car house. Mrs. Brewer is burned badly about the face.

Friday, June 1 ∽ Warmer; awfully smokey. Must be a fire near us. Ruby and Baby went home this morning. Two years today since Ruby was married. I was over to the cook car to see Mrs. Jackson. *[The annual railway repair crew travelled along the railway to where they were needed. Their train consisted of a cook car, at least one sleeper car, and a materials/tools car.]*

Tuesday, June 5 ∿ Awfully dark with smoke. I painted hall and sitting room; first coat of ground paint. It's raining some tonight. All are glad.

Wednesday, June 6 ∿ A lovely warm day. I varnished the sitting room and went to W.A. this afternoon. I stayed to Wardlow Birds for tea. Ethel came down to corner with me.

Saturday, June 9 ∿ Cold and windy. Trying to rain. Didn't write Saturday Night. Couldn't get over the varnished paint. We had to sleep down stairs. I have finished the painting and papering. Was up to Ruby's between trains. She has the linoleum laid upstairs. It's great; also her dining room alabastered. I have been to the corner. It's late.

Monday, June 11 ∿ A terrible wind and a bad fire some place; awfully smokey. I painted and varnished all day. Mrs. Durant asked to go out in their car, so we were up to Ruby's. Stopped at corner for ice cream.

Thursday, June 14 ∿ The lovely rain has come. Was needed so badly. I hope it rains all night to put out the awfully fires. Have finished two white dresses for Mona.

Saturday, June 23 ∿ A lovely day, but rain badly needed. I finished Ruby's gingham dress. Ruby and Mona came down tonight. We have all been to corner. Mona had a great time. *[Gingham is cloth with a square design that is still available today.]*

Sunday, June 24 ∿ A lovely day, but so dry and windy. Terrible for the forest fires. We were up the corner for a walk with Mona and down to Randolph's for the milk.

Monday, July 2 ∿ Lovely; quite hot. This evening is beautiful. I washed and finished Ruby's voile dress. Quite a number from F'ton spent the

[July 1st] holiday at the corner.

Wednesday, July 4 ◡ Have just got home from the social; it's very late. I went up on train to Ruby's this morning. Has look showery all day. Our baskets sold very well. Merle stayed all night at Ruby's.

Saturday, July 7 ◡ Been awfully cold all day. It's like October tonight. Have been up to corner tonight. Mrs. Durant asked me to go to F'ton with them, but it's so cold I didn't want to go. *[Some of the earlier cars did not have heaters.]*

Sunday, July 8 ◡ A lovely day. Merle was to Sunday school. We don't get to church very often this summer. I was up to Baptist this afternoon. *[They often walked at least two miles to their church, so if it's raining, very windy or cold, they stayed home.]*

Monday, July 9 ◡ A very hot day. I washed. Merle and some more boys went to Douglas to pick strawberries for Emerson Hawkins. Came back tonight until some more are ripe. Frank Graham died very suddenly yesterday; so sad. Was buried few minutes after he died of diphtheria *[so the disease wouldn't spread to anyone else in the community].*

Tuesday, July 10 ◡ Very warm; looked so much like rain this morning. Cooler tonight. I preserved fifteen boxes of wild strawberries and made my voile dress. *[Although they could get cultivated berries, people made use of every available item they could to preserve food for winter.]*

Friday, July 13 ◡ Awfully warm, and so dry. Merle went to Douglas again today. Ruby is still here. They have started closing the stores three nights out of the week. Started Wednesday, July 11th. Don't know how it will work. *[Times were getting tough because New Brunswick was in a post-war recession.]*

Tuesday, July 24 ◡ A lovely day. Went to visit Jeddie Brewer. They bought the Charlie Burtt place after their home burned.

Friday, August 3 ◡ Very hot. Albert is learning to run the truck *[may-*

be his own, or the one for the store where he worked]. I was out with him today. Went down around by Colter's bridge.

Sunday, August 12 ∿ Very dull and cold. Ruby and I went to church and left Mona with Albert, and poor little thing cried after us. Awful poor girlie.

Saturday, August 18 ∿ A lovely day and little shower this afternoon. The rollers *[Members of the Pentecost church were sometimes referred to as the Pentecost Holy Rollers because of their very active singing.]* are at the corner tonight. Ruby and Mona came down on train. We were all at the corner.

Wednesday, August 29 ∿ been a close muggy day rained hard this morning. We have all been to the hall to a social for Pearl Bird. Made $57 dollars.

Saturday, September 1 ∿ Cold; showery at times. Have been to the corner. The rollers were there again tonight.

Monday, September 3 ∿ A windy warm day. I washed, and done a peck of cranberries into jellie. It's raining a little now.

Wednesday, September 5 ∿ Another lovely day. I ironed and made bread and bean salad. I'm awfully tired and sleepy. The disciple church are having a chicken supper tonight.

Saturday, September 8 ∿ Another lovely day. We have had the last band concert of the season. Horace Morehouse family were here today.

Tuesday, September 11 ∿ A lovely day. Ruby and I had Mona to town to have her pictures taken. She was a lovely girl. Grace came tonight. She brought Mona a lovely new dress.

Thursday, September 13 ∿ A cloudy, foggy day. We have been to Ruby's all day. Didn't get home until late. Mrs. Durwood Allen has another daughter; born today and I guess Mrs. Urban Haines. Mrs. Sandy Jones died today.

Saturday, September 22 ᕼ A lovely day; a perfect night. Went up to Ruby's. Merle came on his wheel. Albert came after work was done in store. Rena Estey and children also came up to Ruby's.

Monday, September 24 ᕼ A very nice warm day; tonight is perfect. I have done a whole lot of work today. Washed and scrubbed, ironed a little, made cake and cookies and cut my tomatoes up. I'm so tired, I can hardly get ready for bed.

Monday, October 1 ᕼ A terrible cold day. A heavy frost last night. Rain, wind and cold today. I washed and had to bring the big things like sheets and blankets in awhile. Ruby and Mona came tonight.

Tuesday, October 9 ᕼ A lovely day. I made bread and cookies, ironed and made cake. Mr. and Mrs. Coy and Elsie spent the evening with us.

Wednesday, October 10 ᕼ A beautiful day. I have been to Ruby's all day. We had a farewell party for Mr. and Mrs. Spencer *[the minister and his wife]* tonight. Had a nice little time. Gave him a lovely reading lamp, and she a nice puff.

Friday, October 12 ᕼ A lovely summer day. I cut Merle two pairs of sleepers, and knit some on his sweater. Merle shot a partridge tonight.

Sunday, October 14 ᕼ Very nice and warm. We were all to church, morning and evening. Mona too. She was a dear good girl. The church looked nice with its Harvest trimmings. Mr. Spencer's last Sunday with us. We don't like to see them leave for we have liked them very much.

Thursday, October 25 ᕼ Weather unsettled. I was to W.A. Have been down to Tilley Bird's tonight to a house warming *[for their new home, their previous house had burnt down.]* Had a lovely time.

Tuesday, October 30 ᕼ Looks like a storm all day. Started tonight. It's raining, wind blowing, and thunder and lightning. We have been up to Mr. Bubar's to a Halloween party for the Methodist church; a big crowd there. Sold lunches, candy and ice cream.

Wednesday, October 31 ❧ Very nice day. Snowing some tonight for the first. We have been to Willie Crouse's to Pearl's wedding. It was a lovely wedding. The bride looked lovely in white satin and lace and bridal veil. Muriel played the wedding March.

Friday, November 9 ❧ Colder but bright. Mrs. Sam Crouse was in awhile on her way to Mrs. Ben Jones. I cleaned my bedroom today, and baked bread. Was up to see Pearl Bird this afternoon.

Sunday, November 11 ❧ Armistice day. Was celebrated here with a service at Baptist Church; wreaths and crosses of poppies laid on the monument now erected. Was celebrated in F'ton with unveiling of the monument for F'ton boys. It's been a lovely day.

Thursday, November 15 ❧ Very nice day. Cold; looked so much like snow this morning. I have been to W.A. at Ruby's. Mona is such a dear sweet girlie. One of Will Burtt's little girls died this morning. Little Doris was taken to hospital and operated on for something, but she died shortly afterward.

Sunday, November 18 ❧ Raining hard all day. Merle caught a skunk in his trap and the perfume has been lovely all day.

Monday, November 19 ❧ Cold, like winter. I washed and finished Mona's mittens.

Tuesday, November 20 ❧ Very cold all day, but warmer tonight. I fixed a blouse for Merle and a pair of overalls and was down to Mrs. Mac-Donald's awhile.

Monday, November 26 ❧ Cleared off; been warm. Colder tonight. I cleaned the dining room and put clothes to soak *[in the wash boiler]* and footed a sock. *[When the toe or heel of a sock wore thin, Mary would foot it to avoid throwing it away. She would cut out the end of the foot and unravel the yarn back to the straight leg part. Then she picked up the stitches with her knitting needles and re-knit the foot part.]*

❧ *1923* ❧

Friday, November 30 ∾ St. Andrews day. Dull; raining again tonight. I ironed and made Mona's bloomers. *[Frilly underpants that were worn by baby girls over their diapers. Another version had longer legs for toddlers to wear under their dresses.]*

Monday, December 3 ∾ Warm like spring. Raining a little at times, sun shining at times. Looks like rain tonight. I washed and cleaned kitchen, put a border on a handkerchief tonight, and done quite a lot of knitting. Herb Haines oldest daughter is dead; a Mrs. Wilkinson. She was about Ruby's age. Poor little girl leaves two babies.

Friday, December 14 ∾ Colder. Rained all night last night, but it's going to freeze hard tonight. I was up to the store and it's awfully cold. The river boats are still running same as summer. *[Paddle-wheeled boats ran in the Saint John River from Fredericton to Saint John. Car ferries also transported people back and forth across the river in several locations.]* People who remember, say we haven't had a fall like this or winter since 1878; forty years ago.

Saturday, December 15 ∾ Colder, skating today. I made my fruit, nut, and ribbon cake today.

Tuesday, December 18 ∾ Cold; very cold. Our school closed today *[for Christmas]*. I made my xmas pies today.

Wednesday, December 19 ∾ Cold but pleasant. We killed four chickens today. Ruby and Mona are here tonight. Ruby, Hayward and Merle have been to a musical show.

Sunday, December 23 ∾ Dark; snowing a little all day. There was a fire at the corner last night. Howard Burtt's and Howard Gorman's house, store, barn and all their buildings. Started about quarter past eleven. Hayward, Ruby and Mona came down in middle of the night. *[Hayward got there just as the wooden water tower collapsed and fell down over the hill. The community water was piped from a spring about a mile away through a wooden pipeline made from bored-out logs.]*

Monday, December 24 ∾ Xmas eve. A lovely, lovely day. Ruby, Hayward and Mona are here. We have just finished fixing the tree and it's nearly 12 o'clock. Merle has been to a band concert.

Tuesday, December 25 ∾ Xmas day. A lovely day and Santa Claus was awfully good again. We were all certainly well remembered. Mona has had a great time. We were over to Ray's a little while.

Sunday, December 30 ∾ A lovely, wintry day. I was up to Baptist church. Mr. Barton spoke lovely. Merle was up to Sunday school. His gift from the Sunday school was such a nice book; *"If any man sin"*, by Hiram Alfred Cody *[First edition was published in 1915]*. It's great. Merle got another tie and a lovely box of handkerchiefs from the Drs. folk.

Monday, December 31 ∾ The end of the old year which has been a very pleasant one. Many, many blessings have been bestowed on us, which we have not been half thankful enough for. This has been a very cold day to what we have been having. Began to snow about two o'clock; snowed quite a lot. Merle is at the hall to a show. Good bye to the old year with all my failures and mistakes.

1924

Wednesday, January 2 ∾ Very cold; but bright. We have all been to pictures tonight. They were good *"Ten Nights in a Bar Room"*. I was up to Mrs. Bubar's awhile. Merle is in the store helping *[Albert]* while Wassie *[Bird]* is away.

Friday, January 4 ∾ A lovely morning, but cold and blowing this afternoon. Mrs. Bubar and I drove up to Ruby's, and my-oh-my it was cold. The horse merely walking. *[The Bubar's would have put their car in a shed for the winter.]* Beauty *[Mona]* has a cold.

Monday, January 7 ∾ Very cold, I didn't wash. I have a cold and such a sore nose. I made a box for photos, put my clothes to soak, and finished a mitten and other odd jobs.

Thursday, January 10 ∾ Stormy. I have been to Ruby's and to W.A. Dear little Mona has a sore arm. I think a sprain. She is such a dear. George Harris dropped dead today. He was out the Tay *[River]* working in the mill.

Sunday, January 13 ∾ A most beautiful day. G. Harris was buried today. A large funeral; the Masons had charge. We have all been to the Methodist Meeting. A whole sled load with Randolph Maybe's team. Had a good Sermon.

Wednesday, January 16 ⌒ A beautiful day; looks and sounds very much like a storm tonight. Today is Marie's birthday; would have been 22. A year today since Mr. R. MacDonald died.

Thursday, January 17 ⌒ A perfect day; rained last night and today is like last of April. I was in to Mrs. Bird's today and Mrs. Wardlow Bird was here awhile. Merle has just come in from coasting *[sliding]*. The evening is a perfect moonlight.

Friday, January 18 ⌒ A lovely, but pretty cold day. I walked out to Willie Brewer's today. He, Mr. B brought me home tonight. Is lovely and moonlight. The road hill is full of coasters *[people sliding on the main road. The roadways would be snow covered, and the only traffic would be the occasional horse and sled.]*

Tuesday, January 22 ⌒ Very, very, cold. The windows have been frosted all day. *[Their windows would be frosted up because they were single pane glass. Most likely, they also had storm windows on the outside of the house that were attached to the main window frames by metal lever snaps.]* Ruby and beauty went home tonight. The house seems so quiet.

Friday, January 25 ⌒ A big snow storm; worst storm of the season. Cleared off about four. Warm tonight. Merle is up to Bubar's playing games. *[The Bubar's lived on the hill behind the Morehouse property.]*

Sunday, January 27 ⌒ A real winter day; wind blowing, drifting and so cold. We have hardly poked our noses out.

Wednesday, January 30 ⌒ A lovely day. I was up to Jeddie Brewer's for a walk. Lots of people out this afternoon.

Friday, February 1 ⌒ Nice day; cold wind. I finished my ironing, made a clothes pin apron, cut out a house dress, and done some other jobs.

[The clothespin apron was actually two mini-aprons sewn back to back to make a holder for clothespins. The ladies inserted a clothes hanger and hung them near their clothesline to hold clothespins. These were used into the 1960s.]

Saturday, February 2 ∾ Very nice day. I think the woodchuck saw his shadow alright for it was very bright. I have been very busy today. Never got my work all done until nearly four o'clock.

Friday, February 8 ∾ Very pleasant, but pretty cold. I was up to the corner and in to the French peoples. Mrs. Will Burtt has another boy, 12, I think in all. *[Large families were beneficial to maintain the large farms most families managed. The older girls often helped look after the younger children.]*

Saturday, February 16 ∾ Very, very, cold. Edna Wilkins was in. I bought a pretty house dress from her, I'm afraid she suffered with cold before she got home.

Sunday, February 17 ∾ A lovely bright, but cold day. The evening is perfect. I was out just walking to get the air and met Randolph and Stella Maybe coming. They spent the evening.

Thursday, February 21 ∾ It's been a lovely day after the storm. I thought it was going to rain but it's been a lovely day. I was to the corner; got a green check gingham *[cloth]* for a dress.

Monday, February 25 ∾ A very nice day; washed clothes and dried nicely. Mrs. Jewett called and asked me to spend the afternoon with her tomorrow. I covered a large work box today and Merle put the hinges and feet on for me.

Wednesday, February 27 ∾ A beautiful spring day. I ironed and nearly made my cream serge skirt.

Sunday, Mar 2 ∾ A lovely day. We have been up to Ruby's. Willie Brewer and family with a double rig *[sled]* came after us. We had a lovely day. Mona was delightful.

Tuesday, March 4 ∾ A lovely day; snow disappearing with this wind. I have been to the Methodist aid at Mr. Leard's; about 60 there.

Thursday, March 6 ∾ A lovely warm day. I made bread, scrubbed and ironed. Had a nice lot of callers this evening; Mrs. Ambrose Allen, Mable Jones, Ethel Macdonald, Mrs. Willie Jones and Mrs. Coy and Myrtle.

Tuesday, March 11 ∾ Cold and windy; has been all the week. I have nearly made a gingham dress for myself. Had a letter from Annie Weaver. She writes that Uncle James Leckey is dead; the last of four boys in family.

Wednesday, March 12 ∾ Awfully windy and a snow storm has started The Otis train is off the tracks somewhere about upper Keswick.

Saturday, March 15 ∾ A nice but cold day. Hayward, Ruby and Mona came tonight. I have just came home from the Frenchman's. They have a new girl. It's about 1 am.

Monday, March17 ∾ A cold blustery day. Our W.A. Annual was to be today but I don't think it has been. Our school teacher is sick, no school today.

Wednesday, March 26 ∾ Very warm day. A cold night last night, and cold tonight again. Had a letter from Grace. Mrs. Jack Pugh died this morning; only been sick a few days with pneumonia. How the poor crippled boy will miss her. A lot of sickness now. We have colds here.

Friday, March 28 ∾ A very nice day. Mrs. Jack Pugh was buried today. My cold is better, Albert's is not any worse. Merle is dumping tonight *[diarrhea or vomiting]*.

Monday, April 7 ∾ A terrible grey windy day, cold. I washed and never put clothes on line until four o'clock. Thought wind would die down but it's blowing hard as ever. This is our 27 anniversary.

❧ *1924* ❧

Wednesday, April 9 ᑯ A grey rainy morning; nicer toward noon and tonight. I ironed and made doughnuts, done some sewing, and finished a book, *"The Valley of the Giants"*. *[May be an edition by Peter B. Kyne, printed in 1918.]*

Thursday, April 10 ᑯ Warmer and more pleasant today, but cold and grey yet. I have been to the W.A. to Ruby's all day. We were tacking the silk quilt. *[Tacking was very different from quilting. Quilting was a series of small stitches along a line in the quilt design. Tacking was done on two pieces of cloth of equal size laid upon each other with a lining of quilt batting between the two pieces. Then small strips of yarn or thread were pulled through the entire three layers and tied in knots. This was done in a squared or diagonal pattern across the entire blanket. The knots ensured that the blanket pieces stayed together, but the process was not as much work as actual quilting.]*

Sunday, April 13 ᑯ Very nice; chilly wind. I was down to see Mrs. MacDonald dear old friend. I don't believe she's as well as she was.

Monday, April 14 ᑯ A heavy fall of snow last night. Been a fine day, but a cold wind this afternoon. Been no school this afternoon; the teacher is sick. Bruce and Murray Bird were here to dinner.

Friday, April 18 ᑯ Good Friday. I am feeling a whole lot better. My new mattress came today.

Monday, April 21 ᑯ A nice bright day, but mud and snow to your knees. I cleaned my bedroom and Ruby washed for me.

Wednesday, April 23 ᑯ Raining and sunshine mixed. Merle and I between, gave the woodwork in upstair hall the first coat of paint. Water rising today, rained hard last night.

Thursday, April 24 ᑯ Cold; raining quite hard tonight. I have been up to Ruby's all day. We cleaned all of her silver. *[This would be her cutlery and possibly a tea-serving set.]*

Tuesday, April 29 ◠ Nice but windy. I ironed today. Ruby and Mona came down. Hayward, Ruby and Merle have gone to the pictures. Mona has been a dear. Went to bed so good. Said *"Night Mayme." [Mary was known in the community as Mayme. Perhaps it was her granddaughter who gave her the nickname.]*

Thursday, May 1 ◠ Cold rain; all day water rising rapidly, I cleaned Merle's bedroom today and wrote two letters.

Sunday, May 4 ◠ Very nice but raining tonight. We were over at the *[railway]* car and called on Mr. and Mrs. Jackson, and I was down to see Mrs. MacDonald, and tonight we thought we would go to Methodist meeting; got as far as Wardlow's and it began to rain. We came home between showers.

Saturday, May 10 ◠ A very nice day. I have Neuralgism *[neuralgia]* in my head and I sure do some suffering. Mrs. Leard and Mrs. Wardlow Bird called this afternoon.

Monday, May 12 ◠ Very nice day, but cold and raining tonight. I'm thankful for the big days work I've been able to do. I washed, scrubbed, ironed and varnished the woodwork in upstair hall and did some sewing, My head is better. Pearl Kantnor and little Mona K. were in this evening.

Tuesday, May 13 ◠ Raining and cold. I painted all the bedroom floors and done some ironing and different jobs; got the new blinds up.

Thursday, May 15 ◠ Raining all the morning. Merle and I cleaned the shed and we had one busy day. We moved the stove at five o'clock this morning.

Friday, May 16 ◠ I finished the shed. Took me all day to finish. I'm awfully glad it's done. Merle and 4 or 5 other boys have gone to Fish Lake fishing. I miss him.

Tuesday, May 20 ◠ Cold and windy again. We made Mona another bloomer suit today. The dear has done so much walking, I hope she won't be too tired.

Thursday, May 22 ⌒ Awfully cold; raining tonight. We have cleaned the church today, expecting the new minister next week, a Mr. Palmer.

Sunday, May 25 ⌒ Raining all day; a lovely soft growing rain *[for the gardens]*. I've been in the house all day and enjoyed the rest.

Tuesday, May 27 ⌒ A very nice day. I ironed and went up on the train to Ruby's and to church. Mr. Hailstone and Mr. Grey arrived while we were eating supper. They are both very nice. We were all to service. Seven ministers; the dean preached the sermon, Maud brought me home.

Wednesday, May 28 ⌒ Raining all day. I cleaned the upstairs hall, painted the floor and painted the stove pipes and heaters. *[Maybe all the paint, varnish, and cleaner fumes caused her headaches. She seemed to paint or varnish on rainy days when the windows would be shut. The first paints and varnishes contained lead. Any solvents used for cleaning brushes also had strong fumes.]*

Thursday, May 29 ⌒ A lovely day; showery toward night. I cleaned the sitting room. We have 12 new chicks.

Sunday, June 1 ⌒ We have been to church twice. We like the new Englishman fine. Alfred and Edith drove us home.

Monday, June 2 ⌒ Very nice; quite warm. Not so windy. I washed, painted the steps, finished varnishing hall floor. Scrubbed shed and other things. Merle has gone to Fish Lake fishing he and Bill and Luke.

Tuesday, June 3 ⌒ Quite warm, rained this afternoon. I varnished chairs and dining room floor and ironed. Merle came home about half past four. He caught about three dozen fish.

Friday, June 6 ⌒ A very warm day. I cleaned silver and the linen drawers.

[undated and written in the margin of her diary] The new cook house built this year *[for the mill near the railway station].*

Thursday, June 12 ∿ A lovely day but fires are raging at Doyn *[Dorn]* Ridge. The Mill crew and all the men around was ordered out between five and six to fight it. They all came back about nine and are going again in the morning. But it looks very much like rain. I was to town *[Fredericton]* this morning and in to see Mrs. Harrison. *[While she was there, she saw Mrs. Harrison.]*

Friday, June 13 ∿ Looked like rain all day, but none yet. The fire is under control; the men were all out fighting it this morning.

Monday, June 16 ∿ Showery. Lovely growing showers. This is Mona's birthday; two years old. She came down tonight to get her rocking horse we got for her. We have been to corner. 20 years today since my baby was born and died. *[Mary and Albert must have lost a second child.]*

Wednesday, June 18 ∿ A lovely day. Had a shower about noon, but it was a lovely growing shower. Merle, Luther and two or three others have gone away up the creek fishing. Expect to be gone four days. I was over to the cook car to call on Mrs. Kelley. *[The Jackson's may have left or there could be a second cook there.]*

Friday, June 20 ∿ Another beautiful day. I have made a dress today. Mrs. Kelly was over from the car this afternoon. I have been in to Mr. Fowler's and Randolph's tonight.

Sunday, June 22 ∿ Raining this morning a little; cleared beautifully this afternoon. We were to early 8 o'clock celebrations and to half past ten service, and evening service *[three church services in one day].* Mr. Prescott preached tonight.

Monday, June 23 ∿ Warm, the warmer day this summer. I washed, scrubbed and done some sewing, I was at corner tonight and had an ice cream. Merle has been doing the road work today. *[They hired men who* *weren't working to do road work and often it was credited towards their local taxes. Although Merle was only a teenager, he could work for credit towards his family's bill.]*

Saturday, June 28 ⤳ Warm; so dry. We need rain so badly. I was to the corner tonight. The band is out to the Tay or Cross Creek and things are dull at the corner tonight.

Tuesday, July 1 ⤳ A very nice day. The Methodists has had a picnic today in the Foresters Hall. Mr. and Mrs. George Boone are having their 50th anniversary tonight.

Wednesday, July 2 ⤳ Very warm. I was up to the store and helped unpack dishes *[new ones that had come in for sale in the store]*. Ruby, Hayward and Mona were down awhile tonight. We were up to the corner.

Thursday, July 3 ⤳ A very hot day. I was up to Mrs. Ed Brewers to W.A. quilting. Quite a number there. I've been up to the store all the evening.

Friday, July 4 ⤳ Very warm. I made doughnuts and an apron. Was up to the corner tonight. There's a play from Prince William tonight in the Foresters Hall. *[Often church groups from around the county visited other communities and put on plays to raise funds for their church.]*

Saturday, July 5 ⤳ Very hot and dry. We have all been working in the store tonight. Just got home nearly 12 o'clock.

Monday, July 7 ⤳ A lovely day; not too hot. Lovely moonlight night. The band has played all the evening practicing for the celebration of 12th at St. John.

Friday, July 11 ⤳ Lovely today, so cool. We have some woman here tonight. A Mrs. Nerie [?] saleing *[selling]* books.

Saturday, July 12 ⤳ Hot, hot, and still hot tonight. We have just got home from the corner. The rollers sure were there tonight.

Saturday, July 19 ∽ Showery. We have all been at the corner. I sold the ice cream *[at the store]*. The rollers *[referring to Pentecost Holy Rollers]* were at the corner again.

Tuesday, July 22 ∽ A warm day; looks much like rain. I have canned some berries and have started a voile dress for Mrs. Durant. It's a plaid and I've had some time with it. Arthur Pugh and Annie Gilby are married. Don't know when, but we just heard it.

Monday, July 28 ∽ Lovely day. I washed and canned a few sealers of raspberries and finished Mrs. Durant's dress.

Thursday, July 31 ∽ Lovely and cool. Mona and I were to Nashwaaksis in the truck *[with Albert]*. Mona enjoyed it. She and Ruby went home tonight. The house is so lonely without them.

Friday, August 1 ∽ Lovely day. Twenty one year's today since poor mother passed away. Mrs. Palmer and Miss Hailstone were in a little while. Mr. and Mrs. Palmer and Mr. Hailstone and Oscar were swimming. I canned about 3 qts. of raspberries.

Saturday, Aug 2 ∽ Very nice; a few little showers. I went up to Ruby's on the train. I have two boils or something under my arm. We were up the tracks a ways picking blueberries. Hayward took us on the motor. Mona calls them blue strawberries.

Thursday, Aug 7 ∽ Awfully hot; a shower this morning, no thunder, but a terrible thunderstorm this afternoon. Merle just got home as the shower started. The worst shower in years. *[25 mm or almost an inch fell in Fredericton.]*

Friday, August 8 ∽ Very warm but the air is clear. Alfred Hanson dropped dead tonight. Was at the store about seven o'clock, about as well as usual. He has been miserable all summer.

Monday, August 11 ∽ Lovely cool day; a perfect evening. I washed, scrubbed, made pies, and have a dress half made. Have been to the corner this evening. Came home with Alfred and Edith. Merle cut his hand with the axe. He almost fainted.

Tuesday, August 12 ∼ Dull; been raining since about 3 to 8. Merle and some more boys are at Fish Lake again. I finished Mrs. Durant's dress and cut another one out.

Saturday, August 16 ∼ A lovely day. I canned my blueberries today. Merle wheeled to F'ton, was back before one. I have been up helping sell ice cream. It's a perfect moonlight night.

Tuesday, August 19 ∼ A lovely day. I am 49 today. Ruby and Mona gave me two pairs of silk stockings, a book, a bottle of perfume and some money for a sweater. They went home tonight. Mr. and Mrs. Palmer called. *[New minister and wife.]*

Tuesday, August 16 ∼ Rain a downpour. Has been since two o'clock but it's simply poured since four. Hope its cleared by tomorrow. Merle is still at the lake. I cooked for the picnic today. Rolls and two cakes and made a big mess on one cake; spoiled it will have to make another one. I made pies and if fine in the morning and all is well will make the rest.

Wednesday, August 27 ∼ A lovely day. It rained so hard last night *[53 mm or 2 in. in Fredericton]* I thought our picnic was done, but its surely been a perfect day for a picnic. We had a large crowd.

Thursday, August 28 ∼ A lovely day. I was to F'ton this afternoon to have my eyes tested. I don't know whether I should have had it done or not. It is costing $15.00 for just the lens alone *[$211 in today's dollars]*. Merle has gone to the old camp again. I don't know who went with him. He went while I was away. I *[I'm]* afraid they will come in contact with a bear yet for they are very plentiful. *[And they would have both been looking for berries.]*

Monday, September 1 ∼ Cloudy all day. A big picnic for the band this afternoon. We were all up. Orchester *[orchestra]* is up tonight. A big crowd all the afternoon.

Friday, September 5 ∿ Raining; cold. I done pickles and quite a lot of sewing. They didn't clear nothing at the Band picnic; something strange. Took in 5 or 6 hundred dollars. Had a letter from Reuben they have another boy.

Friday, September 12 ∿ Has looked like rain; it's a lovely moonlight night. I have done my chow, must have ten or eleven qts. of it.

Monday, September 15 ∿ A lovely day. I washed and ironed and to-night I have chopped red tomatoes and celery and other vegetables for pickles. Its nearly eleven o'clock.

Tuesday, September 16 ∿ A lovely day. Merle has gone to the Lake again. He went so quickly I hardly knew it until he was gone. There was a man killed in Elwood's mill at Doaktown today.

Thursday, September 25 ∿ A lovely day; very cold last night. Was called up to Ruby's about four this morning. She has a lovely new boy. Am awfully tired. Mona's delighted with the baby. *[Like the first pregnancy, there was no mention of it until the child was born.]*

Saturday, September 27 ∿ A lovely day. I have certainly had some busy day. I scrubbed every room in the house but one, and done cooking and sewing and am going back to Ruby's tonight.

Tuesday, September 30 ∿ I came down from Ruby's today and brought Mona. I have been up there since Saturday night. Ruby is real smart *[alert]*. She had lots of callers Sunday. Mona is a dear. We had quite an earthquake this am. Ruby was very frightened; I slept through it.

Sunday, October 5 ∿ Lovely day; the woods is a picture *[fall colours]*. Ruby is up today and pretty well. Baby is pretty good. Mona was to church with us. I intended to bring her home with me but I wasn't feeling well and I was afraid I wouldn't be able to take care of her.

Tuesday, October 7 ∿ Lovely day. I have been up helping varnish the seats in the church. Was to Ruby's to supper. She and baby are doing pretty good.

Thursday, October 9 ⌒ Awfully cold; such a terrible wind. The pretty leaves are just sailing. I made crab apple jellie and squash pies and bread.

Wednesday, October 15 ⌒ Another lovely day. Merle has worked two weeks picking potatoes. His back gets pretty tired.

Monday, October 20 ⌒ Very cold, and I was up to help Ruby today and found her sick. I brought Mona home with me. The baby is better. The Dr. put him on rice water and he is good, but so poor.

Thursday, October 23 ⌒ A lovely day. I took the beauty home today. Baby was awfully fretful today.

Friday, October 24 ⌒ A lovely day. I think I have finished Mona's coat. Merle shot a partridge today.

Monday, October 27 ⌒ A lovely summer day. I done a big washing. Merle thinks of going to work in the woods tomorrow. Just thinking of it, my wee boy.

Thursday, October 30 ⌒ Lovely again. We heard that Merle is swamping in the woods and likes it. *[Swamping is the action of clearing underbrush and trees in order to make a trail through the woods.]* I called on Edith Bird this afternoon and Mrs. Coy, Jewett and Oliver. Ethel Brewer was here this evening.

Sunday, November 2 ⌒ Warm but looks like a storm. Ruby's baby was baptized this morning and Mrs. Stewart Brewers baby, and Harley Burtt's, Edith.

Wednesday, November 5 ⌒ Cold. Merle came home. His winter's work is done. Older men came in and the boys had to leave. Durant's are moving tomorrow.

Saturday, November 8 ⌒ Awfully cold tonight the wind just lifting *[blowing]* things. Mona is awfully good.

Tuesday, November 11 ∿ Armistice Day. A perfect day. I washed, scrubbed, made bread, two kinds of cookies and biscuits. It's such a beautiful moonlight night; seems too nice to go to bed.

Saturday, November 15 ∿ A lovely day, road like summer. We have all been up to Wassie Birds to hear the new radio but we didn't hear anything *[may have been a reception issue]*.

Sunday, November 16 ∿ A lovely day. They have celebrated armistice day here today such a gathering. *[Sometimes, they held the service in the church on Sunday.]* Was very nice, but very sad.

Monday, November 17 ∿ A great big freezing snow storm blowing and drifting and windows frosted like they would be in January. Surely some change. Merle is out somewhere near Fish Lake trapping. I thought I'd freeze my hands hanging out the clothes.

Tuesday, November 25 ∿ Lovely day; warm. The rain has made much more water in our well. Little Hugh *[Ruby's son]* is two months old tonight.

Saturday, November 29 ∿ Lovely weather; a bit colder. Merle is back again. I wish he would go to school.

Sunday, November 30 ∿ A big blustery snowstorm snowed and drifted all day. We have just sit and lied around all day.

Wednesday, December 3 ∿ Very nice; warmer. I have just about finished Mona's dress. Been stuffing her doll tonight *[likely a stocking doll she would give Mona for Christmas]*. It's a nice moonlight night.

Sunday, December 14 ∿ It's been a cold blustery day. We all hugged the stove. We didn't breakfast until nearly ten, but the day was long but comfortable.

Monday, December 15 ∿ Terrible cold the windows have been white all day *[with frost]*. We, Merle and I dressed five chickens today, I'm so glad it's done.

Tuesday, December 16 ∼ Cold, but warmer than yesterday. My stomach is bothering me but I got the washing done. *[They worked whether they felt well or not. She had handled a lot of raw chicken the day before, so maybe there was a connection.]* Mrs. Harold Jones was here to tea.

Sunday, December 21 ∼ Awfully cold; the windows have been frosted all day. Albert has been to the store three times to build fires. *[There was no hot water or electricity yet in the buildings, so all they would have had for heat would be wood stoves.]*

Monday, December 22 ∼ Cold; very cold, but not as cold as yesterday. I washed. Everything is very dull for xmas times *[still in a post-war recession]*.

Wednesday, Xmas eve December 24 ∼ It's snowed all day. We have a nice xmas tree and Ruby and I have just finish putting the presents on. Nearly 12 o'clock. Ruby has been to a play in the hall.

Thursday, Xmas day ∼ Lovely day. Santa Claus was certainly kind. Mona is delighted with everything. She got a lovely Mauna *[Mona?]* doll. Grace and Hugh sent lovely things. We have had another nice xmas. Mary Jones was here to dinner.

Friday, December 26 ∼ Awfully cold; they say the coldest yet. Baby has been very troublesome today, poor little fellow. We are finding the pleasure of our new *[kerosene]* lamp. Certainly some present. *[Abraham Gesner, New Brunswick's first geologist, discovered kerosene in the 1840s. However another patent was registered before Gesner's, so he lost credit for the invention]*.

Wednesday, December 31 ∼ Last day of the old year. With its pleasures and mistakes. Awfully cold; such a wind.

Chapter 2

1925-1929

NEW BRUNSWICK was still feeling the effects of the post-war recession in the late 1920s, and the forestry industry that many Burtt's Corner residents relied upon was badly affected. Because of the recession there was less work in the local community, so people travelled farther away to places like Detroit to find work. The markets were so poor for the lumber industry that very little was sold for outside shipment. The same was true for the potato markets. Wages dropped significantly because farmers and mill owners received so little payment for the goods they were able to ship.

Money was scarce in the Morehouse family as it was for many during the post-war recession, so they made use of whatever resources they had. For instance, Mary recovered an old couch and remodelled her winter coat with a new collar and new cuffs.

Families in the community continued their normal socializing, and travelled back and forth almost daily to visit neighbours and help those who were sick. Since they walked almost everywhere they went, it didn't cost anything.

Even though there was a recession, the family still managed to acquire a second stove for the shed and they no longer had to move their stove back and forth on a seasonal basis. Now there was a cook stove in the main kitchen and one in the outside kitchen area for summer cooking. Cooking in the summer kitchen eliminated the heat from the main house area when the home was already warm from summer temperatures.

Other home renovations were started and their main kitchen now had a sink drain. Previously, they had washed their dishes in a metal dish pan and tossed the dishwater outside.

The invention of the radio and the ability to purchase one led to another way to entertain. People gathered at a home where there was a radio to spend a few hours or an evening listening to the new contraption. The stories read on radio shows were very popular and continued into the 1950s.

Mail order catalogues provided another option for shoppers who had no means of transportation to major cities. Shoppers received their Eatons catalogue, filled in the order form, and sent it off by mail. Their orders came COD (cash on delivery) by train. This allowed the Morehouse family to purchase items not locally available.

1925

Friday, January 2 ∾ Cold but some warmer tonight. Was out to see Mrs. Lyman Bubar this afternoon. Ruby Bubar has gone to Boston to train for a nurse. Merle and the young folks are enjoying their skating this weather.

Sunday, January 4 ∾ Warm, lovely all day but came four inches of snow last night and roads are heavy. I was out for about three quarters of a hour walking in the cows paths *[trails in the pastures where the cows typically travelled and beat down the snow]* to get the air. Have read a nice book "*The Other Wiseman*".

Monday, January 12 ∾ Nice day, but awfully cold. The coldest yet so they say. I have been up to Ruby's. Baby is no better on the new food. He cryed *[cried]* all day but by my being there Ruby got her washing done and quite a bit of ironing.

Wednesday, January 14 ∾ Cold wind blowing. Merle got about a day shovelling on railroad. I made the baby a night dress and finished Hayward's socks.

Saturday, January 17 ～ Cold. I went up to Ruby's and stayed over Sunday. Baby is gaining fast on Melons *[Mellin's]* Food but crys *[cries]* just the same.

Monday, January 19 ～ Terrible cold. - 40 degrees this morning. *[When the temperature drops to - 40°F, it is also - 40°C]* Baby slept lovely last night but cried all day. Ruby got a good days work done by my being there, but one of us had the baby all the time.

Tuesday, January 20 ～ Cold. Almost as cold as ever, but warmer to-wards night. I washed *[and would have hung wet clothes outdoors when it was - 30° to - 40° Fahrenheit]*.

Wednesday, January 21 ～ Nice lovely in afternoon Hayward was in and said the Dr. was there to operate on the baby to circumcise, and he is ruptured too in the thigh poor child. I came up to Ruby's on the freight *[train]*.

Thursday, January 22 ～ Warmer. Baby cryed all day. Dr. came about one o'clock gave them something to quiet him, I brought Mona home with me; dear old girlie.

Saturday, January 24 ～ Cold. We all saw the eclipse of the sun. It was pretty dark for about an hour and half. Certainly worth seeing. Mona is a good girl; contented and happy. Manser Allen's youngest child died tonight. I didn't know he was sick.

Saturday, January 31 ～ Bright, but blowing and drifting some yet. Merle has shovelled all day on the track. Mona is good. She had her bath and a good sleep this afternoon. Williams is sentenced to be hanged 23 of April It looks very much like a storm tonight.

Monday, February 9 ～ Lovely day. Came home from Ruby's tonight. She got washing and baking done and I made the baby a truss *[A belt-like piece of soft cloth to wrap around the child's stomach/thigh area to hold the rupture in place for healing]*. He is very troublesome.

Wednesday, February 11 ⤳ Rained most of the morning. A heavy mist all day. Snow very soft and is making the water rise. I made yeast today and a night shirt and some other sewing.

Saturday, February 14 ⤳ Lovely spring day; water sounds like April. Ethel Bird was in awhile this afternoon. I made the baby two night-dresses, beside my Saturday work.

Sunday, March 1 ⤳ A fine morning, but the wind began blowing hard about noon. Been cold and grey since. We had a heavy earthquake shock last night about 20 past ten. It lasted a long time. *[This area is on a small fault line and often has minor earthquakes. The latest was in the fall of 2015.]*

Tuesday, Mar 3 ⤳ Awfully cold. Merle and I have been to the City. Got Merle a new suit. I got oilcloth, paper for the kitchen.

Saturday, March 7 ⤳ Lovely day. The Dr. and Maud was here and pulled my under *[bottom]* teeth. Am awfully sick.

Sunday, March 8 ⤳ Nasty, snowing. I am very quite miserable; didn't get out of bed until nearly 12 o' clock.

Tuesday, March 10 ⤳ Cold all day, but is thundering and lightning tonight. So strange as cold as it's been all day. I have been up to Ruby's. Baby was quite troublesome but he takes more notice of things. Mona is fine. I took her some Woolworth Jewellery and she was pleased.

Friday, March 20 ⤳ Very pleasant day. The snow has certainly gone. I finished binding Ruby's quilt and made baby a little one. Called at Mrs. Bubar's and at Mrs. Ray *[MacDonald's]*, cut out a dress and have some done on it.

Monday, March 23 ⤳ Cold wind all day. I walked to church last night and went on up to Ruby's and stayed until tonight. The church was full to over flowing last night. Baby looks much better; have him on malted milk now. Seems to be agreeing with him better.

Thursday, March 26 ∽ A lovely day. I have been to Stella Maybe's to a quilting; the third quilting this week. Had such a nice time.

Friday, March 27 ∽ A lovely day; like summer. Water rising, snow disappearing. Merle has completed a new well box which is a great improvement. [*This well box surrounded the hand dug well in the backyard. Sitting on top of the ground, it prevented anyone from falling down into the well below ground. The small roof that stood on posts a few feet above the well box provided a place to tie off the rope and bucket that was used to raise water out of the well. If the water was close to the ground, it would be easy to just scoop out a bucket of water, but with a deep well the bucket was lowered several feet below ground level to obtain the water.*]

Saturday, March 28 ∽ Another lovely day. The snow is just slipping away. It's like last of April. Merle has been [*working*] in the store all day.

Monday, March 30 ∽ Cold rain. I didn't come home from Ruby's until tonight. Merle has gone to work cooking for Mr. Coy [*at the mill*].

Tuesday, March 31 ∽ Raining, and cold and windy. I washed and went down to see Mrs. [*Evie*] MacLean about going to Ruby's to house clean and I am tired tonight. It's raining hard tonight.

Sunday, April 5 ∽ Awfully cold and windy. Mona and I was over to Mrs. Coys. They move to St. John soon.

Monday, April 6 ∽ A lovely day, but a cold wind again. I took Mona home and we found baby so much better but such a strange thing happened. After being better than he ever was, he took a fit about noon. What a fright it gave us but poor little dear has been alright ever since. [*'Fits' often referred to seizures.*]

Easter Sunday, April 12 ∽ A heavy fall of snow just like winter. I was to church twice; the church was decorated nicely, looked lovely. Albert and Merle couldn't get up at all.

Saturday, April 18 ∽ Cold and windy. I have almost made Mona a dress. We have heard that Mr. John Estey has fell and hurt himself. It's badly; he is not expected to live. So sorry for he is such a nice old gentleman.

Sunday, April 19 ⁓ Cold. We have been up to church in the old truck. The bride and groom appeared out tonight — Jimmy and Opal. Mr. John Estey is still living but going fast I believe. He is 86 years old.

Monday, April 20 ⁓ A terrible cold day; a heavy wind started about eleven o'clock last night, blowed all night and all day. I have been up to Ruby's. She washed but it was too cold and windy to hang out her clothes. Baby seems a lot better.

Tuesday, April 21 ⁓ Warmer, a lovely wash day. Mr. John Estey died last night.

Thursday, April 23 ⁓ Cold; rained a little this morning. We were up to Mr. John Estey's funeral. A large funeral. They feel so badly. Williams was hanged this morning in F'ton for the murder of the little girls.

Sunday, April 26 ⁓ It's been a lovely warm day, just like summer. Mona has been out all day bareheaded and she is just brown. Baby is good. Only his teeth is troubling him now.

Monday, April 27 ⁓ Nice, but wind is cold at times. Ruby and the little dears went home this morning. Mrs. McLean went up to clean the house. Merle is not satisfied with his work. I expect he will leave. So much work, and such small wages.

Wednesday, April 29 ⁓ Awfully cold. I have been to Ruby's all day. Mrs. McLean is more than going through the house. The baby is troublesome and so is Mona.

Saturday, May 2 ⁓ A nice rain, has made the grass so green. Cleared off this afternoon. The mill is down for a few days. Some of Durant's people are sick.

Monday, May 4 ⁓ A lovely day. We were up at four o'clock this morning to get the stove moved before seven; had it moved by half after five. Oh Edith Curry has a daughter.

Tuesday, May 5 ∽ raining and cold. Mrs. McLean has been here and cleaned two rooms papered one, She is certainly a worker.

Wednesday, May 6 ∽ Very nice today. Mrs. McLean cleaned the shed, sitting room and hall, coloured my curtains, finished the dining room and lots of things and has gone up to Ed Fosters to work.

Thursday, May 21 ∽ Ascension Day. Warm but a heavy wind all day. A nice shower about 5 o'clock but it's turned cold again. Ralston Brewer, Howard's boy was hurt badly in the mill today; took him to the hospital tonight.

Friday, May 22 ∽ Cold. Ella has finished my dresses and gone home tonight. Ralston Brewer is doing fine. They operated on him and found his bowels busted.

Saturday, May 23 ∽ Cold. I done some varnishing today. The Brewer boy must be doing well for we haven't heard from him.

Sunday, May 24 ∽ Awfully cold like winter. We have hovered the stove all day.

Thursday, May 28 ∽ A lovely day; quite like summer. I polished hall stove and scrubbed the floor for varnish. Albert put first coat on for it hurts my back to do it. There is a shower tonight at Charlie Allen's for Marg Brewer. She is to be married next Wednesday,

Saturday, May 30 ∽ Rained all day; a nice warm rain. It's quite chilly tonight. I guess I am done varnishing. I oiled kitchen floor today; just finished.

Wednesday, June 3 ∽ A warm day; showery some thunder. Margaret Brewer and Stanley Pugh were married tonight; a church wedding. I guess the church was more than full. I have been out for a walk. Everyone's on the move tonight.

Thursday, June 4 〰 Awfully warm and a terrible wind. I went up to Ruby's on train. We have been to confirmation tonight. It was lovely; everyway a very large crowd there. I think 12 were confirmed.

Sunday, June 7 〰 A perfect day. We have been home all day. Mr. and Mrs. Frank Staples and Bedford were here to tea.

Wednesday, June 10 〰 Cloudy; cleared at noon awfully hot this afternoon. I was up to the Drs. helping to make wreaths for the church. Dorothy came for me and took me up to Ruby's; I came home on train. Dorothy's *[wedding]* presents are wonderful.

Thursday, June 11 〰 Dorothy's *[Dr. Morehouse's daughter]* wedding day. Was married at high noon; everything was lovely. Four ministers, four bridesmaids and I don't know what all.

Tuesday, June 16 〰 Showery all day. This is Mona's birthday; 3 years. I made her a cake with candles on. Ruby and Buddie *[Hugh]* came down and back tonight. Mr. D. Jewett was buried today.

Sunday, June 21 〰 Cloudy this morning; very nice this afternoon. Mona has been a dear. Jimmy came for them tonight. Buddie wasn't too bad. Durant's have returned again. Merle has had the cook house to take care of again. Mr. Coy has been to St. John.

Wednesday, July 1 〰 Showery all morning. Cleared off at noon; cool wind. Lovely tonight. We have all been to the band picnic. and both children were good.

Monday, July 6 〰 Very nice day; since noon. We have all been to a play in the hall. *"Mess Mates"*. It was good. St. Ann's church put it on.

Tuesday, July 7 〰 Rainy; heavy clouds all day, close. Mrs. Byron Gorman was here this evening.

Thursday, July 9 〰 Lovely day. Mrs. B. Gorman and I have been up and spent the day with Ruby. Mona had a good time with Pearl *[Gorman]*. Buddies been good too.

Friday, July 10 ∽ Cloudy until noon. Rained a little, nice this afternoon. I have done some strawberry preserves. Merle has taken the kettle drum *[small bowl shaped drum]* in the band.

Saturday, July 11 ∽ Lovely day; beautiful evening. We have been to the corner. The Durant's have gone home. Got word Mrs. Durant's mother is sick. The mill is down for couple of days.

Monday, July 13 ∽ Lovely day. The 12th [Orangemen's event] is celebrated today in F'ton and other places. Our band is in F'ton. Word came from town that they don't think Pearl Bird will live through the night. Wassie has gone down.

Wednesday, July 15 ∽ Lovely, but hot. The guild girls of the church has a garden party and fancy sale. I was up. Pearl Bird died this morning; poor sufferer.

Thursday, July 16 ∽ Windy and rain. Pearl Bird was buried today. Such a large funeral. They brought her up on train *[from Fredericton]*.

Friday, July 17 ∽ Rained a pour all day. Albert was away up *[Zealand]* Station delivering, so he stopped and got Mona on his way down. She had a great time. I have a big pail of strawberrys *[strawberries]* to preserve.

Sunday, July 19 ∽ Hot but nice. We have set out under the tree all day *[She usually did her hand sewing or knitting while she sat out.]*; had the crib out all day.

Tuesday, July 21 ∽ Lovely day, but awfully warm. Mrs. Estey and I were down to the graveyard. She walks better than I and she is 96 yrs old. Ruby and the dear things went home tonight.

Monday, July 27 ∽ Cloudy this morning; hot this afternoon. Albert has a week off and is putting roofing on the house. It is a hard job and so hot. I washed and scrubbed. Mrs. Caven *[?]* called today.

Friday, July 31 ∽ Lovely day. Albert finished the roof. He expects to go back to the store tomorrow but he can have another day sometime to make up the week.

Sunday, August 2 ∽ Rained all night; a big shower about seven this morning. We were all over to cross roads to church this morning with Mr. and Mrs. Palmer. The scouts were there this afternoon. We were to Baptist meeting, and tonight down to the mouth of Keswick to Methodist with Maybes. An awful big shower on way home.

Tuesday, August 4 ∽ Awfully hot again. I canned some fruit and ironed this morning. Have set under the trees and sewed this afternoon. It's a beautiful moonlight night and nice and cool.

Thursday, August 6 ∽ Hot, but not as hot as yesterday. I have been up to Ruby's helping her make bean pickles. We done 10 pickle bottles. I brought Mona home with me.

Sunday, August 9 ∽ Hot. The Orangemen marched today; band played. We had Mona up to the corner to hear the band play.

Monday, August 10 ∽ Rained all day. It has been election day — the conservatives are in. *[The 16th NB General Election. Political Parties still had no standing, but candidates declared their affiliation anyways. The Conservatives took 37 seats, the Liberals, 8. Peter Veniot (a Liberal) had been the incumbent, but he lost to John Babington Macauley Baxter, a Conservative.]*

Wednesday, August 12 ∽ A lovely cool day. I have been to W.A. at Mrs. Eddie Brewers. Opal Crouse has a pr of twin girls born last night. Merle has got paint to finish painting the house; a pretty thoughtful boy.

Friday, August 14 ∽ Raining all day again. I made about 8 pts. of bean pickles today.

Sunday, August 16 ∽ Lovely day, but so hot. We have been up to Ruby's. Baby is awfully troublesome again. Rilla is very low. She has a boy baby and is in convulsions. Have had Dr. Van Wart. Dr. Morehouse is away.

Monday, August 17 ᓚ Lovely day; but very hot. What haymakers need. I was up at five o'clock. Had a big wash and scrubbing done by ten.

Tuesday, August 18 ᓚ A lovely day again; but pretty hot. I ironed this morning and Mrs. Staples made a date cake this afternoon. Wassie took us over to Willie McKeen's in his car. Albert came for us with the truck. We came home around by Colter's bridge and up the main road. I called on Mrs. Tripp and Mrs. Frank Coburn and the other Mrs. McKeen.

Wednesday, August 19 ᓚ Cloudy, cool. It's my birthday 50. Ruby and children came down on the motor this morning. We had a nice day. I got so many nice gifts. Ruby and Hayward went back before the train came and after they left, I was so uneasy for fear they'd met the train. They shouldn't have done it. I didn't think how near train times it was until they started. *[The motor Mary refers to is a motorized cart used on the railway to do repair work. The wheels were similar to a train and fit the width of the rails. It was heavy and would be difficult to move it off the railway if they heard a train approaching. Hayward's family used this because it was quicker to travel along the railway with the motor instead of walking on the tracks or taking the longer route around on the regular roadway.]* A shower was coming and they thought they would go before.

Friday, August 21 ᓚ Cool and cloudy like fall. I have made a dresser scarf *[piece of linen with hand embroidery designs]* today and covered a box.

Saturday, August 22 ᓚ Lovely, but cold tonight. Feels like frost. Merle and I were up to the corner. A band concert and the Ministers that are at the corner spoke in the *[band]* stand. Albert is down Nashwaaksis to some kind of a meeting.

Sunday, August 23 ᓚ A beautiful day. We have been home all day. There was a big immersion right here this morning. There was 9 or ten baptized. I was down to see Mrs. John MacDonald's new baby; Edith Cavell.

Monday, August 24 ⌇ Hot, very hot. But its cooling off nicely now. I washed and done a little sewing. Mr. Tom Gilby is dead; died today of heart trouble. Only been real sick about a week.

Sunday, August 30 ⌇ A warm day. We have just arrived home from church. We have been on a long drive today. We were just starting to go to church this morning, but there wasn't any anywhere and Hayward and Ruby came. We went down to the Mouth of Keswick and over to McKeen's Corner, over through Bear Island and up through Springfield and lower Caverhill, Hainesville and down home. The disciples *[Church of Christ]* baptised 35 or 40 this afternoon.

Wednesday, September 2 ⌇ Turned cold again; a lovely cold moon-light night. I have been to W.A. Oscar came down for me. I went up to Ruby's afterward. Mona is miserable just dumping *[diarrhea or vomiting]*. They took her down to the Dr. tonight. I do hope she soon gets better.

Saturday, September 5 ⌇ Lovely day; a perfect night. We have been up to the corner to a band concert.

Sunday, September 6 ⌇ Lovely day. Hayward, his father/mother, Albert and I went away down to lower Gagetown. We went about a hundred miles altogether. It was pretty cold coming back; so windy. We got home about 3:30.

Monday, September 7 ⌇ A perfect day. I washed, covered a box, had callers Mrs. Johnny Brewer and Margaret Morehouse, Mrs. Palmer and Mrs. Nelson Brewer. Edith McKeil is married today at Fairville. The Drs. folk are down to attend it. Mother would have been 81 yrs today.

Wednesday, September 9 ⌇ A lovely day. Quite cool. I have done some plum preserves and got pickles put in salt. Made Buddie a pair of bloomers. Washed his coat and cap. Little Pauline Coy was killed with a live wire. *[They had moved to Saint John, so there must have been electricity there.]* Was brought to Jeddie's today.

Monday, September 14 ∽ Such a rain; rained a pour all night and until noon today. Had a letter from Grace. My hat has come. I guess I will have to send it back. *[All women wore hats to church and often dressy long-sleeved gloves.]*

Thursday, September 17 ∽ Cloudy; looked like rain all day. Hayward, Ruby and the kiddies and I were to exhibition. The children were fine. We didn't get home until nearly eleven o'clock.

Friday, September 18 ∽ Still cloudy; looking like rain anytime. I expect that Mona and Buddie has been troublesome today for yesterday's goodness *[being out so late and behaving so well]*.

Tuesday, September 22 ∽ Cold all day; real cold. I am making Mona some night dresses and bedroom slippers.

Wednesday, September 23 ∽ Awfully like November We moved the stove in today. It's a great thing accomplished. It is so cold in the shed in the mornings. I was all day fixing things around and washing up. Merle has started working for Spencer Brewer *[on his farm]*.

Friday, September 25 ∽ Cold awfully; cold. A heavy cold wind. I was down to Mrs. MacDonald's for some buttermilk. This is Buddies birthday, one year.

Monday, September 28 ∽ Lovely day from noon, rained all night. I washed and cleaned up the house and made a call. Merle is not picking potatoes today as it's too wet.

Wednesday, September 30 ∽ Very nice day; cold. I went up to Ruby's and to W.A. Eletha Brewer and Archie Campbell fellow is married this evening. I made Mona a hat this evening. Little Hugh is a dear good baby now.

Thursday, October 1 ∽ A lovely day. I have been busy all day. The Durant's have came back again for the winter. Her mother is dead.

Saturday, October 3 ∽ Raining all day and simply pouring tonight. I'm afraid potatoes will be ruined, so many rotting now.

Sunday, October 4 ∽ Raining a little until noon. We have been to church and up to Ruby's a little while. Mr. and Mrs. Campbell appeared out tonight.

Monday, October 5 ∽ Dull, raining again tonight. Merle has been digging potatoes today. I guess the mud is fierce. He is up to the pictures tonight.

Tuesday, October 6 ∽ Quite fine; warm, but cloudy. Merle is very tired digging potatoes. They have to dig by hand. The ground is so wet. I have been to the Methodist aid at Mrs. Birds.

Friday, October 9 ∽ A nice day; but has looked like rain all day and it's raining quite hard tonight. Merle is better. I was down and called on Mrs. Dawson Pugh this afternoon. Have had word that Grace and Hughie are coming Sunday if it doesn't rain.

Monday, October 12 ∽ It was a perfect morning, but it clouded up and snowed before noon. It's been drizzling and cold and dark all day. Yesterdays snow hasn't all gone yet. Merle is still feeling miserable. The new bookkeeper, Miss Pond, came for the Farmers Store today.

Tuesday, October 13 ∽ Cold and windy. Merle is digging potatoes today in Birdton. The snow is 3 ft deep I guess.

Wednesday, October 14 ∽ A lovely day; first for a long while. Ruby, Mona and Buddie came down today are here over night. Mona and I were to the corner and Bubar's called this afternoon.

Tuesday, October 20 ∽ Cold and squallie. Blows like snow tonight. *[Many people could tell by wind directions and other signs what was coming for weather.]* I was up to the corner this afternoon. Dave Burtt was here to supper.

Thursday, October 22 ∽ A lovely day and nicest for a long while. Merle said they used the *[potato]* digger; today first time in two weeks. Bernice Burtt and Perley Gilby are married tonight in the disciple church. They looked lovely.

Thursday, October 24 ∽ Cold but sunny. Merle has finished his potato digging tonight. The dear boy has earned 46 dollars and some cents. He has had a hard drill.

Monday, October 26 ∽ Turned cold and windy before morning, and the wind has been terrible all day. I have been to Ruby's, I covered a big bedding box for her and she washed and between us we done a big days work. Buddy's been awfully good.

Tuesday, October 27 ∽ Quite a pleasant day, but cold. I washed and the clothes froze as I put them out. Mrs. Cook was in today taking orders for toilet articles. I never looked any worst in my life when she called, for I hadn't got the house cleaned up from washing.

Friday, October 30 ∽ Cold, but the wind has gone down tonight and it's a perfect moonlight. Our Eaton's order came tonight and everything is lovely. The little crippled Pugh boy is dead.

Saturday, November 7 ∽ Very nice day. Merle was out *[working]* in the woods for John McDonald.

Monday, November 9 ∽ Thanksgiving and Armistice Day. Pleasant but cold; heavy wind. I called on Mrs. George Brewer our new neighbours and Mrs. Stanley Pugh, and Mrs. Bubar. Merle is out to McDonald's Camp. He and Irvine are to came *[stay]* there for the week if all is well.

Thursday, November 12 ∽ A lovely warm day. Mona and I were up to the corner and down to Maybe's for the milk. She has had a great day.

Saturday, November 21 ∽ Fine. We have just finished bathing and its nearly 12 o'clock. The Queen's Mother died yesterday *[November 20]*. Little Murray Pugh died this morning.

Monday, November 23 ⌢ It's been warm all day, and now pouring rain tonight. My wash is out in it.

Wednesday, November 25 ⌢ Very cold last night. I went up to Ruby's this morning to W.A. meeting this afternoon. Home with Maud. Mrs. George Brewer called just as I got home. Didn't get to bed until eleven o'clock. Charlie Pugh came for to ask if Merle would go up in the morning to be the second cookee *[for his woods crew]*.

Thursday, November 26 ⌢ Cold, an awful wind. Merle went to the woods this morning. I feel lonesome. I have been to the corner and sold 4 church calendars and collected two and a quarter dollars for the organist.

Wednesday, December 2 ⌢ A lovely warm day like October I cleaned the upstairs hall, and the hall and front room downstairs. I'm awfully tired tonight; haven't been feeling well today anyway. I also made bread and scrubbed the kitchen. I didn't have to get any dinner for Albert as he was to town.

Thursday, December 3 ⌢ A lovely day. We had a social tonight at John Brewers. Money *[will be used]* for xmas tree for school.

Friday, December 4 ⌢ Another lovely warm day. Our xmas order came. It's alright. I was at the corner this afternoon. They are fixing the things for xmas at the store. I have collected $3.50 from Kathleen and sold 6 calendars.

Saturday, December 5 ⌢ Another nice warm day. I went up to Ruby's on one train and back on the other. Little Hugh is just a dear. He is so fat; he's like a rolly polly. Mona is great too.

Monday, December 7 ⌢ It looks like more rain. I done a lot of little jobs. Albert has been home this evening. Has worked all the evening on the Forester Books.

Friday, December 11 ⌢ Not so cold. Got cute garters for little girlies xmas gifts. I had a letter from Merle tonight. My first letter from him. He is getting on fine up in the woods. Likes the older Cookee.

Sunday, December 13 ⁓ Snowed this morning and it's blowed the rest of the day. Quite cold tonight. I have written some letters and addressed some xmas cards.

Wednesday, December 16 ⁓ Very pleasant. Quite a cold wind. I was up to the corner. I have made some cute bibs from salt bags. *[They used every bit of cloth they could find. Food bags were often cleaned and used for cloth items around homes.]* I have made a little fruit cake and finished little Hugh's booties.

Friday, December 18 ⁓ Lovely day again. We have certainly had a lovely week. I received my first xmas present today from May *[Ferguson]*. I haven't opened it yet.

Monday, December 21 ⁓ A great big snowstorm. We dressed our three chickens today so that nasty job is done. I have all of my parcels mailed. 23 years tonight the poor Bertie passed away.

Tuesday, December 22 ⁓ Warm; half rain all day. I have just been doing odd jobs. Merle came home tonight. I was so glad to see him, the dear. It's been four weeks since he went away.

Thursday, December 24 ⁓ Lovely and bright, but very cold. Merle and I have been to town. It's after 12 o'clock and we have just got things fixed for xmas day.

Friday, December 25 ⁓ xmas day. A very cold morning. Was a very cold night. We have had a lovely xmas again. We didn't think that Ruby could get down at all, but about quarter after eleven they drove down. My we were glad. We all got lovely presents and Grace and Hugh's presents were beautiful. Mona got two lovely dolls and dishes and everything to please her. Little Hugh got nice things too. We could only have gotten to church, our day would have been complete. Only I'd like to know where Reuben is.

Sunday, December 27 ∽ Cold and blowing. Merle has suffered all day with something in his eye. It seems to be out now. He expects to go to the woods in the morning. I am beginning to feel lonesome already. Willie Brewer was here awhile this afternoon. He brought me a letter. Mrs. Willie will go and help Ruby out if no one is sick at home. If she can't get Evie.

Monday, December 28 ∽ Been so cold, but blustery. Merle has gone back to the woods. I have been up to Ruby's all day. Got quite a lot of little things done. The Dr. is away again until Wednesday, I hope all will be well until then.

Thursday, December 31 ∽ A lovely day. Very clear, cold weather but nice and bright. I believe last night was the coldest yet. The last of the old year. With all pleasures and mistakes it has been a very happy year.

1926

Friday, January 1 ∽ A brand new year. Warmer I think; another snow storm on hand. Dr. Jewett is at the corner tonight. I feel safer. I wish Ruby knew it. *[With this entry and the one on December 27th, it seems like Ruby may be expecting again.]*

Sunday, January 3 ∽ A nice bright day; cold. I have been sick. Have stayed upstairs on my aching back all day. We had quite an excitement this morning and an all day one for the boys. A potato car burned right here in the switch with a hundred barrels of potatoes in it. *[They would have had to heat the cars to keep the potatoes from freezing.]*

Tuesday, January 5 ∽ A nice warm day; snowed a little wet snow. Ruby has a new boy baby *[LeBaron]* this morning. I've been up all day. They have Florence McKeil and Mrs. Willie Brewer. I brought Mona home with me. They had Dr. Jewett and liked him very much.

Thursday, January 7 ∽ A terrible wind all day; just lifting things to-night. I washed, hanged my clothes out and they dried and I got them in. Mona is making out fine I guess. Everything is well at Ruby's.

Sunday, January 10 ⁓ A beautiful day like a March day. Mona and I were down to see Mrs. MacDonald and then we went over to Durant's awhile. Mona took her dolls over to show the children.

Monday, January 11 ⁓ Another lovely day. Mona and I have been up to Ruby's. Things are coming on pretty good and the little baby is awfully good.

Wednesday, January 13 ⁓ A lovely day. Mona has had a great outing today. She was [out] about an hour this morning and right after dinner I took her to the corner and let her slide down the corner hill. If she wasn't delighted. Then we were in to Mrs. Byron Gorman's a little while. I brought her home and she slept nearly three hours, and was out awhile again and she had a great romp later this evening and went to bed about 8 o'clock.

Friday, January 15 ⁓ A heavy fall of snow last night. Warm today; snowing a soft snow tonight. I have been up to Ruby's; Mona and I. Things are coming on fine.

Saturday, January 16 ⁓ Another lovely day. 24 yrs today since little Marie was born.

Sunday, January 17 ⁓ Another lovely day. We didn't get up until ten; didn't have breakfast until eleven. Mona and I were down to Mrs. Mac-Donald's awhile. It's only eight o'clock and I am making preparations for bed. I feel sleepy but don't know whether I can go to sleep this early or not. I should have written a letter to May Ferguson.

Tuesday, January 19 ⁓ Rained all night and until nearly noon today. Very bad travelling so much water under the snow. It's warm still tonight. Mona couldn't get out today. Mary Jones was in awhile waiting for the train. Ruby's baby is two weeks old today.

Thursday, January 28 ⁓ A lovely morning; started snowing about noon and we have had a heavy fall of snow since blowing and drifting. Mona and I have been up to Ruby's. She is alone now. Baby is good day time, but pretty fussy nights. Little Hugh is quite troublesome — cutting teeth.

Sunday, January 31 ∾ Lovely day. We didn't go any place today, only a little walk as far as the mill. Newt Bird *[Newton, the blacksmith]* died this afternoon. I was surprised and Cobie Allen is very sick I guess. Has been for a couple of weeks. Poor Mrs. Bird left with four small children all under ten years.

Monday, February 1 ∾ Cold with a raw wind all day. I didn't wash. They have taken Cobie Allen to the hospital today. A big storm on tonight.

Tuesday, February 2 ∾ A big storm; snowed and blowed all night and snowed all day but its mild. Newt Bird was buried this afternoon. *[There was no such thing as a vault to store the deceased until spring.]*

Thursday, February 4 ∾ Rained all day. Snow and blowing a gale tonight. I have taken Mona home and left her. We surely feel lonesome. Ruby is fine and baby has been awfully good today.

Saturday, February 6 ∾ A lovely day. Was expecting Merle tonight but he didn't come. I feel disappointed. I had made fudge and other things he likes. He sent a letter saying he'd be down next Saturday He is eighteen years old today. I called on Mrs. Bubar today. She has blood poison in her foot but it's getting better.

Sunday, February 7 ∾ Nice bright sun. Wind has blowed all day. Drifted quite a lot. I was up to see Mrs. Newton Bird this evening. Poor woman; I feel so sorry for her.

Monday, February 8 ∾ Blustery; it's drifted all day but a very bright sun. I have started to look over my patch work pieces. My head and eyes bother me so much.

Tuesday, February 9 ᴄ᷈ Cold and windy; bright sunshine. Mrs. Ambrose Allen called. Mrs. Durant was in for quilting frames. I had a letter from Aunt Sarah in Duluth and one from Grace *[in Maine]*.

Saturday, February 13 ᴄ᷈ A lovely day; like spring. I have been very busy patching and washing Merle's clothes.

Sunday, February 14 ᴄ᷈ Beautiful day. I was down to Mrs. MacDonald's awhile. Little Carman is five years old today. I give her the candles for her cake. It's seemed nice to have Merle home today.

Monday, February 15 ᴄ᷈ Snowing and blowing as mad this morning, but got milder through the day. I'm glad for I felt bad for Merle to take the long walk back to the woods in such a wild snow for he has a cold. I intended to go to Ruby's today but thought it too cold to leave the house *[She had to tend the fires to keep house heated.]* Fred Burtt was in to heat his tea and he said Mona said the little baby had their tongue clipped last week. *[The condition is commonly referred to as tongue-tied. Everyone has the membrane that attaches the tongue to the bottom of the mouth. In tongue-tied babies, the membrane prevents easy movement of the tongue. Clipping the membrane allowed the baby to raise his or her tongue to make it easier to feed.]*

Friday, February 17 ᴄ᷈ A lovely day. I washed and got my clothes all dry in a few hours. I have made a striped quilt this evening. Pink and white. Ruby and I are going to give it to the W.A.

Thursday, February 18 ᴄ᷈ A fine day. Mary Jones was in. I was over to Mrs. Howard Brewers for a walk. A man was killed at Charlie Pugh's camp yesterday; Perley Gilbert from up near Zealand. A tree fell on him I think. I think it's the first man ever killed up the creek since the lumbering started and it's been a good many years. Merle will have cause to remember well the first winter he worked in the woods.

Friday, February19 ᴄ᷈ Another big snowstorm. Hailing this afternoon. Warm tonight. Another sad thing happened yesterday. Mrs. Harley

Crouse dropped dead on their way from the woods yesterday. She had been cooking for Harley all winter somewhere near Charlie Pugh's camp.

Tuesday, February 23 ∾ Cold; awfully cold. I believe the coldest day yet. I have made a pretty bassinette for the baby. I'm real proud of it. I started to wash my feather pillows, but found I couldn't or thought I couldn't so I put them in bags to air and am washing the ticks. *[Ticks were the earliest form of mattress. People filled a cloth casing with feathers, straw or other soft materials. There were no box springs in this time period, so the tick was often laid on either a metal spring or on a series of ropes stretched across the bed frame.]* Mrs. Casey and Mrs. Durant spent the evening. I send to Eatons for paper for the halls and sitting room, tan and oatmeal.

Thursday, February 25 ∾ A very nice day. Much warmer. Mrs. Brewer and I were up to Ruby's today. The children were all good. The baby is a sweet thing; good as he can be. So thankful.

Saturday, February 27 ∾ Mild; a little flurry of snow this evening bright moonlight now. I have cut out a house dress for Mrs. Durant. Had a letter from Merle. They think they will finish in the woods next week.

Monday, March 1 ∾ A very frosty morning. I started out bright and early to ask some women to a quilting for Wednesday, Only 8 o'clock when I started, I have 6 or 7 asked and there is a big snow storm on tonight. I done some cooking this afternoon. Mrs. Byron Gorman was in this afternoon.

Tuesday, March 2 ∾ It was a little windy this morning; began snowing and blowing about noon and it's been a fright since then. I have my quilt on ready for a quilting. I washed today, scrubbed and done a number of things.

Wednesday, March 3 ∾ Nice and warm; the storm wasn't so bad after all. Everyone I asked to my quilting came. Nice; got the quilt done and another one pieced. We had a great time.

Thursday, March 4 ∿ Blustery. I have been up to Ruby's. Baby has been awfully fussy all day. Mona has a bum arm. Buddies *[Hugh's]* alright, only he's lost his bootees.

Friday, March 5 ∿ Cold and blustery. I was to the store; first time for a long while. I got a new dress. They have very nice new goods in. *[The local stores carried everything because people weren't able to travel far outside the village.]*

Saturday, March 6 ∿ Very nice day. I thought maybe Ruby would come down but she didn't. Merle is still in the woods. Most of the crew have come *[back to the community].*

Sunday, March 7 ∿ Another big snow storm and cold. We have hugged the stove all day. It's howling fierce tonight.

Monday, March 8 ∿ Snow and blow last night; was the worst storm of the season and it snowed and blowed a fright all night. I have finished setting a quilt together and made Mona and Buddie a pair of stockings.

Wednesday, March 10 ∿ Lovely day. Have been to Mrs. Maybe's to a quilting. Merle came home today. 40 yrs today since we came to Keswick.

Thursday, March 11 ∿ A lovely day. I finished stitching a quilt on the machine. *[This would have been be a treadle sewing machine. It had a mechanism that connected the needle to a large grated steel pedal near the floor. When Mary rocked the pedal back and forth with her foot, the needle would go up and down and make the stitches.]* Vera Allen was married tonight to a fellow from Millville. A big crowd gathered at station to give them a send off

Sunday, March 14 ∿ Cold; awfully cold. The windows was frosted more this morning than any morning this winter. Baby is quite troublesome, I don't think the milk agrees with him. *[Ruby and her children were visiting.]*

Monday, March 15 ∽ A terrible cold morning. We have washed and done a quite a lot of work. Ruby had Hugh and Mona to the corner this evening. The children are doing very well. They have a new baby at Frenchman's; for Mrs. Durant's sister, Mrs. Richard.

Wednesday, March 17 ∽ Lovely day; thawing. I called on Mrs. Fred Allen and Mrs. Ambrose Allen. And the new French baby. I was invited to a quilting, but Merle or Albert neither one told me until tonight; a pretty time to tell me.

Friday, March 19 ∽ Lovely day. I done Saturday work. I expect to go up to Ruby's tomorrow as the wood sawers will be there. *[The women prepared meals for the men working in the woods.]*

Saturday, March 20 ∽ Snowed some this morning. A lovely afternoon. I went up to Ruby's but they didn't saw after all. Would have stayed up for church in morning, but there won't be any service. The baby has been awfully good. Albert was to town today and to a Farmer's Meeting tonight.

Sunday, March 21 ∽ A beautiful day. I was to Mrs. MacDonald's and away up the track for a walk. Stella and Randolph was here this evening.

Monday, March 22 ∽ A lovely, lovely day. I washed and it was such a pleasure to hang them out. Merle got the big drift shovelled and I got some out and side places cleaned *[of snow]*. It's a lovely evening.

Tuesday, March 23 ∽ Mild; looks as if it would rain most any time. I have another quilt on. Expect to have a quilting tomorrow if all is well.

Wednesday, March 24 ∽ Rained hard until noon, then stopped. Nine women came to my quilting; all I asked. Got quilting finished and one bound, and a stocking leg knit.

Thursday, March 25 ∽ Quite nice; rained a little this afternoon. Mrs.

Ambrose Allen was here and helped me tack my puff. We had it done by half passed two. Started half passed 12. I am crocheting Mona a hat.

Friday, March 26 ⌒ Lovely day; snow going fast. I washed some feathers *[feathers she saved when preparing chickens for cooking. The feathers were used to stuff pillows.]*; and finished Mona's hat. Ironed and was over to Mrs. Ray MacDonald's awhile.

Saturday, March 27 ⌒ Cold wind all day. Merle and Charlie Pugh settled today. Charged him $30 for 70 gals. of molasses he lost. *[while working as camp cookee. That's a lot of molasses to lose. Maybe he spilled them.]*

Monday, March 29 ⌒ A terrible windy, cold day. Worst than yesterday. I washed but didn't hang my clothes out. The *[railway]* station burned down about five tonight. Hayward has just gone home, eleven o'clock. Merle is to watch awhile *[for flare ups]*. I expect Ruby will be awfully worried not knowing whether we were burned or not.

Tuesday, March 30 ⌒ Windy but not so cold as yesterday. Maud was here this evening. We went up to the Milliner store. I got a big black silk Hat. *[A milliner designed, made, and trimmed hats for everyone].*

Wednesday, March 31 ⌒ Was a lovely day. I have quite a sore throat. Mrs. Ray MacDonald cut and fit my rayon crepe dress. They put an old car *[boxcar]* in here tonight to serve for a station house until a new one is built.

Good Friday, April 2 ⌒ Very pleasant. There has been two services in the church but of course we couldn't go. There was a service in the Baptist church, tonight the Methodist Church. I didn't know it until afterward.

Sunday, April 4 ⌒ Easter Sunday. An awfully big snowstorm. I went up to Ruby's last night to be there for Easter and Albert and Merle were to come up this morning, but they couldn't so we were all disappointed. Just like last year and two years ago and three yrs ago. I went down to church. The church was half full and 32 or 33 for communicant *[Com-munion?]*. Thought it lovely for the awful day. Merle and I were to town yesterday. The day being lovely. I had the impression of my lower teeth taken. They cost $20. Merle got a stove for the shed. Got it at Uncle Sam's a second hand. So nice of him. *[Now they had a stove in the main kitchen and one in the shed for the summer kitchen.]*

Monday, April 5 ∿ Cold, a very strong wind. Mrs. McLean is papering the halls. Ruby's baby *[LeBaron]* is three months today.

Wednesday, April 7 ∿ Not so cold; wind not blowing. Mrs. McLean has finished papering. It's great. She goes to McDonalds from here.

Monday, April 12 ∿ Awfully cold; wind blowed all day. Bitter cold last night. I was up to Ruby's. Little Hugh is awfully troublesome; more trouble than two like the baby.

Tuesday, April 13 ∿ It's been a lovely day, but cold tonight and grey. Looks like a storm. I washed and I have another cold tonight. Maud was here this evening said there would be a social at her place tomorrow night.

Wednesday, April 14 ∿ Very nice; snow going fast. Roads terrible. Muriel came for me this afternoon to go to social. Albert and Merle came up tonight. We just got home. Wasn't many there. Made about $14 dollars.

Monday, April 19 ∿ A very pleasant day. I washed. The new manager has gone in the store today. *[Not sure which of the several stores has the new manager.]*

Wednesday, April 21 ∿ Cold wind, but not as cold as yesterday for the sun is bright and the snow has thawed a lot. I was up to the corner. Had a little gold braid put on my hat *[at the milliner store]*.

Thursday, April 22 ∿ Quite a warm day. Looks very much like rain tonight. I cleaned the clothes room today and Merle got some of the upstairs windows washed on outside.

Saturday, April 24 ∾ Nice and warm; the wind hasn't blowed for three days. Merle has been painting the house. He has one side done first coat. Myrtle Brewer was in awhile this morning waiting for the train.

Sunday, April 25 ∾ Cold and raining. It is Ruby's birthday *[27]*. Hayward came down for us. Hugh is troublesome. I made a birthday cake with 27 candles. The children were pleased.

Monday, April 26 ∾ Very nice day. I done a big wash and it's been beautiful for it. Merle has given the side of the house another coat of paint. It looks nice. Mrs. MacDonald is real bad again. She is over to Ray's.

Tuesday, April 27 ∾ Cold and grey. I have cleaned the front bedroom and painted the floor. Merle painted one side of shed. Mrs. McDonald is better.

Wednesday, April 28 ∾ Nice morning. Heavy wind this afternoon. Raining since four pm. Merle has cleaned the dooryard so nicely. I ironed and made half of a pair of curtains. Mrs. MacDonald is better.

Thursday, April 29 ∾ Rainy; rained hard last night. We have got the *[new]* shed stove up.

Saturday, May 1 ∾ Nice pleasant. Quite a cold wind. There was may poles on the ice today. They say the first in 60 years. *[The only explanation found for may poles is the phenomena of ice spikes or poles that are formed when water freezes so quickly that it is forced upward in the middle to form a frozen spike of water. According to weather sources for that date, the temperature dropped from 13°C to -2°C.]* I was up to Lucy Gorman's this evening to see her mother.

Monday, May 3 ∾ Lovely warm day. I done a big wash and nearly finished cleaning the shed. Merle went to the *[log]* drive this morning. I felt lost without him.

Thursday, May 6 ∽ Lovely day. I ironed and painted two bedroom floors. Mrs. Durant and Mrs. Casey and baby called. I was over to see Mrs. MacDonald this evening.

Friday, May 7 ∽ Quite a nice day. I finished cleaning upstairs, all but painting the hall floor. Merle came home from the drive; no work.

Wednesday, May 12 ∽ A terrible cold, windy day. I washed. Tried to hang out my clothes but couldn't keep them on line so I didn't get them hanged out until tonight. Merle is cleaning the yard just fine. It's a very cold night.

Thursday, May 13 ∽ A lovely day. I was up to the corner this afternoon and down to Maybe's for milk tonight. Merle has the sink running and a lot of other things done. *[The house didn't have running water yet, so this sink drained out under the house through a pipe or ground ditch which would freeze up during the winter. When it did, they had to toss their dish water out the door.]*

Saturday, May 15 ∽ A nice warm day. I went up and brought Mona down. We have been at the corner. She had ice cream and a dandy time.

Sunday, May 16 ∽ Lovely day. Just like summer. You could just see things grow. Mona has had a lovely time. We were over to Mrs. Mac-Donald's this morning.

Monday, May 17 ∽ Windy, cloudy; a bit cold at times. I washed a good wash today. Mona is fine. Merle has gone to Dorn Ridge to cut cord wood with some other boys. Hope he strikes a good job.

Tuesday, May 18 ∽ Cold; sometimes hot. Sometimes the wind blows awful cold tonight. Albert has left the store. Couldn't agree with new manager. I'm awfully sorry he has lost a good job.

Wednesday, May 19 ∽ Very cold this morning. Lovely this afternoon and evening. We have been up to the corner. Mona had a great time. The bigger girls played with her. She has quite a cold today. I've had her up to Dr. and I hope she will be better in morning. Elwood *[Burtt]* hired Albert to work in the planner mill.

Thursday, May 20 ⌁ Cold and rainy. I have finished two suits for Mona. Mrs. Palmer and Mrs. Harry Bird and Kathleen were here this afternoon.

Friday, May 21 ⌁ A terrible cold, windy day. Albert has been painting the house. The lemon *[yellow]* trim is looking nice. I am making Mona another suit.

Tuesday, May 25 ⌁ Cold and grey. I have been up to Ruby's. I thought she was coming down so I took Mona up to help her down *[with the other children]*. But she couldn't come. I brought Mona down to stay until they get their varnishing done.

Wednesday, May 26 ⌁ Cold and grey. We have been to a play in the hall. It was great. Mona enjoyed it as well as the rest.

Friday, May 28 ⌁ Not so cold as yesterday. Mary Jones has been here for dinner. Mona has played all day with the French children *[next door]*.

Saturday, May 29 ⌁ Lovely and warm. Mona has had a good play with the French children. Then we went up on the afternoon train to Ruby's and stayed all night. The mill broke down at noon.

Sunday, May 30 ⌁ Lovely day. The trees and grass are beginning to look beautiful. We were at early service this morning. Hayward brought us down on the motor car this evening.

Monday, May 31 ⌁ Very pleasant; only such a cold strong wind again. I washed and done some odd and ends. Merle has been painting the house today. *[This family took great pride in their home. They worked constantly to make it look nice, both inside and out.]*

Tuesday, June 1 ⌁ Dull, grey; looked like rain all day. 5 years tonight since Ruby was married. How time flies. Merle is doing fine painting. I have cleaned the dining room today and done some painting.

Thursday, June 3 ◠ Cold again; rained last night. I have been cleaning the kitchen, and painting. Cooking and a little of everything. I'm awfully tired. I have taken a lovely bath just now and feel much better. Hope it will make me sleep good. Merle has the house nearly all painted. He's doing a good work.

Friday, June 4 ◠ Cold wind; awfully cold. I have finished the kitchen at last and done some varnishing. Oiled the kitchen floor and lots of other little jobs. We have a new black kitten. Merle got it at MacDonald's. My new coat arrived today. I like it.

Monday, June 7 ◠ Raining a pour all day. Cold and is blowing tonight. I have painted and varnished all day. Such a bad thing has happened. Florence Brewer, Rankine Brewer's wife died last night. Leaves three little children about the age of Ruby's, and her sister, Wilder Brewer's wife is in hospital, not expected to live. Merle has gone back to the camp tonight. I feel sad thinking of those two poor women. Florence was married only five years ago, same summer Ruby was.

Tuesday, June 8 ◠ Raining this morning; cleared this afternoon but showery. I am still varnishing. Have heard today that Wilder Brewer's wife is better.

Wednesday, June 9 ◠ I cleaned and mopped the shed. Varnished 8 chairs and cleaned and painted stairs. Baked bread and cake.

Thursday, June 10 ◠ Nice day. I ironed and sewed some. Ethel Hawkins and a Mrs. Wheeler were here awhile this morning. They promised to spend the day at Mrs. Harry Allen's. There is a Sunday School convention at the corner today.

Saturday, June 12 ◠ Lovely day and evening. We have been to the first Band Concert. It's getting quite cold now.

Sunday, June 13 ◠ A lovely day. We have been to church tonight. Mr.

Durant kindly took us in his car and came after us again. Two of Harley Burtt's boys were baptised tonight. Today is Grace's birthday; 39 yrs.

Tuesday, June 15 ∿ Rain cold and damp. I ironed and made Mona two night dresses and finished her dress and bloomers for her birthday tomorrow, and made her a cake.

Wednesday, June 16 ∿ Today is Mona's birthday. I took her a cake and some more things. Merle and I fixed the grave some today. Merle sodded *[laid new sod on]* Mother's grave. It looks better.

Thursday, June 17 ∿ Another lovely day. I have done some pressing and mending. Merle is working with potatoes for Howard Gorman. *[The men worked wherever they could find work on a daily or weekly basis. Most was labour work, so they didn't need special education.]*

Wednesday, June 23 ∿ A beautiful day. I painted bedroom second coat and sewed quite a lot. Winslow and Hattie came down and took us for a drive this evening.

Thursday, June 24 ∿ A lovely day. I have painted some more and made Mona a bloomer suit. Merle is helping some boys with pulp wood for a few days.

Saturday, June 26 ∿ Hot and smokey. Looks much like rain tonight. We have been to corner to a band concert.

Sunday, June 27 ∿ Lovely day. We had a big shower sometime in the night. Refreshed everything wonderfully. We were over to Mrs. George Brewers this evening.

Tuesday, June 29 ∿ Quite a nice day. A heavy shower this evening. Hail in places. I have been to Ruby's. She and the children came down with me tonight.

Wednesday, June 30 ∿ Awfully hot and showery. Buddie is getting more used to everything and isn't so troublesome. The baby is the sweetest thing. So good. Just lays in his basket all day and all night. I made Ruby a dress today. She made a few calls tonight.

Friday, July 2 ⤳ Hot, showery. Ruby went home tonight. I miss them all so. Buddie cries so much. He bewilders me. But feel awfully lonely after they go. The little baby is a dear. Mr. and Mrs. Durant took them home.

Saturday, July 3 ⤳ Lovely day, a shower early this morning. Mrs. Coy was here for supper. Merle caught a lovely bunch of trout; one a foot long.

Sunday, July 4 ⤳ A lovely cool day. Almost cold. We haven't been any place and no one has been here. It's seemed lonesome.

Monday, July 5 ⤳ Perfect day. I washed this morning and this afternoon. I was to Marysville and F'ton with Bubar's. Mrs. Tillie Bird went too. Mrs. Bubar went to Marysville to an uncle's funeral and they asked me to go for the drive, and I certainly enjoyed it. We were to see Mrs. Jewett and Mrs. Fred Bird.

Wednesday, July 7 ⤳ Lovely warm bright morning. Cold this afternoon. Feels like frost tonight. I have enamelled *[painted]* some and made myself a dress.

Thursday, July 8 ⤳ Warm and bright this morning, but cold and windy this afternoon. I have finished enamelling the bedroom. I am thankful today.

Friday, July 9 ⤳ Very warm, but cool. Almost cold tonight. I saw Clifford Ferguson marriage in the paper tonight. He only the age of Merle, 18.

Saturday, July 10 ⤳ Raining all day. Merle is in town to a circus. I expect he will be staying down.

Monday, July 12 ⤳ A perfect day. We have all been to the hall to the Orangemen's picnic. Mona was good. I'm tired.

Tuesday, July 13 ⌒ Lovely day. I washed and preserved half pail of strawberry's.

Thursday, July 15 ⌒ Lovely day. Real warm this afternoon. I took Mona home today. I preserved another three pails of strawberries this morning. The little field ones, they are very plentiful.

Friday, July 16 ⌒ Dark and raining. I tore the old couch to pieces today to cover new. It was some job. *[They wasted nothing. If the frame was good, they would recover it with new materials instead of trying to buy a new one.]*

Tuesday, July 20 ⌒ Lovely day. Merle picked a 3 lb lard kettle of wild strawberries today. Tomorrow the church girls have their social. Hope it's fine. I have made a cake for it and made some *[pot]* holders *[to sell]*.

Wednesday, July 21 ⌒ Rain this morning; a heavy shower rained until noon. Intended to go up to Ruby's on train and to the girls garden party this afternoon but Mr. Palmer came after me about six tonight *[probably for a social as she had mentioned the girls making money.]* Had a enjoyable time. They made $86 dollars.

Thursday, July 22 ⌒ Hot and heavy shower this afternoon. Hail and wind. Thunder and lightning. It's raining now tonight and thundering, lightning. Hope it won't be heavy. I have been up to Ruby's. She is feeling better than she was last week. I'm so glad the children haven't same colds. We have stemmed 20 boxes of berries this evening.

Saturday, July 24 ⌒ Was up to Mrs. Lawrence's to get her to see Dr. Jewett about having Merle's tonsils out. *[Dr. Jewett lived in Burtt's Corner at one time and later moved to Millville. It's possible that Mary went to see Mrs. Lawrence because they may have had a phone. Her husband was the undertaker as well as a merchant. Most doctors had phones and it's possible a call had been made from the store to the doctor in Millville.]*

Tuesday, July 27 ⌒ Very hot. We were to Millville and had Merle's tonsils out. Brought him home tonight on train. He's vomited a lot tonight. Dr. Jewett has been here twice. Percy Crouse had his tonsils removed today too.

Wednesday, July 28 ∽ Hot if anything. Hotter than yesterday. Merle is feeling pretty miserable. He hasn't been dressed all day. Just drinking thin soups and boiled water.

Friday, July 30 ∽ Cooler; had a little rain early this morning. Merle's better today. Mrs. Bev Lawrence called tonight.

Saturday, July 31 ∽ Hot. Merle is better today but throat still very sore. We have been up to a band concert.

Monday, August 2 ∽ Wasn't feeling well past couple of days, but feeling better today. Done 6 pts. of gooseberries. Merle's throat still very sore.

Wednesday, August 4 ∽ Lovely day. I feel much better. I ironed and done some preserves and made a little jellie and pie. Merle's throat is getting a little better each day.

Thursday, August 5 ∽ Lovely day; real cold last night. Some being afraid of frost. Have been to Ruby's all day. Had green peas and new beets for the first *[time]* this year.

Friday, August 6 ∽ Lovely day, but very dry. Have just about made a dress today.

Sunday, August 8 ∽ Very hot; a lovely shower this afternoon. Mr. and Mrs. Frank Staples and Bedford were here for tea.

Monday, August 9 ∽ Such a lovely rain. I catched *[caught]* such a lot of water for my wash, and the gardens needed rain so much. Our well water is getting good again. *[Many people kept a rain barrel outside to collect rain water. It was a source of good clean water because any dirt or silt would fall to the bottom of the barrel.]*

Tuesday, August 10 ∽ Lovely day. Merle picked about 13 qts of rasp-berries and I picked two.

Wednesday, August 11 ∽ Warm. I done a lot of jellie and canning again today. Grace came tonight.

Wednesday, Aug 18 ∽ A lovely but cold day. Frost last night again. Grace went home this morning. I feel lonesome. Have been to Ruby's all day. Was to the W.A. Merle is to F'ton tonight getting measured for a suit for the band.

Thursday, Aug 19 ∽ Quite cool again. Annie Staples came up this morning. This is my birthday. I got some nice presents. 35 years today since Annie was married. I have had a busy day today.

Friday, August 20 ∽ Quite a cool day. It's very cold tonight. Will be a heavy frost. We have done bean pickles today.

Sunday, August 22 ∽ A perfect day. We have been to church twice. Mr. Palmer's last Sunday here. We feel bad because he is going. Everyone likes him. Hayward came after us this morning and we were with Ruby all day. Maud brought us home tonight. Lovely moonlight night.

Tuesday, August 24 ∽ Raining all day. This was to be our Sunday School picnic day. Picnic will be tomorrow.

Thursday, August 26 ∽ Lovely day. I ironed and tidied the house, washed yarns and done lots of odd jobs this afternoon. I was down to McDonald's and picked cherries *[likely wild chokecherries for jelly]*.

Friday, August 27 ∽ Raining this afternoon and evening. Merle and I picked about 10 qts of cherries for jellie. I only picked two qts. Merle picked the rest.

Saturday, August 28 ∽ Raining most of day. I made a lot of jellie and preserved some rhubarb. We have been to the store. I got a little felt hat. *[This would have been an everyday hat. She would have had a few good ones for church or other outings.]*

Monday, August 30 ⌒ Cold sometimes; the sun came out tonight but it's windy and cloudy. I done a big wash, made cake and doughnuts.

Thursday, September 2 ⌒ Have been to F'ton since Aug 31. Merle started Business College yesterday. I was over to town all day yesterday. Stayed two nights at Bedford's. Saw Mable McLaggan and Mrs. Will Cummings. Came home this afternoon. *[Merle stayed in the city through the week for school. Only major centres had high schools and colleges in the 1920s, so anyone fortunate enough to attend one had to board in the community during the week because it was too far to travel.]*

Sunday, September 5 ⌒ It's been a perfect day. The Orangemen marched today and played. Tomorrow is the Orangemen picnic if all is well. Mona has been a dear good girl today.

Monday, September 6 ⌒ Rained a pour all the afternoon. They had the band picnic. Set the tables in the planning mill. A big crowd too for all the rain.

Friday, September 10 ⌒ A beautiful day. I have made a lot of mustard chow. Ironed and done some more odd jobs. Merle hasn't come home tonight.

Monday, Sept 13 ⌒ Rained hard this morning until about 10 o'clock. Merle went to F'ton with the Drs. Mona and I have been for the milk. It's a very cold moonlight night. Will be a big frost. 24 years since little Marie passed away.

Tuesday, September 14 ⌒ A lovely day; a very cold morning. A heavy frost last night. I was over to see Bessie Allen this afternoon. She is in bed with heart trouble, poor woman. Mona and I have been for the milk again.

Thursday, September 23 ⌒ Another beautiful day. I have fixed my winter coat today. Put a new collar and cuffs on. We have been to the corner and down to get milk. The moon is lovely now.

1926

Friday, September 24 ∼ Rained all day. I have been making my flannel dress over a little today.

Sunday, September 26 ∼ Very pleasant, but cold. We had a heavy shower last night, a terrible heavy rain and wind but not much thunder and lightning. We were to Baptist church this afternoon and then went out to Willie Brewers to tea. They took us out and brought us back tonight. I believe it's the first time Mona was driving with a horse and wagon. *[She always travelled in the motor car, on the train, or walked with her grandmother.]*

Saturday, October 2 ∼ Dark and gloomy all day. Merle has been digging potatoes for the Bubar's today. Mary Jones was there for dinner.

Saturday, October 9 ∼ Cold and disagreeable. Rained a little every few minutes. Merle came home this morning. Has been working for Bubar's all day. He is going to Night School now; two nights a week.

Sunday, October 10 ∼ A cold windy day. Brighter toward night. Merle wheeled *[bicycled]* to town and I suppose Elwood did too. The leaves are falling fast. It looks so lonesome.

Wednesday, October 12 ∼ Lovely day. I took Mona home as carpenter work is done at Ruby's. I've been to W.A. Buddie is walking and baby's standing by things.

Friday, October 15 ∼ Cold, rainy and disagreeable. I was up to see Mrs. Bubar. She's awfully miserable. Merle wheeled up tonight from town *[Fredericton]*; the roads are awfully muddy. There was a heavy wind in his face. He was awfully tired. *[It would be about a 20-mile or 32-kilometre bike ride.]*

Monday, October 18 ∼ Cold. Wind blowed after it cleared off and dried the roads. Merle wheeled to town this morning. I washed this morning and went out to Mrs. Cooks to try my dress this afternoon. *[Mrs. Cooke would be helping to fit it properly because Mary wouldn't be able to check the fit in the back.]* It's a lovely moonlight night.

Tuesday, October 19 ∾ Cold but such a perfect moonlight night. I done a nice lot of sewing today. I was down for the milk tonight. Mrs. Byron Gorman and Pearl was in awhile tonight.

Thursday, October 21 ∾ Our first snow storm, and a good cold one. Everything looks very wintry.

Friday, October 22 ∾ Warmer, snow most gone. I done quite a lot of my Saturday work. Expect if nothing happens, to go to help Ruby and children down. Merle wheeled up tonight.

Saturday, October 23 ∾ Warm, I went up to help Ruby down with children. We had a circus with Buddie on the train.

Saturday, October 30 ∾ Very nice all day, but looks like snow or rain tonight. Merle is at the hall to a Halloween social.

Saturday, November 6 ∾ Cold, awfully cold. I have had a busy day. It's eleven o'clock now and I've just finished all my little jobs. Merle earned a dollar today trapping.

Sunday, November 7 ∾ Warmer, but very muddy. We were up to Baptist Church; a big crowd there. Quite a number home for Thanksgiving.

Monday, November 8 ∾ Raining and warm. Merle went down on the train tonight. He has such a sore leg. Hurt it on a wire fence the other night. I do hope it heals without any trouble.

Tuesday, November 9 ∾ Foggy, disagreeable all day. Everyone has clothes on the line. I have been to Ruby's to help her with her ceiling. White washed it. The children were fussy.

Sunday, November 14 ∾ A fairly nice day. We were up to Baptist church to Armistice sermon *[where it]* was preached. Mr. and Mrs. Willie Brewer and children were here to tea and Muriel called. Merle and Elwood wheeled to town.

Wednesday, November 17 ∾ Last night was a wild night. The wind blowed a gale but today has been like summer. Just as warm and sunshiney. I put the border on Merle's bedroom. We made mincemeat tonight. There is a bean supper at Oliver's tonight for the church. It's moonlight and warm as September

Saturday, November 20 ◒ A lovely day. Merle wheeled up this morning; some muddy wheeling.

Monday, November 22 ◒ A lovely day. Cold tonight. We have been to a play at the hall for Wilder Brewer. Quite a lot of his work was sold. *[Mary doesn't elaborate, but it's possible that Wilder wasn't able to work at this time. Wilder repaired furniture so he might have made some furniture that was sold during or after the play.]*

Tuesday, November 23 ◒ A cold but pleasant day. I have been to Ruby's. Got the kitchen wall murescoed a little. The baby has stuck to me like a burr *[burdock]* all day. He's beginning to talk at ten months. *[Muresco was a powder that mixed with water. It acted as an early form of paint before oil, wax, or milk paints existed.]*

Wednesday, November 24 ◒ Snowed quite a dust until noon. It's rained all the afternoon but it's turning cold again tonight. I cleaned the clothes closet today and a few odd jobs. Went to *[post]* office and mailed my xmas Eaton order.

Friday, November 26 ◒ Warm, raining tonight. Merle came home. Started to wheel but busted a tire at Mouth of Keswick. He had to walk and lead the wheel, and the night so dark and roads so slippery. He was very tired.

Sunday, November 28 ◒ Cold; real winter weather. Merle started to wheel to town, had to turn back. The roads are a fright. Can hardly get a car or anything else over them. Maud was down awhile with the horse and wagon. We went for a drive it was a good rough one.

Monday, November 29 ◒ Such a grey gloomy day, just dark all day. We have had a long day. Merle walked to town; some walk *[about 20 miles*

or 32 kilometres] and he set the alarm for half after four and it alarmed half after 3. We were all awake then until we got up at five. I washed and it's pouring rain again tonight. I bet Merle's tired tonight, dear old boy. Roy Burtt met him below Curry's *[Currie's]* Mountain sometime between seven and eight. He started half past five.

Thursday, December 2 ∽ A cold snow storm blowing in and freezing. I haven't done five cents worth of work today. I guess I'm lazy. Had a letter from Grace. Mrs. Casey was in awhile.

Friday, December 4 ∽ Awfully cold; it's just fierce cold tonight. Merle came home this morning. He's taking a cold. He got a lovely lot of wood in the shed today.

Sunday, December 5 ∽ Cold last night frightfully cold. I had a call from Trilby *[local hobo]* this morning.

Wednesday, December 8 ∽ Snow storm again. Warmer but the wind has started tonight. I have finished cleaning the house for a little while. Wrote a letter to Grace tonight and finished LeBaron's mitty and worked a dishtowel.

Thursday, December 9 ∽ A lovely day. I have been out as far as Ben Jones collecting for Kathleen Bird.

Friday, December 11 ∽ Warm, snowing this afternoon and evening. The wind is beginning to blow now nearly eleven o'clock. I made my xmas doughnuts today and some gingersnaps. I miss Merle not coming today. Miss him so much this evening the first time he has stayed down on Sunday.

Monday, December 20 ∽ Not so cold, real pleasant. We killed five roosters today; a great job done. *[They would pluck the feathers and prepare the birds so they could cook them for Christmas.]* I was very tired. I done up a few xmas parcels and received a few.

Tuesday, December 21 ∽ Snow this morning. But it was warm. Mona

142

and I were down to Maybe's for milk. I made more sausage meat.

Wednesday, December 22 ⌒ Lovely morning. Another little dust of snow and it's blowing real cold this afternoon. Merle came home this morning. We popped some corn tonight. *[They dried their own corn. To pop it, they would heat the corn with a bit of butter in a covered pot on the stove. They swished it back and forth so it wouldn't get too hot and stick to the pot. If they couldn't tell by the sound that the corn was finished popping and lifted the lid too early, popcorn would fly everywhere.]*

Friday, December 24 ⌒ Lovely day; very cold morning. I went up on one train and back on the other for Ruby and the children. We have had some busy day.

Saturday, December 25, Xmas Day ⌒ Beautiful like spring. Santa Claus was wonderfully good again and had a nice xmas, if I only knew how it was with poor Reuben *[She hadn't heard from her brother in a while.]* It's nearly 12 o'clock and I'm still up. It's turning real cold.

Tuesday, December 28 ⌒ A big snow storm on this afternoon. Ruby went home. I went up with them. There was a big box of toys for them up there from Grace, and Mona is so excited from it all that she's just cross and whiney. It's still snowing hard now; eleven o'clock at night.

Thursday, December30 ⌒ Merle is working with Arthur Allen cutting pulp.

Saturday, December 31 ⌒ Rained all day; cold tonight. Feeling some better. The last of the old year with all its joys and mistakes, it has been a happy year. We have all been blessed with health and plenty. It's been a nice day. Merle has been working today again. Good bye old year.

❦ *1926* ❦

1927

Wednesday, January 5 ∽ Very mild; rained all day. I have been up to Ruby's. It's LeBaron's birthday; one year. He had a cookie with a candle in it for he don't eat cake, but cookies.

Thursday, January 7 ∽ Another lovely day. The wind a little cold. I have sewed a little; made Buddie a pair of rompers, and went down for milk.

Saturday, January 8 ∽ Another lovely day, but colder. Real snapping cold tonight. I have painted and varnished the rocker that Wilder Brewer re-bottomed *[out of wicker or thin wood]*. It looks great. He, Wilder brought some of his work down to the store tonight. I guess he sold quite a lot of things.

Tuesday, January 11 ∽ Cold; snowing a little all day and blowing. Mrs. Macdonald is very low; expecting her death any time. Mrs. Bubar was there last night and she said she slept lovely all night. I'm so glad. I had Trilby for dinner which I enjoyed very much.

Wednesday, January 12 ∽ Poor Mrs. MacDonald died last night about nine o'clock. I'm glad she's at rest but how we will all miss her. One of the best women I ever knew. Albert and I spent the evening with them tonight.

Friday, January 14 ∽ Warm; a big thaw on. Mrs. MacDonald was buried today *[funeral at the house].* A big funeral. It don't seem possible that she's gone. There is a lot of sickness, grippe. Mrs. Casey and the little boy are both sick and Mrs. Durant's baby.

Thursday, January 20 ∽ Another big thaw, and it's been just like an April day and still warm tonight. Mrs. George Brewer was in this afternoon. I have been making sash curtains for the kitchen.

Monday, February 7 ∽ Done a big wash, scrubbed and varnished a chair and sideboard. Then went to see Mrs. Allen and back again after noon.

Tuesday, February 8 ∽ Tried some lard and had 13 lbs taken out of my old hog at store. *[They would have slaughtered a pig and melted the lard from the pig fat.]* I've painted a chair and hem stitched a pillow case.

Saturday, February 20 ∽ Merle was at Bev Lawrence's and heard a Church of England *[service]* on the radio. A baby was baptised and he could hear it fret. *[Some people in the community have a new form of communication — the radio.]*

Saturday, February 26 ∽ Was to the city. Got a lovely new bedstead, mattress and springs. I got alabastine (blue), and border for dining room and my bedroom.

Wednesday, March 2 ∽ I have finished painting my bedroom floor. They were gassed at the Drs. last night. Wouldn't have taken much to kill them I guess. *[Nitrous Oxide, or laughing gas, was the most common gas used for medical and dental procedures after 1900. It can be deadly because it is combustible if near a heat source.]*

Thursday, March 3 ∽ Made $31 at the church social.

Wednesday, April 26 ⌒ Merle got the old flue torn down and ready for the new one. I got the screen doors and windows down and cleaned them. *[The windows were made of single pane glass and had no screened section, so wooden frames with screens were fastened to the windows for the summer months. In the fall, the screens would be removed and replaced with storm windows for the winter.]*

Tuesday, May 4 ⌒ We are cleaning the dining room. Merle white washed it and helped me paper it. We are going to put fibre veneer *[a form of wainscoting]* on tomorrow.

Tuesday, May 27 ⌒ I washed, make over curtains for Merle's bedroom, painted the hall floor up stairs, scrubbed the kitchen and made Buddie a pair of stockings.

Sunday, May 29 ⌒ Were to Baptist meeting twice 115th anniversary. Great crowds.

Wednesday, June 8 ⌒ Mrs. Will Burt has another set of twins. A boy and girl; making 16 children. *[Not an unusual size for families in this time period.]*

Thursday, June 9 ⌒ Merle put a new roof on the house. Yard full of old shingles.

Friday, June 10 ⌒ Merle cleaned up all old shingles and piled three loads of wood.

Thursday, June 16 ⌒ Mona is 5 today. My baby would have been 23.

Monday, June 30 ⌒ Band practicing for big celebration; 60th year of Confederation tomorrow July 1st.

Tuesday, July 1 ⌒ Merle went with the band. The mill is down as most everyone is in the city.

Tuesday, July 12 ⌒ Merle to Pokiok to play in band for Orangemen's picnic. Showers sent them home early.

Wednesday, July 13 ❧ Strawberry tea on Rectory grounds. Made nearly $50.00.

Monday, August 22 ❧ Went to town to see a picture, *"The Four Horsemen"*.

Thursday, September 1 ❧ Making new siding for the station *[likely wooden slab siding from the mill]*.

Monday, September 5 (Labour Day) ❧ We all went to the big picnic at the corner. The band played; big crowd.

Wednesday, September 21 ❧ Merle is at the exhibition. I wash, scrubbed, ironed and preserved apples, and did some pickles.

Friday, September 24 ❧ I had a busy day. I'm awfully tired. Dressed 4 chickens, cooked, cleaned the house and other things.

Monday, September 27 ❧ Mill broke down so won't be work for some time.

Friday, September 30 ❧ Merle has been picking potatoes for Dell Pugh again.

Tuesday, October 4 ❧ Keswick Fair started.

Saturday, October 29 ❧ Mill finished sawing today. *[The men would be heading back to woods soon for the winter.]*

Saturday, November 5 ❧ Terrible storm; lots of washouts in places. Terrible train accident near Woodstock from a washout. 3 men killed.

Friday, November 18 ❧ I have boiled down 16 lbs. of lard. Some hot job.

Wednesday, November 30 ❧ Made big jars of mincemeat.

Friday, December 16 ❧ Jaundice in BC *[Burtt's Corner]*. Jim Jewett's family all sick with it. *[Jaundice is a disease that gives the skin a yellowish tinge. It is often caused by an elevated level of bilirubin in the blood.]*

Friday, December 23 ∾ Dressed 5 chickens. *[They may have used all of them for Christmas dinner if they were small chickens. Often people traded or bartered at the store for other items they needed, so she may have traded some. Some families cooked chickens, some turkey and some goose. It depended on what they raised at home.]* Took bath early to avoid rush.

Saturday, December 31 ∾ Albert done in the store tonight. I'm sorry business so slack.

1928

Thursday, February 2 ∾ Albert working for the mill unloading oats for the mill and it's a hard heavy job. *[The oats would be feed for the work horses.]*

Friday, February 3 ∾ Albert finished unloading oats.

Thursday, February 9 ∾ Been to Jim Jewett's to a knitting party.

Monday, February 13 ∾ Albert's been scaling some pulp for Howard Gorman.

Wednesday, February 15 ∾ Jim Logan been here tonight. Has been working on a bridge out the Forks.

Tuesday, February 28 ∾ Merle and I are papering, murescoed the ceiling in the kitchen. It's lovely and white. We have it all papered but the border. The men are putting the fibre veneer on tomorrow.

Tuesday, March 6 ∾ Merle is helping Ralph Bubar racking potatoes.

Saturday, March 10 ∾ Merle got his papers for Detroit but won't be going for awhile. *[This was the second person going to Detroit for work.]*

Tuesday, March 13 ∾ People are hauling car loads of potatoes and selling at $3.00 per barrel.

Wednesday, April 4 ∾ Maddie Jewett and I were up to the barber to have our hair cut. *[The community barbershop provided service to men, women, and children.]*

Thursday, April 5 ∾ The mill started up.

Sunday, April 8 ∾ High water. A big washout on rail just above here. Hayward has been out all the afternoon. The logs run out *[of the mill pond]* and all over and people figure they will be gone *[down the river]* by morning.

Monday, April 16 ∾ Mill started again today; if it can only stay going.

Monday, April 30 ∾ We put the moulding on the kitchen and dining room today.

Wednesday, June 20 ∾ Merle has Detroit fever again. He and Holly Pugh are going soon.

Friday, June 22 ∾ Albert has been to town to get his teeth made.

Tuesday, June 26 ∾ Merle and Mona and I went to an ice cream social at the hall.

Friday, June 29 ∾ Merle is packing his suit case tonight *[for Detroit]*.

Monday, July 2 ∾ Merle has started for Detroit. It was so hard to part with him.

Tuesday, July 3 ∾ They expect to arrive in Detroit at one or half after tomorrow morning; Wednesday,

Monday, July 9 ∾ I varnished the screen door, painted the sink *[would likely be cast iron, but possibly still wood]* and scrubbed.

Thursday, July 12 ∾ Heard from Merle. Was to start in a factory last Monday.

Saturday, July 14 ∾ Got a card from Merle tonight. Says he's working 13 ½ hrs a day in Detroit.

Thursday, July 26 ∾ Have been to F'ton to a carnival. The band is playing.

Thursday, August 2 ∾ Done up 6 pts. of gooseberries and some raspberry jellie.

Tuesday, August 7 ∾ Went to aid out Birdton to Densmore Bird's. Went with the Bubar's. *[Birdton is about 5 miles or 8 kilometres north of Burtt's Corner at the intersection of Route 617 and Crow Hill Road where 617 turns east towards the Route 620 which leads to Stanley, New Brunswick.]*

Friday, August 10 ∾ Had a letter from Merle. He is out of work.

Saturday, August 11 ∾ Letter from Merle. Has found more work in another small factory.

Sunday, August 19 ∾ My birthday. Ruby gave me a lovely apron and a dollar. Albert gave me a purple umbrella. Merle sent me some money. Grace gave me a pretty dress and the women that came to visit with her gave me a little cream set.

Tuesday, August 28 ∾ I ironed and preserved a basket of plums.

Sunday, September 2 ∾ Went to F'ton. Hayward had to take a man to catch the Montreal train.

Thursday, September 13 ∾ 26 years today since little Marie went away.

Wednesday, September 26 ∾ Was a man shot at Brewer's Mills today. Perley Graham.

Wednesday, October 3 ∾ Went to barbershop for haircuts.

Friday, October 12 ∾ I cut out and made myself a warm house dress, dressed a fowl, finished a set of curtains, scrubbed my kitchen floor.

Sunday, October 21 ∾ Went to Lucy Gorman's awhile this afternoon, but she was ready to go on a nursing case *[as midwife]*.

Wednesday, October 25 ∾ A typewritten letter from Merle.

Tuesday, October 30 ∾ Changed the summer and winter curtains.

Wednesday, October 31 ∾ I have just got home from a bean supper at Dunk Brewer's. We made 17 dollars. Had a letter from Merle; he's homesick. He has had a piece of steel in his eye.

Friday, November 23 ∾ Durant's have moved away. *[They lived in Burtt's Corner from spring to fall while the mill was in operation.]*

Friday, November 30 ∾ I have embroidered a set of pillow cases.

Sunday, December 2 ∾ We went down to George Brewer's to listen to radio.

Sunday, December 23 ∾ We had first car incident today down Douglas. Roads slippery and car slurred and over she went. My neck and shoulder a little stiff and Ruby's elbow. Bruises but no major injuries. But children awfully scared and no wonder.

Monday, December 31 ∾ It has been a pleasant year gone with all my mistakes and faults, and all its happiness as well as the lonely days since Merle left. But so thankful that he is well and has work.

1929

Wednesday, January 2 ∾ Albert worked in the potato house.

Thursday, January 10 ∾ Had letter from Merle. He thinks there must be 5000 out of work in Detroit.

Friday, January 11 ∾ Henry Bird died. *[Nicknamed Harry, he was the local shoe maker.]*

Friday, January 18 ∾ Albert has been helping with potatoes.

Saturday, January 19 ∾ Water everywhere. Albert's working in store as Wassie went to town. So much water and roads dangerous so Wassie came back home by train.

Tuesday, January 22 ∾ There was a big fire in F'ton today. Queen Street from Woolworths to Edgecombe's. Terrible day for a fire with big wind. *[The buildings were all connected to each other and the only heat source was wood or coal. Flue fires were common because stovepipes were made from a single layer of metal and the hot pipes close to walls and ceilings often caused fires.]*

Monday, January 28 ᴄᴡ Albert still working in potato house, and loading potatoes in boxcars.

Wednesday, January 30 ᴄᴡ Albert working at Spencer Brewer's today.

Thursday, February 7 ᴄᴡ We're putting oilcloth in bedroom, and painted the front bedroom.

Tuesday, February 12 ᴄᴡ A social. Made cookies and made fudge for the social. Made over $30.00. *[Possibly at a Valentines Social.]*

Thursday, February 21 ᴄᴡ Up to Mrs. Will Hagerman's to a quilting.

Friday, March 1 ᴄᴡ Mona and I had lovely walk on the log roads over nearly to J. Curries. Five or six slides on hills behind Curries. When we came back, couple of children was playing on ice under the bridge so I let her play there awhile. After supper she was sliding with Beth Bubar and Pearl Gorman.

Monday, March 4 ᴄᴡ Was over to Lloyd Woodworth and had my hair trimmed.

Saturday, March 23 ᴄᴡ Finished stitching some tablecloths.

Thursday, March 28 ᴄᴡ Finished my quilt, baked two kinds of bread and made tiny Easter cookies for the children. And some fudge.

Wednesday, April 10 ᴄᴡ Albert working on road for J.D. Brewer.

Monday, April 22 ᴄᴡ Mona started school today. Hope she will like it and the walk won't be too much for her. The mill started today. The big mill, the planning mill has been running for a week. Albert to start work there in the morning.

Saturday, April 27 ᴄᴡ High water so mill is down.

Saturday, May 4 ᴄᴡ The mill down again due to high water.

Wednesday, May 8 ᴄᴡ Put up dining room curtains and re-dyed my other curtains. My new armchair came today.

Friday, May 10 ～ I varnished my bedroom floor and cleaned out some more boxes and drawers. And cleaned the kitchen sideboard. Went to corner tonight and re-seated a leather bottomed chair.

May 18-20 ～ ground white with snow.

Friday, May 24 ～ The young folk have taken their play to show in Millville.

Wednesday, June 5 ～ Just got home from oyster supper at Dunk Brewers. Quite a crowd.

Friday, June 7 ～ Was to town in the truck with Albert. Got a *'ready-made'* black silk dress. *[She had been making all their clothes.]*

Monday, June 17 ～ Bobby Durant came today. He is here part of the time.

Friday, June 21 ～ Bobby finished piling the last of the wood.

Saturday, June 22 ～ Methodists had a food sale at Hagerman's Store.

Friday, June 28 ～ Went to high school closing. *[This would be in Fredericton as Burtt's Corner didn't have a high school until 1948, with the first five graduates graduating from the IOF Hall location in 1949.]*

Wednesday, July 24 ～ Had ice cream social here under the trees.

Thursday, July 25 ～ Mona and I were up to Tom Fowler's tonight.

Friday, July 26 ～ Mona, Mrs. Morehouse and Mr. McQueen went to F'ton to see a circus parade.

Monday, July 29 ～ Have been to Forester hall for pictures *[movies]*.

Wednesday, August 14 ～ Little Lebaron nearly drowned while they were bathing *[in the creek]* and he got out in deep water. Went down three times before Ruby got him.

Monday, August 19 ～ Albert is in the store as Wassie has gone peddling today. *[Wassie would have travelled around selling merchandise* *from the store.]*

Sunday, August 25 ～ Picked some cranberries. Hope I didn't do wrong picking on Sunday. *[Many believed that Sunday was a day for Church and rest.]*

Tuesday, August 27 ～ I've made 17 bottles of jellie, cranberry, grape and black current.

Friday, August 30 ～ Albert is at the hall to a lecture.

Sunday, September 1 ～ Went for a walk on the flat. Then went up to the Orangeman sermon at the hall this afternoon.

Tuesday, September 3 ～ election; went up to vote. We both went.

Thursday, September 19 ～ Mill burned today, a number of board piles, and I don't know how much more if the fire motor *[fire truck]* from F'ton hadn't have come. People were here from far and near. *[to help. This was the first time the new Fredericton fire truck was used.]*

Monday, September 23 ～ Albert worked half a day on the bridge. *[This could have been the covered bridge next to the mill.]* He is at the lodge tonight.

Tuesday, October 1 ～ Been to town for my glasses. Work is done on the bridge for the men around here.

Wednesday, October 2 ～ Albert is at the *[Forester]* hall as he is now caretaker.

Tuesday, October 8 ～ Albert has another job; finishing the potato house.

Thursday, October 10 ～ I called on the two families in the Coy House.

Sunday, October 13 ～ We got a big fire scare last night. The church bell rang at quarter of one but it was only Harry Elliot's empty house. Had everyone out of their beds running and frightened. *[The church bell* *was the quickest way to alert the community of an emergency.]*

Monday, October 14 ∽ W.A. sold our rug by tickets. Hazel Estey got it.

Wednesday, October 16 ∽ Walked from Maud's up and collected the "Mite Boxes". *[The mite boxes were common in the Protestant Women's Aids organizations where each woman got a box to collect funds for church needs or service projects.]*

Thursday, October 17 ∽ Cleaned the stove pipes and moved the kitchen table in from shed *[summer kitchen].*

Saturday, October 26 ∽ The old cook house started *[to burn]* the way of the mill, but was put out.

Monday, October 28 ∽ Cold. I washed and the clothes froze as quick as I hung them out. I ironed 7 pairs curtains today. Albert working at the potato house.

Tuesday, October 29 ∽ very cold, done a day's work of odds and ends, put up clean curtains, went to corner, mailed Eaton order. Stopped at Maud Jewett's. Had her tonsils removed. Albert worked at potato house again today.

Wednesday, October 30 ∽ fine and cold. At W.A. at Duncan Brewer's quilting. Kathleen Brewer and Elmer Jones married tonight in the church. Albert still at potato house.

Thursday, October 31 ∽ Damp, raw day. Been up to Ruby's; had Merle's letter. He's still working. Poor old Trilby is dead. *[Local hobo woman]*

Tuesday, November 5 ∽ Ironed my embroidered bedspread and two pairs of curtains.

Thursday, November 7 ∽ The mill barn burned tonight, another strange fire, added to the list, I had lots of callers on the strength of it.

Monday, November 11 ∽ Armistice Day with a little celebration at the monument. Quite a few there. This is also Thanksgiving Day.

Saturday, November 16 ∾ We have had about 30 in for a musical evening.

Monday, November 18 ∾ A big snow storm, and an earthquake shock.

Wednesday, November 20 ∾ Merle arrived home from Detroit by train; shipped his motorcycle.

Saturday, November 23 ∾ Another lovely musical evening at Johnny MacDonald's.

Tuesday, November 26 ∾ Merle and I have been to town. He got me a pair of $7.50 shoes and a pair of stockings, and a new white enamel sink.

Friday, November 29 ∾ Merle has gone again to Detroit. Albert drove for our pump, but something is wrong and he has worked so hard. *[Mary was referring to the process of driving a point into the ground to hit water. They dug a hole with picks and shovels until they hit water. Then they inserted a tapered metal and mesh rod shaped like a pencil with a pointed end. They attached piping that ran into the house to the hand pump. The water would filter through the mesh into the piping. When they moved the hand pump handle up and down, the water was forced up through the piping and out the spout into the sink.]*

Monday, December 2 ∾ Earl Burtt was here for dinner and supper. He is in the station learning telegraphy. He will be here quite a lot. *[Telegraph communication used short and long taps on the coding machine or 'key' to relay messages. The series of dashes and or dots represented each letter of the alphabet. One example is ··· ––– ··· for SOS. The other telegraph operator on the receiving end could tell from the taps what letters were being sent to make up the messages. Telegraphic messages (or telegrams) were sent from one railway station to another to warn of washouts, trains delayed due to weather, and other necessary communi-*

cation. The messages travelled along wires similar to the telephone wires used today.]

Wednesday, December 4 ◠ A wild time with the *[hand]* pump. Struck quick sand and been pumping it up all over the floor and everywhere. Willie Gilby was here to supper helping with the pump. *[They would have likely lifted some flooring too.]*

Thursday, December 5 ◠ The pump is surely a failing.

Monday, December 9 ◠ We got the pipes and point jacked out today.

Wednesday, December 18 ◠ A terrible snowstorm. Just got home from Hazel Wallace's wedding. She looked fine in white silk and lace veil and orange blossoms.

Thursday, December 19 ◠ Still storming; roads heavy. Ruby has gone with Mona to school closing. It will be a hard walk.

Friday, December 20 ◠ Rain freezing as it comes. Terrible travelling.

Saturday, December 21 ◠ The crust shimmering like ice everywhere. Terrible for the horses *[pulling sleds]*.

Monday, December 30 ◠ An awful big snowstorm; big drifts. Sadie Smith was here waiting for morning train. Came from Birdton in the storm.

Chapter 3

1930-1934

THE TRAIN was still an important way of travel for people, and initially the Burtt's Corner station was as busy as ever. Either the waiting room at the station wasn't heated very well or people were just anxious to socialize, because the location of the Morehouse home next to the railway provided the perfect spot to stop for a cup of tea or hot soup while they waited for the train.

The Woodstock to Fredericton train cut back to one round trip daily. Nothing in Mary's journal suggested why, but, by the 1930s, the railway was in financial difficulties and started cutting staff, services, trains, and routes.

The market crash of 1929 sent many countries into a state of financial depression that continued into the 1930s. In addition, Western Canada was hit with a drought which ruined many farms. The extended period without rain turned once-green farmland into acres of dust and the term *The Dirty 30s* became a household phrase. Eastern Canada offered help in any way possible, and Mary noted that a car load of vegetables was headed west from the Burtt's Corner station. Some of the local farmers also struggled, and farm auctions in York County are mentioned in the diary. In December, 1932, the Canadian churches proposed an International Day of Prayer for World Depression, but had no luck getting one set aside.

Originally, Canadian Thanksgiving was the same week as Armistice Day, with Thanksgiving being on the second Monday in November and Armistice Day, the Monday before November 11th. For many years, the two fell on the same day. This caused some concern with Thanksgiving being a time for celebration and Armistice Day commemorating a solemn event. On March 18, 1931, A.W. Neil, MP for Comox-Alberni in British Columbia, introduced a motion in the House of Commons to have Armistice Day observed on November 11 and on no other date. It was then that the name was also changed to Remembrance Day in order to honour the veterans who lost their lives as opposed to the actual signing of the

Armistice. Thanksgiving Day was also moved to a Monday in October at this time, and it no longer coincided with the date in the United States.

Burtt's Corner residents still got their medicine directly from doctors instead of a pharmacy. Old diseases such as tuberculosis and diphtheria returned to the province and clinics were set up for diphtheria vaccinations. Those suffering with tuberculosis had to get treatment at a hospital.

The community continued to support both girls and boys baseball teams which competed against other communities. The church groups from Burtt's Corner and surrounding communities still used their travelling plays as fundraising events. A young people's group started at the church for teens.

1930

Tuesday, January 7 ᔕ Tillie Bird has his *[potato]* car loaded so he won't be back for awhile.

Wednesday, January 8 ᔕ Albert hurt his back at the potato house today.

Thursday, January 23 ᔕ Over to Mrs. B. Gorman's having our hair trimmed.

Sunday, February 2 ᔕ Earl *[Burtt]* and I drove up to Zealand to supper; did enjoy the sleigh drive.

Saturday, February 8 ᔕ Made ice cream tonight. It's lovely.

Saturday, February 15 ᔕ We were over to Mrs. George Brewers tonight to listen to the radio. It wasn't any good tonight. *[She could refer to the signal and not hearing it well as it was very weak when they first started listening in the area, or it could be that the program they listened to wasn't any good.]*

Friday, February 21 ᔕ In to Mrs. Allen's and heard Arnold Jones give an address over the radio from the high school. It was good. About F`ton being a good sight *[site]* for an airplane port *[airport]*.

Sunday, March 9 ∿ Rained last night. Raining a little now. Water all over the flat. Pulp piles *[8-foot logs for the mill]* falling down.

Wednesday, March 12 ∿ A heavy rain storm last night. Water everywhere; everyone travelling over the hill. *[The regular road was along the brook, but, during high water, there was a temporary road along the hill behind the Morehouse property from the station to the Keswick or main road through the community.]*

Thursday, March 13 ∿ Still lots of water everywhere.

Friday, March 14 ∿ A terrible cold windy day, and tonight the wind is nearly lifting things.

Wednesday, April 9 ∿ Earl is at a dance to Stanley Pugh's.

Thursday, April 10 ∿ Was up to the millinery store tonight.

Saturday, April 12 ∿ Was up to the millinery store again a big crowd there. *[The ladies always tried to have a new spring hat for Easter, which may explain the crowded store.]*

Sunday, April 13 ∿ We all went to the Methodist Church. *[The Morehouse family are Anglican but they go to church anywhere whenever they can attend.]*

Wednesday, April 16 ∿ Tillie Bird was here for supper; staying all night looking after a potato car.

Sunday, May 11 ∿ The first they *[Hayward and Ruby]* have had their car out this year. Mona was vaccinated this week.

Thursday, May 22 ∿ Earl, Anna Lovegrove, Albert and myself were down Keswick tonight looking for greens. *[It was very common for people to search for spring fiddleheads around the Keswick and Burtt's Corner area. The Indians also used to set up camp for weeks on the islands in* *the Saint John River just below the intersection with the Keswick River to harvest fiddleheads.]*

Friday, May 23 ∼ Albert has been helping haul boards to F'ton *[Fredericton]* all day for Elwood Burtt.

Sunday, May 25 ∼ We were down to the airplane port this afternoon, up above the city. *[There was a small airport north of the main city (off what is now Sunset Drive) before the current airport in Lincoln opened.]*

Wednesday, May 28 ∼ Albert's been loading a car of lumber.

Wednesday, June 4 ∼ Merle fishing and caught 70 fish. Albert started work on the road today.

Saturday, June 14 ∼ Walked down to Mrs. MacLean's this afternoon for a sitting of eggs. Mrs. Wilkin's went with me.

Wednesday, June 18 ∼ Albert to the hall tonight for a lecture. *[Probably election candidates speaking.]*

Thursday, June 19 ∼ Election day. The conservatives in again. *[This was the 37th NB Parliament. Conservatives got 31 seats; the Liberals, 17.]*

Wednesday, June 25 ∼ Been up to the graveyard doing a little work. Saw such a horrid big snake in our lot, we couldn't half work. Had a letter from Merle. He is working in Carabo *[Caribou, Maine]* on B&A railroad. *[The one on the Monopoly game board was named after it.]*

Monday, June 30 ∼ Albert not working on road today, so put the pump down in the well.

Tuesday, July 1 ∼ The United Church had a big picnic, we just got home 12pm.

Tuesday, July 8 ∼ Had our strawberry supper on Ruby's verandah. A good crowd turned out. Cleared $18 *[for the Woman's Aid].*

Monday, July 28 ○ Election day. Hanson got two hundred votes, Wilson only 93 or 98. *[This was the federal election and she must have been reporting for the local polling station where Ruby sometimes worked. Hanson, the Conservative cadidate got 10,666 total votes while Winslow, the Liberal candidate got 3,207.]*

Sunday, August 3 ○ Mrs. Tom Colter and Guida were here awhile.

Saturday, August 16 ○ Mona and I went down on the steam boat to May Ferguson's *[She lived at Lakeville Corner. Steam boats were still running on the Saint John River.]*

Saturday, August 20 ○ Clarence Burtt died tonight from injuries received yesterday from runaway horses.

Monday, September 1 ○ Baptists had their picnic at the hall today, so we were all up.

Friday, September 26 ○ Albert got a job today on the bridge by Maybe's. *[This wooden covered bridge replaced the first wood structure over the Jones Forks Stream.]*

Monday, October 13 ○ Just wonderful, I washed and steamed pillows, made a pine needle pillow and made cookies.

Wednesday, October 15 ○ Albert made potato inspector. *[He later inspected potatoes in Keswick, Kingsclear, Devon, Woodstock, Millville, Fredericton, Longs Creek, Prince William and Hartland.]*

Thursday, October 16 ○ Albert is away tonight; up Perth getting instruction for the potato business.

Monday, November 3 ○ We have been to a concert by the Devon Quartet.

Tuesday, November 18 ○ We have a new boarder for a few days; a station agent.

Thursday, November 20 ○ Very tired. Been busy all day, and made meals for my four men *[boarders that stayed until November 22].*

Friday, December 19 〜 I made doughnuts and ribbon cake. Earl has been down to Peter Christie's helping dress chickens.

Saturday, December 20 〜 Tom Brewer died today. *[He owned T.M. Brewer Store in the main village.]*

1931

Thursday, January 8 ᴄᴡ Mrs. McLean was in awhile this evening waiting for train.

Tuesday, January 13 ᴄᴡ We have an invitation to the Governor's Ball. *[probably as a result of Albert's potato inspector job. Unfortunately, Mary doesn't mention actually attending the ball in her diary.]*

Friday, January 16 ᴄᴡ Cold but bright. Albert walked to Keswick and back. *[He was at the Keswick Station to inspect potatoes. In January, this was likely a cold walk along the railway bed, because it would be about 7-10 kilometres one way.]*

Friday, January 30 ᴄᴡ A heavy fall of snow.

Saturday, January 31 ᴄᴡ Merle was on the road shovelling all the morning. *[Merle came home from Detroit for Christmas and stayed.]*

Friday, February 13 ᴄᴡ I got a valentine from the children. Quite a lot of hauled potatoes today.

Saturday, February 14 ᴄᴡ A big rain all day and half of last night.

Sunday, February 15 ∾ Some water coming in well since rain. *[They had gone back to the outside well because of all the problems they had trying to install the hand pump.]*

Tuesday, February 17 ∾ Merle is at the Young People's meeting to-night.

Wednesday, February 18 ∾ A storm brewing tonight. I walked up to Dr.'s and had my medicine bottle filled.

Tuesday, March 3 ∾ Albert was at Keswick all day. Smith, the head man *[for potato inspection]* was here.

Sunday, March 8 ∾ We were over to see Mr. Brewer, still wandering in his mind.

Tuesday, March 10 ∾ Bubar has got the farmer's store. *[He had taken over ownership. There were several stores in the community at this time.]*

Friday, March 20 ∾ The first team broke through on the ice road *[shortcut on the river]*, so people will have to drive around by the Dr.'s. It was Bubar's team.

Monday, March 31 ∾ Albert was at Keswick. Merle went after him. The first *[potato]* car was out. *[Being a "first car" of potatoes out, these would have been seed potatoes for farmers anxious to start their new crop. Albert was the potato inspector and had to approve the quality before the potatoes were loaded at the station.]*

Tuesday, April 1 ∾ I crossed on the new bridge for the first.

Saturday, April 4 ∾ The band had a supper at the hall tonight. Made about $40.

Tuesday, April 7 ∾ We have been married 37 years today.

Wednesday, April 8 ∾ Albert was to Hayne, Canfield, Keswick and Zealand.

Tuesday, April 14 ∿ There's a fire out the forks; don't know just where.

Wednesday, April 15 ∿ It was Stanley Pugh's house burned last night. There is a dance in the hall tonight.

Friday, April 17 ∿ Out to Willie Brewers for butter. Merle has been with others getting lumber for to build a house for Stanley Pugh.

Sunday, April 19 ∿ Hayward and Ruby came down on motor to dinner. We went up to Tilly Hughson's funeral. A large funeral. The war veterans were up. *[These were WWI vets.]*

Tuesday, April 21 ∿ Howard Bird's house and barn were burned today.

Wednesday, April 22 ∿ We have had a social here tonight. Quite a crowd took in about $22.

Thursday, April 23 ∿ Have house all put to rights again *[after rearranging it for the social]*. Men putting steel roof on shed.

Monday, April 27 ∿ They're loading potatoes here *[at the station]*.

Wednesday, April 29 ∿ A dance in the hall tonight.

Friday, May 1 ∿ I cleaned the clothes press today.

Thursday, May 7 ∿ I stretched 3 pairs of curtains.

Saturday, May 9 ∿ Byron Gorman moved today in the Orange Hall. Ray and Ethel will move in soon. *[Likely while they built a home or prepared to move in somewhere.]*

Tuesday, May 12 ∿ Merle fixed the shed with building paper. *[He had covered it with the black tar paper that was used prior to attaching shingles or wood siding.]*

Tuesday, May 19 ∿ Merle drove Edna Wilkins to F'ton to take train for Connecticut.

Friday, May 29 ∿ The Dr. met at the hall this afternoon to give the treatment to prevent Diphtheria. 195 *[people]* had it done.

❧ *1931* ❧

Wednesday, June 3 ∿ There is a band concert social or something at the hotel tonight.

Sunday, June 14 ∿ Been to church twice and took a little drive around Jewett's Mills and Tripp Settlement.

Thursday, June 18 ∿ The boys are practicing tonight for to go to camp. Merle is to have a horse *[to work with this time]*.

Friday, June 19 ∿ They had the diphtheria clinic today again.

Thursday, June 25 ∿ The boys are training on the horses tonight.

Friday, June 26 ∿ The boys went to camp this afternoon on the horses.

Sunday, June 28 ∿ Was to early service, then down to the Military Service. It was in the Park and we were late; just in time to hear the King played. *[God Save the King, the National anthem at the time because King George V was on the throne.]* We saw Merle March past.

Friday, July 10 ∿ The last diphtheria clinic today.

Thursday, July 23 ∿ We were to F'ton to see the water sports. Very nice.

Saturday, Aug 8 ∿ Oliver Morehouse's store was robbed last night.

Thursday, August 20 ∿ I've canned chard and made cranberry jellie.

Saturday, August 29 ∿ We drove to F'ton, then I took boat for McGowan's. Albert came by car; met us at wharf. Drove out to May's *[Ferguson at Lakeville Corner]*. The men have been to Minto to see the new electric plant. *[It burnt coal to create electricity.]*

Wednesday, September 16 ∿ Mrs. Bubar and I were to the Passion Play. It was wonderful but awful.

Sunday, September 20 ∿ Went down to the *[Fredericton]* flying field this afternoon.

Wednesday, September 23 ∿ Bishop was up and consecrated the new burial ground *[by the Anglican Church in Zealand]*.

Tuesday, September 29 ∽ We have been to the Keswick fair, quite nice.

Wednesday, September 30 ∽ Old Mr. Hagerman passed away last night.

Thursday, October 8 ∽ They took the brick burner down today *[for the mill]*.

Saturday, October 10 ∽ Merle is picking potatoes for Gordon McLean.

Sunday, October 11 ∽ We have been to church four times today. Took Mr. McQueen to Caverhill and Brewer's Mills, then two services in our own church.

Tuesday, October 20 ∽ Merle is working on Keswick Ridge.

Thursday, October 22 ∽ Merle is done at Jewett's tonight.

Friday, October 30 ∽ Merle has been in town drilling *[with the marching band]* last two nights.

Saturday, October 31 ∽ Halloween, I hear lots of whooping.

Thursday, November 5 ∽ Was over to Edith Curries and collected last of little helpers money. Went to corner and sent it away.

Wednesday, December 2 ∽ Very cold. We have been to church this afternoon. A day of Prayer set for the World Depression.

Friday, December 11 ∽ Albert's been out to Henry Brown's to look after some of their things that are to be sold. *[This could have been an estate sale or they may have sold their farm because of the Depression.]*

Tuesday, December 15 ∽ An awful storm. It's terrible cold. Blowing and drifting. Feel uneasy about Merle staying tonight in Hayward's old house on the ridge. He only has one quilt and not sure how much wood is there. He's one old pair shoepacks and I expect his feet are in bad condition.

❧*1931*❧

Wednesday, December 16 ᴄᴡ Hayward was to Birdton to see about Brown's goods for the auction.

Thursday, December 31 ᴄᴡ It's been another lovely year. Have had many lovely pleasant days. God has been good. I don't like to see it go. Hope the new year will bring lots of employment and the world find its way again. Good bye old year with all its pleasures and all our missteps.

[There is a note to someone in the house on the back of the 1931 journal]
"I may not be back to supper. Use this little loaf of bread on the table, apple sauce on the stove, put the yeast cake to soak about half after five in warm water, set this brown bread mixture where it will keep warm when the fire is going down, won't need any fire after five. Keep her boiling until then."

1932

Saturday, January 9 〜 We have just come home from a concert at the hall. It was good. Hall was full.

Saturday, January 16 〜 Merle has been up to the doctor's to have 7 teeth pulled. Today is little Marie's birthday.

Sunday, January 17 〜 Been out to Willie Brewer's for supper.

Monday, January 18 〜 Been to Stella Maybe's and Mrs. Wilkins this evening.

Tuesday, January 19 〜 Merle has a very badly swollen face from the teeth pulling.

Thursday, January 21 〜 Been to Mrs. Albert Estey's to visit.

Saturday, January 23 〜 Johnny and Myrtle Albright were here waiting for the train this evening.

Monday, January 25 〜 They took Howard Bird to the hospital on Sat; something the matter with his head. He is very low.

Tuesday, January 26 ∽ Howard Bird is dead.

Wednesday, January 27 ∽ Rained all day. Were going to go on a driving party tonight, but it's been put off.

Friday, January 29 ∽ Howard Bird buried today. Was snowing a little.

Saturday, January 30 ∽ Bev Brewer died last night.

Monday, February 1 ∽ It blew a gale all day. I did not wash. Bev Brewer buried today.

Friday, February 5 ∽ Mrs. Inch called.

Saturday, February 6 ∽ Merle is 24 today.

Monday, February 8 ∽ A big snow storm. Albert and Merle have been up on Leigh's place to see about wood cutting. Ruby and children came tonight. Merle is at a party.

Wednesday, February 10 Ash Wednesday, ∽ The men have started wood cutting.

Tuesday, February 16 ∽ Bright but cold. Albert's real miserable. The wood is too hard work or the walk.

Thursday, February 18 ∽ Albert no better. He and Merle were to Keswick to inspect a car of potatoes.

Monday, February 22 ∽ Lovely day. First time the clothes have dried outdoors all winter. Jane Burtt buried today.

Tuesday, February 23 ∽ Pretty cold; bright. Merle has been out in the woods again fixing the road a bit. I have been to Mrs. Sheldon Howland's with others making quilt for the Peacock Family.

Wednesday, February 24 ∽ Been to Mrs. Howland's again and helped others to finish quilt.

Thursday, February 25 ∽ Been to Mrs. Sam Crouse's to W.A. Stanley Pugh is hauling our wood.

Friday, February 26 ~ Was down to Stella Maybe's for some butter-milk.

Sunday, February 28 ~ Johnny and Myrtle Albright, Wassie and Cora spent the evening.

Sunday, March 6 ~ Perfect day. Willie Brewer came with a double team *[sleigh]* and we all went up to Ruby's for supper. Ten of us with the baby. It was a lovely drive.

Thursday, March 10 ~ 46 years since we came to Keswick.

Tuesday, March 15 ~ I dyed some rags for mats. Ethel MacDonald was in.

Thursday, March 17 ~ Spent the evening at Byron Gorman's. H. *[Horace]* Gorman's little boy broke his arm.

Friday, March 18 ~ Albert is helping Bubar's saw wood. Mrs. Ambrose Allen and Mrs. G. Brewer called. Some sort of a party at Dan Pugh's potato house.

Monday, March 21 ~ Mrs. Elmer Jones has a new arrival; came Friday, night.

Tuesday, March 22 ~ Big snow storm. Snowed all day. Merle came down from Hayward's tonight for orchestra practice at Fred Allen's.

Wednesday, March 23 ~ Merle went back to work this morning. It's been a hard walk for snow is so deep. Cold night. I made some animal cookies for the children's Easter baskets.

Good Friday, March 25 ~ Lovely day. Was to church at the Baptist this afternoon and the Methodist tonight. Mr. Bubar took a sled load.

Sunday, April 3 ~ Hayward and Ruby were here with children. We made maple candy.

Tuesday, April 5 ~ We have been to a play at the hall. And it was good.

Wednesday, April 6 ᔅ Albert is at the hall; a meeting of Foresters.

Thursday, April 7 ᔅ Merle and others have been cutting wood for the church *[stove]*.

Friday, April 8 ᔅ Been up to Lucy's to quilt. Mrs. Tom Brewer and Mrs. Hagerman were there too. The ice ran out of the creek today.

Sunday, April 10 ᔅ Walked up to Maud's today. Heard a church service from Bangor on the radio.

Tuesday, April 12 ᔅ Been a busy day. Albert murescoed the two hall ceilings and sitting room and we tore off the paper and patched walls and got ready to paper. *[When homes were built in the 1920s and 1930s, sheetrock had not been introduced. Builders covered the walls by putting up the main studs, then putting thin strips of wood, called lath, horizontally across the studs for added strength. Then they covered the entire wall with a layer of plaster. Homeowners would then paper or paint over the plaster. Some older homes still have remains of the lath in their attic spaces.]*

Wednesday, April 13 ᔅ Nice but cool wind. We are just starting paper and patching walls. I done some cooking this morning and went to Maud's to W.A. this afternoon, and over to Ray Macdonald's this evening.

Thursday, April 21 ᔅ A very nice day. We have been to the hall to another meeting for electric lights to see about getting it.

Friday, April 22 ᔅ Albert inspected two potato cars today *[at the railway station]*.

Monday, April 25 ᔅ Ruby's birthday.

Friday, May 6 ᔅ I have ironed all day and made bread. Merle is at a dance at Adie MacLean's. *[They take turns having the dances at different homes in the community.]*

Sunday, May 7 ∽ Hayward and Ruby have been down with the car for the first this year.

Saturday, May 13 ∽ The Hainesville ball team played against Burtt's Corner tonight and beat.

Monday, May 16 ∽ Hot like July. Showers passed all around us. Thunder and lightning. I washed, and washed windows outside. Varnished the sitting room. *[They usually did the floors and the wainscoting.]*

Thursday, May 17 ∽ Very nice. We have finished varnishing sitting room. I canned some fiddleheads today.

Friday, May 20 ∽ Need rain so much; everything so dry. Forest fires in different places. Canned 4 more qts. fiddleheads. Have 14 qts. now.

Monday, May 23 ∽ Merle now working at Spencer Brewer's farm.

Wednesday, May 25 ∽ Lovely day. I finished ironing and cleaned the silver. Mr. McQueen *[Anglican minister]* was here for supper. Burtt's Corner played ball at Hainesville tonight.

Thursday, May 26 ∽ I cut out and partly made a dress and apron.

Saturday, May 28 ∽ Burtt's Corner beat Zealand at ball game tonight. Osborne Brewer died yesterday.

Sunday, May 29 ∽ Osborne Brewer buried today. Large funeral. Band played.

Tuesday, May 31 ∽ Mr. McQueen asked us to go with him to service at the Cathedral. *[This would be Christ Church Cathedral in Fredericton.]* Bishop of Maine, the speaker. 60 Ministers present and such a pretty sight.

Wednesday, June 1 ∽ Found out today that I have diabetes. Not a pleasant thing to find out.

Thursday, June 2 ∽ I'm feeling miserable. Had nothing to eat all day.

Drs. orders.

Friday, June 3 ∽ Another hungry day; don't mind too bad.

Saturday, June 4 ∽ Lovely, day hot. I am feeling fine; had something to eat today.

Tuesday, June 7 ∽ I have ironed, patched and pressed three pairs of pants today. Merle was up and sprayed Hayward's apple trees.

Saturday, June 11 ∽ A lovely day. Was up to see Dr. again. I'm coming along nicely with the diet. Burtt's Corner is at Hainesville playing ball and will have a band concert at the end. Nearly all the corner have gone.

Thursday, June 16 ∽ Ruby had Buddies *[Hugh's]* eyes tested today.

Friday, June 17 ∽ The men are doing their road work. Albert has three more cars *[of potatoes]* to inspect. Devon played Burtt's tonight and beat.

Monday, June 20 ∽ Woodstock Road played Burtt's Corner tonight and beat.

Tuesday, June 21 ∽ Bird Settlement played with Burtt's Corner tonight and BC beat.

Wednesday, June 22 ∽ rainy, we have been to the city. Andrew Currie dead. Merle gone to town tonight with others for Army clothes. Buddie has glasses.

Saturday, June 25 ∽ showery, Merle went to town to camp. Guida is here tonight.

Friday, July 1 ∽ Been to F'ton to watch the boys drilling *[marching]*. To Bubar's tonight to a social.

Sunday, July 3 ∽ cold and cloudy, rainy at times. Merle came home today. Wardlow and Ethel Bird were here for awhile. *[Not sure why Merle went for army clothes or was at camp drilling unless he was possibly* *registered with the army reserves. There were no active conflicts during this time.]*

Tuesday, July 5 ⌒ Devon played with Burtt's Corner tonight and beat, then Hainesville and Devon played afterward. *[There were several locations in the community where the teams played ball. Many of these ball games took place in the field next door to the Morehouse home.]*

Thursday, July 7 ⌒ We had our strawberry supper and picnic combined.

Saturday, July 9 ⌒ Boiled 26 pts. of strawberries. *[They had no electricity or freezers so they prepared everything for storage in canning jars.]* We were over on Sisson Estey's to a ball game.

Sunday, July 11 ⌒ lovely, we were to Willie Brewer's for supper and to church tonight. The holy rollers have started today at the corner.

Monday, July 12 ⌒ Washed and canned 4 qts. of *[Swiss]* chard *[a leafy vegetable similar to spinach.]*

Thursday, July 15 ⌒ Merle was over to Keswick Ridge to tennis court; a truck load of boys and girls and they had a picnic. Mouth of Keswick played with the home *[baseball]* team here tonight.

Friday, July 16 ⌒ Merle and Albert sprayed Hayward's potatoes.

Saturday, July 17 ⌒ We have all been over to McKeen's Corner to the ball game. Burtt's Corner and the Indians *[from the Kingsclear Reserve]*. Burtt's Corner beat.

Thursday, July 22 ⌒ Lovely and warm. Mona is bathing *[in the creek]* for the first *[time]*.

Monday, July 25 ⌒ Lovely day. Done a big wash. Preserved a few gooseberries and done a little sewing. Band practicing tonight. Devon played BC here tonight *[baseball game]*.

Wednesday, July 27 ⌒ Merle picked raspberries so I canned 4 pts. and a quart.

Thursday, July 28 ∽ We all went up Stone Ridge raspberrying. Canned 16 pints and a quart and half gal.

Friday, July 29 ∽ Made pies and canned 1 quart berries, since supper.

Sunday, July 31 ∽ We had the outdoor *[church]* service this afternoon. Band played. Had a nice crowd. A band concert tonight at the corner. People from all over.

Saturday, August 6 ∽ I made raspberry vinegar and done my Saturday work. *[This vinegar was probably used on salads, similar to raspberry vinaigrette dressings.]*

Tuesday, August 9 ∽ I've done beets and more berries. The girls played ball tonite. Burtt's Corner and Zealand.

Wednesday, August 10 ∽ We've been out Nasonworth blueberrying.

Thursday, August 11 ∽ I've canned blueberries and made wine.

Tuesday, August 23 ∽ Nashwaaksis girls played here tonight with Burtt's Corner.

Monday, August 29 ∽ Washed, preserved apples from Ruby's and made cranberry jellie.

Wednesday, August 31 ∽ An eclipse of the sun; was pretty dark. Merle to Hainesville to a ball game and picnic.

Thursday, September 1 ∽ I made mustard pickles and did blackberries.

Friday, September 2 ∽ Very hot. It's been a very stirring day at Burtt's Corner. Two ball games; Burtt's Corner and Stanley this afternoon, and Burtt's Corner and Devon tonite. A band concert tonite and a corn boil at Mrs. Tom Brewer's.

Monday, September 5 ∽ A picnic at Spencer Brewer's and two ball games on.

Tuesday, September 6 ∿ I washed and put some cucumbers in salt. Mattie Jewett here for supper.

Sunday, September 11 ∿ We were to Keswick to an open air Orange Lodge Meeting. Band played; had their new uniforms. Look very nice.

Monday, September 19 ∿ The potato house burned tonite — Daw [*Dawson*] Pugh's.

Thursday, September 23 ∿ Nice. Lucy and I have been on a hike today over Tripp Settlement. Had dinner at Willy McKeen and supper at F. Coburn's and 4 calls besides that.

Friday, September 23 ∿ Rainy. I have done more cranberries and made cakes. Merle is helping R. Maybe dig potatoes. Came home early on account of rain.

Friday, September 30 ∿ Very heavy frost last nite. I am collecting a little of the mite box money. Was to G. Curries today and Mrs. D. Pugh and Mrs. Wilkins.

Tuesday, October 4 ∿ Went to corner and called on Mrs. Inch. We have been exchanging pieces for butterfly quilt. Albert and Merle were to hall this evening for orchestra practice.

Friday, October 7 ∿ Have done most of my Saturday work for I'm invited to a knitting party tomorrow.

Saturday, October 8 ∿ Have been to Mrs. J. Jewett's for a knitting party. Albert and Merle went to Hayward's picking apples.

Sunday, October 9 ∿ Have had the hammock out. It's as warm as summer.

Tuesday, October 10 ∿ Merle was out Fish Lake hunting. Shot a duck this morning.

Thursday, October 13 ᴄᴡ We had a lovely partridge dinner. Merle got 5 yesterday and 3 today.

Friday, October 14 ᴄᴡ Merle got 7 more partridge.

Monday, October 17 ᴄᴡ Washed and I stretched 3 pairs of curtains.

Friday, October 21 ᴄᴡ We killed 10 hens. *[With nowhere to store this many chickens, they would sell or barter with neighbours or local stores.]*

Tuesday, October 25 ᴄᴡ Was out to Charlie Burtt's to a sewing and knitting party. 35 had supper there.

Wednesday, October 26 ᴄᴡ Have been to Mrs. Sam Crouse's to a bean supper *[would be baked beans]*.

Friday, October 28 ᴄᴡ Terrible rain. Freshet water everywhere. All around our house; almost as bad as flood 9 yrs ago.

Tuesday, November 1 ᴄᴡ We have moved from the shed *[summer kitchen]* back into the kitchen.

Wednesday, November 3 ᴄᴡ I put up the sitting room curtains for the winter. *[With little heat in the homes, they had two sets, thin curtains for summer and heavier drapes for winter.]* Put away the rest of the beets and done some ironing.

Saturday, November 12 ᴄᴡ Merle got a deer today.

Thursday, November 17 ᴄᴡ We made sausage meat today *[probably from yesterday's deer. They would can some for winter.]*

Sunday, November 20 ᴄᴡ Was up to Ruby's. They finally have the waterworks all finished *[with an indoor hand pump for water]*.

Monday, November 28 ᴄᴡ Potato market not very bright. Only the car that's loaded is going.

Thursday, December 1 ᴄᴡ Albert's inspecting a car load of potatoes for Clifford Haines. I don't know if they will go or not.

1933

Thursday, January 5 ᴄᴡ The young folks are enjoying the good skating.

Wednesday, January 11 ᴄᴡ Made four nities *[night gowns]* for the children and sent them.

Thursday, January 12 ᴄᴡ Making Buddie a play coat *[to wear around the yard playing]*.

Monday, January 16 ᴄᴡ 31 years since Marie *[her daughter]* was born; 10 yrs since Mr. MacDonald went away *[died]*.

Wednesday, January 18 ᴄᴡ Everything a glade of ice. Mona has had Merle's big boots and skates, and for all they're so big for her, she's learning fine. Went W.A. at Mrs. Albert Estey's. Only Maud and I for it's so icy. Too icy last week for any *[Women's Aid]* too.

Monday, January 23 ᴄᴡ Snowed and rained last night. Windy. Nice wash day. Albert is up to a business meeting at the church.

January 31 ᴄᴡ Was feeling sore, Ruby is sick and Hayward called for the doctor.

Sunday, February 5 ∿ Took a car ride up the road, got stuck in a drift by Campbell's. Had to get Ed Jewett to pull us out.

Sunday, February 12 ∿ Merle gone to Hayward's to cut ice this week. *[They cut ice blocks from the rivers and put them in a small shed-like building called an ice house. They covered the ice with sawdust from the local mills to keep the ice from melting. The ice often remained solid until fall or the next winter.]*

Tuesday, February 14 ∿ Had Buddie to Dr. to see about his throat; painting it with iodine to see it if will check it. *[There was an iodine solution used to coat sore throats, and it was also used for tonsillitis.]*

Friday, February 17 ∿ Was over on woods road. Charlie Pugh loading his timber.

Monday, March 6 ∿ Merle and Randolph out for wood. Charlie Pugh crew loading their lumber. What an excitement for these dull times.

Sunday, March 26 ∿ We walked to church on the crust.

Wednesday, March 29 ∿ Beautiful day. Ethel, Lucy and I were sliding on the crust for two hours this morning. Then W.A. afternoon. *[Even the grown women took time to play.]*

Thursday, March 30 ∿ Mrs. Tom Colter and Guida was here this afternoon.

Sunday, April 2 ∿ Quite heavy fall of snow last night. Was up to Bubar's to hear a service on radio this morning.

Monday, April 3 ∿ Merle went back to Ruby`s to the wood splitting. School started up there today; first since xmas. *[There must not have been any teacher available.]*

Wednesday, April 5 ∿ Water everywhere; water over road in so many places.

Friday, April 7 ∿ cleaned the clothes press.

❦ 1933 ❧

Sunday, April 9 ∾ I called on Mrs. G. Brewer, Mrs. Ambrose Allen and Mrs. Maybe, Mrs Wilkins and Fowler. *[They are still doing lots of visiting back and forth between residences.]*

Tuesday, April 11 ∾ Been to Maud`s quilting. Want it done to fill an order before Easter. *[Selling quilts to raise funds for the Women's Aid, W.A., for short.]*

Friday, April 14 ∾ Albert was to Keswick inspecting a car of potatoes; another one started here. I went to Mrs. Bubar's to hear a service. None broadcasted this morning *[on radio].*

Tuesday, April 18 ∾ The Woodstock train only making one trip a day now. *[This could be due to economy or that people are now using cars and trucks more.]*

Friday, April 21 ∾ They are loading another car of potatoes. *[The potatoes stayed fresh in the potato house because the earthen floor kept the temperature stable so the potatoes didn't freeze over the winter. If small sprouts were just starting to grow on the potatoes because of warmer spring temperatures, the potatoes were still okay for seed potatoes. Original potato houses were built so they appeared to be dug into a side hill. Quite often their roof touched the ground with only the door of the building visible. The potatoes stayed hydrated because of the moisture from the floor.]*

Monday, April 24 ∾ Lots of potatoes loading today.

Friday, April 28 ∾ I cleaned cupboards, and drawers and book cases. Albert is in Keswick inspecting again.

Monday, May 1 ∾ Squire Fowler died this morning.

Wednesday, May 3 ∾ I finished the *[spring]* house cleaning, all but the varnishing.

Saturday, May 6 ∾ Couple of hobos *[usually travelled by train]* here to supper. The ball games have started.

Tuesday, May 9 ∿ They are fixing walks in the new burial ground today. Albert has been up to help.

Thursday, May 11 ∿ Up to Maud's to get insight into the mail as I will look after it while she is away. *[Before post office buildings existed, the local mail was sorted and delivered from the railway station. In later years, it was taken to an assigned home or store for sorting and delivery from there. In this instance, Maud, the doctor's wife, was handling the mail because she was considered to be a respectable member of the community and responsible enough to handle the mail.]*

Sunday, May 14 ∿ Mother's day. Lovely dinner. Had the rooster roasted.

Sunday, May 21 ∿ Mrs. Sam Gilby is dead. Had a son born Thursday. *[Quite often women died during or after childbirth from complications.]*

Friday, June 2 ∿ Our new student *[Minister]* arrived tonight. I guess I'm to board him. A Mr. Tom Hawkins from Newfoundland.

Monday, June 5 ∿ Mr. Tom Hawkins seems like one of our own.

Sunday, June 11 ∿ Mr. Hawkins preached at St. Paul's and All Saints today.

Wednesday, June 14 ∿ We cleaned the church.

Sunday, June 18 ∿ Mr. Hawkins preached at Brewer's Mills and Caverhill today.

Tuesday, June 27 ∿ The men all away to dinner. Mr. Boyle here for dinner; a telephone man or something.

Monday, July 3 ∿ A ball game; the Barber's from F'ton up. BC beat them.

Monday, July 10 ∿ The men made me two nice lawn chairs.

Tuesday, July 11 ∿ Canned and preserved a crate of berries, did 5 lbs of gooseberries. Made bread and made Mona a pair of bloomers.

Wednesday, July 12 ⌒ Real nice. The band had their picnic. A play up tonight from the city *[to perform in the hall]*.

Tuesday, July 18 ⌒ Was a ball game tonight Fredericton and Burtt's Corner; the Corner beat 20-3.

Wednesday, July 19 ⌒ Most all of BC has gone to Stanley to a ball game this afternoon and evening. The band will play there tonight. Merle's been splitting wood for H. Gorman 3 days now.

Thursday, July 20 ⌒ lovely perfect night to Duncan Brewer's to W.A.

Friday, July 21 ⌒ quite hot. Mona has had a lovely bath in the creek.

Saturday, July 22 ⌒ quite nice and warm. Merle finished wood. Hayward and Ruby down tonight. Maude, Clara Boydd *[Boyd]* down tonight.

Sunday, July 23 ⌒ rained again last night. Cloudy this morning. Ruby had a new daughter *[Carol]* born this morning. I have come up and expect to be here nearly two weeks. The baby is a dear and Ruby is fine.

Monday, July 24 ⌒ very hot and everything coming fine. Kate Burtt doing the work. *[Maybe Mary means helping Ruby.]*

Sunday, July 30 ⌒ all coming fine, Albert and Hawkins here for tea. Edith here tonight. We called the baby Carol Deborah. Baby being fussy.

Tuesday, August 1 ⌒ Ruby was up and dressed today. Baby doing nicely, but tongue is tied. Doctor expected up to clip tongue. Doctor didn't come.

Wednesday, August2 ⌒ Doctor arrived and clipped baby's tongue.

Friday, August 4 ⌒ I made bread, and preserves and pickles. And bean salad and doughnuts. Buddie was in *[creek]* bathing. Keswick Ridge girls played our girls tonite. Our girls beat.

Tuesday, August 8 ✺ Albert was out Birdton to George Urquhart's funeral.

Sunday, August 13 ✺ The band played today at Keswick Ridge for an Orangemen's parade.

Thursday, August 17 ✺ A ball game tonight; a picnic at Keswick ridge and ball game. Our girls played Keswick Ridge.

Monday, August 21 ✺ LeBaron and I had a bath in the creek.

Thursday, August 31 ✺ We had our picnic. The last band concert of the year tonight. A corn boil for the young people at John MacDonald's after the concert.

Sunday, September 3 ✺ Such a lovely night. I've been sitting in the yard enjoying the moonlight.

Tuesday, September 5 ✺ I was up to the hall and voted.

Friday, September 22 ✺ Was to the crossroads to Harvest service. The church looked lovely.

Friday, October 6 ✺ We were all at young people's meeting in evening.

Thursday, October 19 ✺ Merle came home with 8 partridge. I canned more tomatoes.

Tuesday, November 14 ✺ Been to city with Maud and Mr. McQueen to hear choir boys from London.

Thursday, November 23 ✺ Have another boarder. A Brewer man from F'ton tallying the xmas trees *[that were being shipped by train]*.

Monday, December 4 ✺ Albert tallying today for Colter.

Monday, December 18 ✺ Killed 3 roosters *[probably for Christmas dinner]*.

Thursday, December 21 ᓚ A terrific big snow storm. The teacher had a *[concert]* program but no one could get there.

Sunday, Christmas Day ᓚ nice, we were all down to the creek. A horse race on the ice *[Keswick River]* this afternoon; a huge crowd.

Friday, December 29 ᓚ Terrible, terrible cold. Haven't had the like in years. Merle and the rest started for the woods. Elwood *[Burtt]* on the train and sent them back. Can't do nothing, the snow so deep.

1934

Monday, January 15 ∾ Have nearly made two night shirts.

Tuesday, January 16 ∾ Was up to Hagerman's to a shower for Dora Bird.

Wednesday, January 17 ∾ Was up to Parker's to see Dora and Bernard Hine married.

Friday, January 19 ∾ Snowed all day again. Men been shovelling roads again.

Sunday, January 28 ∾ Was up to Bubar's to hear a service on the radio.

Friday, February 2 ∾ Mona has been skating all afternoon on the forks *[Jones Forks Stream]* with other kids.

Monday, February 5 ∾ Mona has been skating all day. Merle up to Hayward's cutting ice again.

Wednesday, February 14 ∾ Train didn't get from Otis until nearly 4pm. Grace Jones been here waiting for it all this time. Lucy came and helped me finish the quilt. Mona has learned to quilt.

Friday, February 16 ᐳ Spent afternoon at Mrs. Tom Fowler's.

Saturday, February 17 ᐳ Coldest night yet. Most all my *[house]* plants froze last night. *[If they didn't get up during the night to fill the wood stoves, they had no heat.]*

Monday, February 19 ᐳ Not quite so cold. A number in here tonight waiting for the train. It didn't come until 9 pm. Harry Brewer's little boy died Saturday nite in hospital and I think Lorne Brewer died tonight. They sent for the family this afternoon and we heard he has died.

Tuesday, February 20 ᐳ A big snow storm on; a gloomy windy day. They buried the little Brewer boy and brought poor Lorne Brewer up *[by train]*.

Wednesday, February 21 ᐳ Roads drifted full of snow again. They buried Lorne Brewer today. Albert was to the funeral.

Thursday, February 22 ᐳ Albert shovelled snow all day on the railroad. I finished the binding on my quilt.

Friday, February 23 ᐳ Started piecing my sunflower quilt.

Tuesday, February 27 ᐳ Cold and blowing all day; everything drifted full. No train this afternoon or tonight. Merle's been shovelling on track.

Tuesday, March 6 ᐳ It was little warmer so I did washing in the shed today.

Thursday, March 8 ᐳ Lizzy Jewett and Ethel Brewer were here to tea.

Monday, March 12 ᐳ Covered the old kitchen couch *[with new fabric]*.

Thursday, April 15 ᐳ Was up to the corner; first time in ages. Sold some tickets on W.A. quilt.

Monday, April 23 ᐳ Albert's been to Keswick. Lots of loading *[potatoes]* here now. Merle racking potatoes at Dell Pugh's.

Thursday, May 3 ᐳ Raining most all day. I cleaned upstairs hall and varnished front bedroom floor.

Friday, May 11 ᕲ Lots of potatoes loading here and at Keswick.

Monday, May 21 ᕲ I washed, washed windows on outside and cleaned screen doors.

Friday, May 25 ᕲ I had my quilts out airing.

Saturday, May 26 ᕲ Albert's been tallying lumber for Colter and inspecting potatoes too.

Wednesday, May 30 ᕲ Potato market at an end for awhile.

Thursday, May 31 ᕲ Sparrow *[?]* was up trying to arrange a singing school.

Friday, June 1 ᕲ Such a wind; fires awful in different parts of province.

Wednesday, June 6 ᕲ Mona, the Wilson children and myself have joined the singing class. Duncan Brewers house burned today.

Monday, June 18 ᕲ Albert was out to Birdton scaling some lumber.

Tuesday, June 19 ᕲ Albert's been out Dorn Ridge scaling lumber for R.B. Hanson *[A future leader of the Federal opposition]*. Merle helping paint the bandstand *[in the village]*.

Wednesday, June 21& 22 ᕲ The men doing their road work.

Sunday, June 24 ᕲ Church. Professor Pugh was there, played organ and spoke on the Boy Scouts.

Wednesday, June 27 ᕲ Been to W.A. and singing class.

Saturday, June 30 ᕲ Albert's inspected last load of potatoes today.

Sunday, July 1 ᕲ Dominion Day celebration at Hall this afternoon. Band played and school children marched and Boy Scouts there.

Friday, July 6 ᕲ Canned a crate of berries and baked two batches of bread.

Monday, July 9 ∽ Washed and canned 6 qts of rhubarb.

Thursday, July 12 ∽ Over to Keswick Ridge to Orangemen picnic.

Friday, July 13 ∽ Ruby and children came down on the train. Albert's been to rectory shingling

Monday, July 16 ∽ I washed, and made bees honey. *[The family either had bee hives or made their honey from clover that grew in the fields.]*

Tuesday, August 7 ∽ A political meeting in the hall.

Saturday, August 11 ∽ The band has gone to play in Hartland.

Monday, August 13 ∽ The Women's Institute was organized today.

Thursday, August 16 ∽ I canned a gal. of chard.

Monday, August 20 ∽ Albert and Merle up to finish shingling the rectory. Also mowed our lot *[in the graveyard]*.

Wednesday, August 22 ∽ Had our Sunday school picnic today and our last singing lesson tonight.

Monday, August 27 ∽ Merle cutting or sawing wood for Mark Shephard.

Tuesday, August 28 ∽ I canned 5 bottles of beans.

Friday, August 31 ∽ Merle sold car few days ago, and bought a motorcycle today.

Monday, September 3 (labour day) ∽ Tom Fowler dropped dead today.

Wednesday, September 5 ∽ Tom Fowler buried today.

Monday, September 10 ∽ I washed, made jellie and canned.

Tuesday, September 11 ∽ I canned more beans and made jellie and cut tomatoes for 10 bottles of chow.

Saturday, September 15 ∿ Hunting season opened today.

Tuesday, September 25 ∿ Merle out to Stanley fair with the Band.

Wednesday, October 3 ∿ Merle loading lumber today. Keswick fair started.

Monday, October 8 ∿ Thanksgiving; made tomato mincemeat and apple jellie.

Tuesday, October 9 ∿ Albert up to Sam Crouse's painting.

Friday, October 12 ∿ Terrible cold and our first snow with terrible wind.

Friday, October 16 ∿ Albert was up working in the graveyard. I made crab apple jellie.

Saturday, October 20 ∿ Ruby and children down. Carol *[fourth child]* looks cute in new knitted rompers.

Wednesday, October 31 ∿ They are loading a car of vegetables for the west. *[During the Depression, Western Canada experienced several years of drought. The ground dried up from lack of rain, and the crops that farmers depended on for both food and income failed to grow. Many Canadian agencies set up appeals for food and clothing for these farmers and their families. It's possible that the car loads of vegetables that Mary spoke of were part of these efforts. These years of drought became known as The Dirty Thirties because the ground dried up, the foliage died, and the Prairie winds blew the soil around as dust.]*

Thursday, December 6 ∿ Made mincemeat and fruit cake.

Friday, December 14 ∿ Made cookies and pies, and sewed and knit today.

Monday, December 17 ∿ Hayward bought their first radio today.

Saturday, December 22 ∿ Made doughnuts and other cooking.

Chapter 4

1935-1939

THE MOREHOUSE FAMILY continued to upgrade their home during this time period. House insurance became an option, and they were approached to buy coverage for their home. They seemed to be doing ok financially as they either earned money through various jobs or bartered for goods with other residents. Not all families were this fortunate during the 1930s. People learned to do a lot of different tasks because they couldn't afford to hire someone. Throughout the next few years, Albert's health deteriorated and Mary's continued concern for her beloved *"Ta"* is evident in her diary entries.

Special meetings were held at the Independent Order of Foresters IOF Hall to discuss the possibility of installing electricity and electric lights in the community. In September of 1936, electric lights were turned on in the community hall and local businesses for the first time. Improvements to equipment allowed motorized plows to take care of the winter roads, and the horse teams were only pulled out to plow on occasion.

Better road conditions also allowed people to begin winter travel by car. They still attended various socials and entertained at individual homes, and a Young Ladies Women's Aid had been started. Outdoor activities like skating, baseball, and bathing or swimming in the creek remained favourite pastimes.

Many people were interested in the Royal family and events which affected them. Mary made note in her journal when King George V died on January 20, 1936. His successor, son Edward VIII became King, but abdicated in December of that year, leaving the throne to his brother King George VI. In the next few years, King George VI and his parliamentary members would prepare for another war.

The First World War was supposed to be the war to end all wars, yet after the Armistice (agreement to cease war), tensions were still high in Europe. In the mid-1930s, Germany's Hitler rose to power, causing concern in Europe and elsewhere. Talk of war built up and went down a few times. Canadians, like others, listened closely, while going about their daily lives. The Second World War broke out on September 1st, 1939 when Hitler invaded Poland. Britain declared war on September 3rd. As things escalated in Europe, the Canadian government declared war on September 10th. Thousands of Canadians enlisted from either loyalty or because they needed employment, just like many from Burtt's Corner.

1935

Tuesday, January 1 New Year`s Day ⌒ Dr. Morehouse Sr. passed away *[on the anniversary of his father, Elisha's death in 1920]*. Young Oscar 28 years on Wed. Jan. 9.

Wednesday, January 2 ⌒ Brought doctor up last night by train but we were all in bed. *[He must have been in the hospital or living in the city.]* They felt bad.

Thursday, January 3 ⌒ The doctor buried today.

Friday, January 11 ⌒ I had tea with Mrs. Herb Haines.

Sunday, January 20 ⌒ Was way out on the ice road for a walk, and visited Mrs. Squire Fowler.

Monday, January 21 ⌒ Mona came down on train. Train very late; nearly 3pm. Should have been here at 11am.

Thursday, January 24 ⌒ A terrible storm. The 3pm train never arrived until 10pm.

Saturday, January 26 ⌒ Merle came home tonight. All done yarding *[logs]* and he was one of those laid off. *[During the winter, men cut trees in the woods and hauled them by horse to a "yard" or staging area close to a stream or river. Another work group removed all of the tree limbs. In the spring, the crews then rolled the logs into the river so the current would transport them to the local mill.]*

Sunday, January 27 〰 Mona and I took a walk out on the log road to Jim Jewett's.

Tuesday, January 29 〰 Mrs. George Lovegrove and Theora called for tea.

Friday, February 1 〰 Mona and I walked over to Mrs. Eldrick Staples on the lumber road. Myrtle Albright here waiting for train.

Friday, February 8 〰 Up to Ruby's. Came home on noon train.

Tuesday, February 12 〰 Merle was out Birdton breaking a road *[cutting down trees and building a road so they could get to the stand of wood they planned to harvest]*.

Monday, February 18 〰 Had 4 railroad men for dinner. Merle been shovelling on railroad again.

Monday, February 25 〰 Merle went up as cookee for Charlie Pugh *[at the woods camp]*.

Thursday, February 28 〰 Mona and I walked to Zealand *[only five kilometres]*.

Tuesday, March 5 〰 Buddie and I were to Maybe's for some buttermilk.

Thursday, March 14 〰 Been to *[Women's]* Institute at Will Hagerman`s.

Tuesday, March 19 〰 Lucy and I was over to see Mrs. Bird and to Perley Brewer`s. Done a little sliding in the meantime.

❧ 1935 ❧

Friday, March 22 ⟋ Albert real miserable. Had a bad heart attack last night. Dr. Jewett to see him tonight.

Wednesday, April 3 ⟋ Lucy was in and a hosiery woman selling stockings. *[There were a lot of people peddling goods from community to community to earn income.]*

Saturday, April 6 ⟋ Dr. was in today and found Albert's heart better.

Thursday, April 11 ⟋ Was sliding this morning, to Institute tonight at Mrs. Inch's.

Wednesday, April 16 ⟋ Maud has her car out for the first *[women were also driving]*.

Wednesday, April 24 ⟋ Was to Maud's to our W.A. oyster supper. Took in $23. Don Haines hurt bad when horses ran away.

Monday, April 29 ⟋ Lovely and warm. I washed. We cleaned stove pipes and tore plastic off the kitchen. *[This sounds like it was inside, but many people stretched plastic around the bottom two or three feet of their homes and banked it with sawdust or sand to keep the floors warmer during the winter. There were no basements.]* Ready for Muresco and Merle did the ceiling.

Wednesday, May 1 ⟋ Finished the kitchen, and got little bit more done on shed.

Saturday, May 4 ⟋ quite nice, cold wind

Sunday, May 5 ⟋ lovely morning. Hayward came down for me. Ruby has a new boy *[Minot]*.

Monday, May 6 ⟋ quite nice, cold rain. The King's Silver Jubilee. We heard the King's speech. Ruby fine, baby fussy.

Tuesday, May 7 ⟋ cold. Things coming on fine.

Wednesday, May 8 ⟋ cold. Very good. Carol likes the new baby.

Friday, May 10 ∿ cold. Ruby good. Baby quite troublesome.

Wednesday, May 15 ∿ awfully cold. Ruby downstairs today. Baby quite fussy last night. Lebaron has a bad cold. I came home tonight. I miss the little baby too, but will be glad to get a good night's sleep.

Thursday, May 16 ∿ Merle working at loading lumber this afternoon.

Tuesday, May 21 ∿ Have been to a play in hall. Bear Island put it on.

Monday, May 27 ∿ Washed, and washed 4 floors to get ready for varnish.

Thursday, May 30 ∿ I've coloured *[dyed]* and ironed, and put up curtains and planted flower seeds, and odds and ends of everything.

Monday, June 3 ∿ Our garden all in.

Thursday, June 6 ∿ There is a lecture in the hall. The liberal party, so the men are there.

Wednesday, June 12 ∿ Was to W.A. and a political meeting in the hall.

Wednesday, June 19 ∿ Was to corner to an ice cream social for the Institute.

Friday, June 21 ∿ Albert is to be in Bubar`s store a few days. Luther and Winnifred going to Boston.

Tuesday, June 25 ∿ Another political meeting in the hall tonight.

Wednesday, June 26 ∿ Wasn't to W.A. The hens got out, and *[I]* ran after them all afternoon. Was to a political meeting tonight.

Saturday, June 29 ∿ First band concert of the season.

Monday, July 1 ∿ Have all been to the hall to a strawberry tea and play.

Thursday, July 4 ∿ I canned strawberries and some rhubarb. Merle came home with some beautiful trout.

Friday, July 12 ∿ Awfully hot. Albert tallying here for Colter. Merle gone with band to a picnic in Millville.

Monday, July 15 ∾ Both Merle and Albert at the lumber loading.

Thursday, July 18 ∾ Oscar *[doctor]* has been in and left my insulin.

Friday, July 19 ∾ Started insulin today.

Friday, July 26 ∾ I've gained 5 lbs. Was down to Maybe's and got weighed. *[They had a large scale to weigh potatoes or meat for the farm.]*

Saturday, July 27 ∾ A social at the corner for the tennis club.

Monday, July 29 ∾ Harry Bird died. *[He owned one of the shoe repair shops].*

Thursday, August 1 ∾ Garden near burned up. Carried 25 pails of water *[to the garden].*

Monday, August 5 ∾ Merle gone out to the woodlot again to cut wood.

Monday, August 12 ∾ Merle was out to woodlot but came in around noon. Cut his foot; Dr. put 3 stitches in it. Beautiful moonlit night. Out in the yard all evening; hated to come in.

Thursday, August 15 ∾ Hot and dry; every day hotter. I got a lot of *[choke]* cherries for jellie, and made cabbage relish.

Saturday, August 17 & Sunday, August 18 ∾ Terrible hot, 106°F *[37°C].* The hottest I ever remember.

Monday, August 19 ∾ Lot of big fires in different parts of the country. My birthday today and I am 60. Got some nice gifts.

Tuesday, August 20 ∾ Still terrible hot and dry. The men doing their road work, very smokey.

Wednesday, August 21 ∾ Terrible wind. Over 60 fires in the province, some terrible ones.

Friday, August 23 ∾ I made cherry jam and a nice lot of it. Also made bread and cookies.

Friday, August 30 ∿ Merle came home and found the cows had been in camp and ate all their food, so he walked all the way home after work.

Monday, September 3 ∿ Albert tallying a car of lumber.

Sunday, September 8 ∿ Mona, Neva and Fern walked down to get their school books. *[School books arrived by train until the mid-1960s, but the girls may have picked up theirs at the school and strolled farther down the corner hill for a visit with Mona's grandmother, Mary.]*

Monday, September 16 ∿ I washed and canned a gal. of apples, and made jam from the peels and cores.

Tuesday, September 17 ∿ Gone to Albert Estey's and picked a pail of crab apples. *[These were cooked with a sauce and canned.]*

Thursday, September 19 ∿ Heavy thunder shower tonite; the heaviest one of the season. Have been to Mrs. Bev Jones to Institute, and to a very interesting political meeting tonite. R.B. Hanson the speaker. *[He was their member of Parliament and was the Minister of Trade and Commerce for the Bennett cabinet during this time period.]*

Thursday, September 26 ∿ I canned 7 pts. of applesauce.

Monday, September 30 ∿ Merle gone to Burtt Lake loading lumber. Albert tallying here.

Thursday, October 3 ∿ Have been to F'ton to hear *[Prime Minister]* Bennett's speech.

Saturday, October 5 ∿ Moved everything around for our winter quarters *[back into main kitchen]*.

Tuesday, October 8 ∿ Carl Macdonald died yesterday and they brought him down to Ray's tonight. Funeral tomorrow.

Thursday, October 10 ∽ Albert and Merle working on the road today. Was down to see lovely flowers on Carl's grave.

Saturday, October 12 ∽ Heard that Beth Bubar has been asked to leave school, that she has TB. Hope it's a mistake. *[They were neighbours; the Bubar's living on the hill behind the Morehouse property.]*

Monday, October 14 ∽ Election day. Hanson leading here. Was up to the hall to vote and then I took care of children so Ruby could go.

Tuesday, October 15 ∽ Hanson not elected here. *[William George Clark, the Liberal candidate got in instead, but he only beat Hanson by 254 votes, so it was a close race. Nationally, Mackenzie King and the Liberals were back in power.]*

Monday, October 21 ∽ I washed and went to corner. Called on Mrs. Harry Allen and Mrs. Herb Haines. Knit a sock leg this evening.

Wednesday, October 22 ∽ Merle went to the woodlot to finish cutting limbs. Albert had another heart attack last night. Hadn't been taking his tablets for some time and been doing too much lifting I think.

Thursday, October 24 ∽ Merle had 3 lovely loads of wood hauled today.

Wednesday, October 30 ∽ Merle has been over to Don Pugh's helping thrash. I called on Mrs. Bubar. Such a shock, Beth having TB.

Saturday, November 2 ∽ Was an earth quake Friday about 2 am. We never knew but quite heavy in F`ton.

Tuesday, November 5 ∽ Warm and close. Have finished cap and made two pr bloomers for Carol. They were down tonight.

Sunday, November 10 ∽ An Armistice Service in hall today. Packed full, four or five ministers, band quartet, large choir.

Monday, November 11 ∽ Real Armistice Day. Merle out on the big hill tonight hunting and trapping. He and Arwood. Will stay in Johnny

McDonald's camp.

Tuesday, November 12 ∽ Merle came home with a deer tonight. Made over 3 gals. of mincemeat.

Friday, November 15 ∽ Merle loading lumber here at station.

Wednesday, November 27 ∽ To Maud`s. Also sold $2.60 cents worth of Mrs. Wilkins fancy work.

Wednesday, December 4 ∽ Merle's been to town selling his wood. Nearly froze.

Friday, December 6 ∽ Merle been helping load Veneer Wood *[at the station]*.

Thursday, December 12 ∽ I made a dark fruit cake and a white one. Called on Mrs. Bubar. I baked two little cakes for Beth for Xmas. She has started the new treatment. Poor Mrs. Bubar misses her so much.

Monday, December 16 ∽ A terrible big snow storm and I never saw trees loaded so in my life. Merle cutting wood for Mr. Parke. He went down but they didn't work; storm so bad. *[25 cm of snow recorded in Fredericton at the University of New Brunswick.]*

Tuesday, December 17 ∽ Merle been shovelling snow on railroad. We killed 4 chickens.

Sunday, December 22 ∽ Very cold windy day, but bright. Been all day with bedroom slippers on.

Monday, December 23 ∽ Very cold. I done some odds and ends of sewing. Had the xmas tree brought in. Several people in waiting for the train this am.

Wednesday, December 25 ∽ Ruby and kids all here. She and children to a little concert tonight at Baptist Church.

❧ 1935 ❧

1936

Monday, January 6 ∾ Albert and Merle loading lumber. The children are starting school at Upper Keswick *[after their Christmas break]*.

Wednesday, January 8 ∾ The men finished loading lumber. The roads are perfect. Been plowed with the big road plow. Cars going to the city.

Thursday, January 9 ∾ Merle was out over the hill to check his traps; caught a bob cat.

Sunday, January 12 ∾ Was down to Mrs. Fowlers to get some milk and have some *[fresh]* air.

Monday, January 13 ∾ Merle loading pulp this afternoon for Willie Brewer.

Tuesday, January 14 ∾ Hate to see Mona start out to face that wind to school. Wassie's children didn't go. *[They would have been walking from Zealand to Upper Keswick; a minimum of three miles.]*

Wednesday, January 15 ∾ Merle to town to sell his bobcat *[hide]*.

Saturday, January 18 ∾ Buddie *[Hugh]* suspected of having TB. Ruby taking him to town Monday, if all well.

Monday, January 20 ᗢ Such a wild nite last night. The plow went over the *[rail]* road early so the trains were on time. Merle been shovelling on railroad today.

Tuesday, January 21 ᗢ The King died last night. *[This would have been King George V. His successor was his son Edward VIII.]*

Wednesday, January 22 ᗢ No results yet from Buddie's x-ray.

Friday, January 24 ᗢ Just got word of Buddie's x-ray not very satisfactory. Mona is here tonight.

Sunday, January 26 ᗢ Was to a memorial service for the King at Baptist Church, and called on Mrs. Inch.

Tuesday, February 4 ᗢ Oh we have good word about Buddie. He is alright what a relieve *[relief]*.

Saturday, February 8 ᗢ Wassie and Cora in waiting for train.

Tuesday, February 11 ᗢ The train has started going up and back every day for awhile. Mona is peppered with measles.

Friday, February 14 ᗢ Another storm blowing in. Was in to Lucy's and Stella's and Mrs. Fowler's. She is very sick.

Tuesday, February 18 ᗢ Mrs. Squire Fowler died this afternoon.

Thursday, February 20 ᗢ Mrs. Fowler laid to rest. The rest *[of Ruby's children]* have measles now.

Monday, March 2 ᗢ Was down to help Stella hook her mat all afternoon and evening.

Friday, March 13 ᗢ We have had another flood; an ice jam in the Forks. *[On March 12, the recorded rainfall at UNB Fredericton was 44 mm.]* And we have surely been flooded here. Water was in shed. Expected it to be in the house but was lucky. But we lost 7 hens which is too bad; were all laying so good.

Monday, March 16 ∽ Merle's been cutting ice cakes on forks road. Making a channel or something *[to force water to run away from the house. They had another 23 mm of rain recorded on this date.]*

Tuesday, March 17 ∽ Went to Maud's to W.A., then to Lucy's and helped hook on her mat.

Thursday, March 19 ∽ Rain again. Ice jam running and jamming. *[Another 13.5 mm recorded so no wonder they were dealing with ice jams and flooding.]* A wash out on the railroad tonight at Albert Estey's. No train yet, nearly 11pm. Hayward is going up and down with the motor car checking. Merle's been racking potatoes at Perley Brewers *[farm on McLean Settlement Road]*.

Friday, March 20 ∽ The Woodstock train never got here until tonight. A train from Minto came to meet it this am and took the passengers to town. The Otis train came too. The F'ton railway bridge was out yesterday. The floods are terrible everywhere.

Saturday, March 21 ∽ Merle been working on the railroad today. There is fear that the people of Maugerville are all drowned.

Sunday, March 22 ∽ Clara Haines and I were down to Mrs. Daws *[Dawson]* Pugh to see if she knew anything about the people of Sheffield, Maugerville. She has a sister there; she knows nothing. Can't hear or get in touch with them. She's awfully worried and no wonder.

Monday, March 23 ∽ Washed and put another quilt on. Mona here tonight and helped quilt. The people at Maugerville alright. Merle working on railroad again today.

Tuesday, March 24 ∽ Merle worked on railroad until noon. I had my quilting here; 7 came this afternoon and 8 here this evening. We finished it.

Thursday, March 26 ∽ I finished the binding on my quilt and put on a little mat. Got a lot of knitting done on my sweater.

Monday, April 6 ∾ I washed and I had to bring it in off line and put it back in the tub. A terrible rain and wind. The Chipman train started today.

Thursday, April 9 ∾ The men are jacking the shed up. *[to put a higher foundation underneath as added protection from flood waters. Some homes in this period had four foot concrete walls without any basement.]*

Easter Sunday, April 12 ∾ Heard 3 men entombed in a gold mine in NS. *[Unsure how Mary knew about this unless it was wired to the train station or through someone she knew from other parts of the Province. She was referring to the Moose River Gold mine disaster that happened on that date. Sometimes if she had been away, she wrote a couple of days at a time and got the information mixed up and crossed out dates, so that may be the case here.]*

Monday, April 20 ∾ Merle is up to Ruby's taking off outside windows. *[He exchanged the storm windows for summer screens, which were held in place the same way as the storm windows.]* I washed and the men cleaned the stove pipes.

Tuesday, April 28 ∾ Beth Bubar came home today. *[She had been away for TB treatment for almost six months.]*

Thursday, April 30 ∾ I ironed curtains and cleaned the old cupboard in the shed. I called on Beth tonight; she is fine.

Monday, May 4 ∾ Rained all day and so cold. I washed and we moved the table to the shed and got the old desk moved to the summer quarters, and the stove cleaned and oiled and lots of odds and ends.

Wednesday, May 6 ∾ Merle at Hayward's putting in garden. Albert planted our peas and lettuce.

Monday, May 11 ∾ Very nice. Did a big wash. Merle bought 15-5 week old check *[chicks]*. He put garden in today. I have sitting room and hall ready to clean. Curtains down and washed and the heater cleaned. Hayward has a new car. They were down tonight. It's surely a beauty. *[He would have done well, working regularly for the railway.]*

Wednesday, May 13 ～ Merle started peeling pulp out Dorn Ridge. I guess I've finished sitting room all but varnish and settling *[putting things back in place]*.

Friday, May 15 ～ Awfully cold, froze ice last night. Done more varnishing and stretched five pair curtains. Fixed some chairs and lots of little jobs. Merle working at the pulp. Howard Hagerman has taken *[ownership of]* Arnold's store.

Tuesday, May 19 ～ Rained all day. Albert tallying for Colter. I varnished dining room, and ironed.

Sunday, May 31 ～ Real nice day. Hayward and Ruby and children here for supper. They brought fiddleheads.

Thursday, June 4 ～ A train wreck at Marysville and poor Murray Hoyt *[the engineer]* was killed.

Friday, June 5 ～ Very nice and warm. The men are making a new hen yard and I guess Merle is done with the pulp. I've been painting chairs all day.

Monday, June 8 ～ We have *[been]* to rectory to a meeting about electric lights.

Wednesday, June 10 ～ Very hot. Albert still tallying. Pie social for the band at the hall tonight.

Saturday, June 20 ～ A big frost last night; many things frozen. Albert tallying for Colter's.

Sunday, June 21 ～ Came home to find Merle has gone to St. Stephen to peel pulp for a month.

Sunday, July 5 ～ There was a car accident up in Zealand bridge tonight. Dave Bird's boy run into another car. Some people hurt in that car. *[Many had started to drive, but there was no such thing as driving lessons. When people bought a car, they received their driver's license.]*

Tuesday, July 7 ⌒ Merle came home early from St. Stephen. The mill that Brawn has been building started today.

Wednesday, July 15 ⌒ Lovely and cool. Merle went over to Earl Jewett's to hay.

Thursday, July 16 ⌒ Hayward needed men so we drove to Earl Jewett's to get Merle so he could work on railway.

Friday, July 17 ⌒ Merle working on railroad. I made bees honey.

Wednesday, July 22 ⌒ Lovely day. Went to Mrs. Bev Lawrence's helping quilt on an Institute quilt; tulip pattern for exhibition.

Monday, July 27 ⌒ Albert been working at the little mill here. We had new potatoes and peas for first *[this season]*.

Thursday, July 30 ⌒ Albert finished at the mill.

Friday, July 31 ⌒ Merle finished on the railway.

Wednesday, August 5 ⌒ A man here today; something about electric lights.

Saturday, August 8 ⌒ The cook cars put in here this afternoon for railway *[for the annual repair work]*.

Wednesday, August 12 ⌒ Lovely day. Merle helping hay at Jeddie Brewer's.

Tuesday, August 18 ⌒ Had a letter from Grace with $5 for my birthday. Our spring pullets *[hens]* laying now.

Wednesday, September 2 ⌒ Albert has made a banister for the stairs. *[People learned to do many different tasks.]*

Friday, September 4 ⌒ Had my jaw x-rayed found a small piece of root. Went down in bus. Back with Ruby. *[The bus was now running from Millville to Fredericton.]*

Thursday, September 10 ∽ Ruby has Erysipelas in her leg and will be in bed sometime. *[Erysipelas is a streptococcus bacterial infection that affects the upper layer of skin. It causes red patches, fever and general overall illness.]*

Friday, September 11 ∽ Rilla is taking care of Ruby. Ethel McKeil doing her work.

Wednesday, September 16 ∽ A crowd of men; about 25 are here in cook cars for railway. They surely a lively bunch.

Friday, September 18 ∽ Getting hall wired today. Turned the lights on at corner tonight for the first *[time]*.

Monday, September 21 ∽ Cold and dark. I washed and canned 4 qts. crab apples.

Thursday, October 1 ∽ I made chow and relish. A show in the hall.

Friday, October 2 ∽ Hayward's lights turned on tonite for the first. He came down for us *[and took us up to their place]* to see them.

Tuesday, October 6 ∽ very nice. I've had the kiddies all day. Ruby and Mona were to town. Elsie Bird died last night. A large earthquake shock all nite so they say.

Monday, October 12 ∽ Albert has been up to church with *[Mr.]* Rideout. Rideout is putting the lights in.

Sunday, October 18 ∽ Our new lights in church tonite for first. They are lovely.

Saturday, October 31 ∽ Hayward and children were down; the kids all dressed for Halloween.

Wednesday, November 18 ∽ A terrible cold blustery day. Windows white with frost.

Friday, November 27 ∾ Made 3 gals. of mincemeat.

Thursday, December 10 ∾ The King has abdicated. *[King Edward VIII abdicated the throne and married Wallis Simpson, a twice-divorced American woman.]*

Saturday, December 12 ∾ Our new king *[King Edward's brother]* George VI takes the throne today. *[He was father to the current Queen Elizabeth II.]*

Friday, December 18 ∾ Killed 3 chickens and done some cooking.

Sunday, December 20 ∾ Wrote 3 letters and done up some xmas cards.

Wednesday, December 23 ∾ I done some washing, and made six pies, steamed the fowls *[chickens]*.

Thursday, December 24 ∾ It's 11pm and I'm tired but so thankful we are all together.

1937

Friday, January 8 ∾ Lovely snow to make travelling good *[by sled]*.

Friday, January 15 ∾ Poured all last night, and today a glade of ice. Bubar men all sent home but 4. Merle stayed.

Tuesday, January 19 ∾ Our new station agent and wife arrived, living upstairs in station. Glad to see a light there again. *[Max and Peggy Spears moved in and remained there until the 1950s.]*

Sunday, January 24 ∾ called on our new neighbours, the Spears.

Saturday, February 20 ∾ Over to see Mrs. Spears. Their maid is sick.

Tuesday, March 2 ∾ Was up to store, in to Mrs. Inches. Was weighted *[at the store]*; I hundred 26 ¼ lbs. *[Mary was a tall woman. But she walked miles every day.]*

Wednesday, March 17 ∾ Water over the road and ankle deep everywhere.

Friday, March 19 ∾ Merle shingling the barn for a hen house.

Wednesday, March 31 ∾ Merle helping with the wood cutters at Ambrose Allen's. *[The men went from house to house to help one another.]*

Monday, April 5 ∾ Men are papering overhead *[ceiling]* in the shed.

Wednesday, April 7 ∾ Our 40th wedding anniversary. About 20 came and gave us a lovely surprise party with lovely presents and a lovely lunch.

Friday, April 9 ∾ Mrs. Wilkins gave me another piece of enamelware making several nice pieces for our anniversary. *[The enamelware was quite new and fashionable in the 1930s, but it is now used for camping.]*

Saturday, April 24 ∾ Merle at Charlie Pugh's racking potatoes.

Sunday, May 9, Mothers Day ∾ Hayward and Ruby down with children. Got a lovely red rose and some fruit.

Tuesday, May 12 ∾ Very nice. Coronation day. Many have gone to the city. I've been varnishing all day. Merle and Albert working on the barn. Merle bought 16 chickens. Mill not running today.

Tuesday, May 25 ∾ Merle helping load lumber for Byron Boone.

Friday, May 28 ∾ Aired all the bedding and done Saturday work.

Tuesday, June 8 ∾ Merle at Dorn Ridge mill loading ties *[squared timber that was tarred for railway ties and then placed under the steel rails to support the railroad]*.

Saturday, July 10 ∾ Albert and Merle been to Caverhill this am with Boone loading lumber.

Friday, July 30 ∾ Albert and Merle both working with lumber; Merle with Boone, Albert with Brawn

Friday, August 6 ∾ Mrs. Spear and I had a lovely bath in the creek.

Tuesday, August 10 ∾ Very hot. I canned 6 pts. of beets.

Monday, August 23 ∾ Washed, and fixed pickles in salt.

Thursday, August 26 ❧ Been to the supper and play in hall.

Friday, August 27 ❧ Merle been working on the wharf [*in Frederic-ton*].

Monday, August 30 ❧ Very hot and dry and smokey. Washed, canned tomatoes and plums.

Friday, September 3 ❧ Merle and Albert working at lumber for Boone.

Tuesday, September 7 ❧ Election day. Cyril Brewer elected. [*Suspect that this was a parish or county seat being filled.*]

Wednesday, September 8 ❧ School not opened. A number of cases of infantile paralysis in NB [*and across Canada. Infantile paralysis, also known as poliomyelitis or polio, was a serious disease that could cause paralysis or death.*]

Friday, September10 ❧ Canned some crab apples and made pumpkin pies.

Monday, September 13 ❧ Canned some rhubarb. 35 yrs since Little Marie went away.

Wednesday, September 15 ❧ Canned more apples and made more pickles. [*She continued to prepare lots of food for the winter.*]

Saturday, September 18 ❧ Evelyn Macdonald married this pm at Rays. [*Home wedding instead of church.*]

Tuesday, October 19 ❧ we sulphured 4 gals. of apples. [*This process kept the apples from darkening if stored for long periods. It made the apples look fresh so people would eat them. They removed the peels and cores, sliced the apples by hand or machine, steeped them in a solution of three pounds of salt to a gallon of water for two or three minutes, spread them on wooden trays, and subjected them to sulphur fumes for a few minutes. Then they were placed in the sun to dry.*]

Sunday, November 14 ❧ Had Remembrance Day service in the hall today. Rained all day and so cold. *[They usually held it on the Sunday, not necessarily on November 11th.]*

Wednesday, November 17 ∿ A missionary service at the church. It was fine, on *[about]* China. Had a basket social at the United church.

Tuesday, November 23 ∿ Merle still racking potatoes at Charlie Pugh's.

Monday, November 29 ∿ Albert finished tallying at noon. Merle going to woods in black's harbour tomorrow with 16 or 17 more from here.

Tuesday, November 30 ∿ Albert tallying for Robbie Currie.

Monday, December 6 ∿ Wonderful day like fall. I washed and hanged clothes out without cap or sweater on.

Thursday, December 30 ∿ Had lots of callers today. 10 plus Mr. Jack Brawn here for supper.

218

1938

Tuesday, January 13 ∽ Nice. Merle went to Barton today to work for Ashley Colter.

Thursday, January 19 ∽ Been to Ethel's. She's helping me with a knitted skirt.

Friday, February 4 ∽ Lyman, Lucy and Dorothy Saunders were here playing monopoly tonite. *[Patented in 1935, this would have been a relatively new game for them.]*

Wednesday, February 9 ∽ Been to W.A. Maud took the horse and we had a lovely sleigh ride.

Saturday, February 12 ∽ Nice, roads good again

Saturday, March 12 ∽ Jack Burtt's house in Zealand burned today.

Wednesday, March 23 ∽ To Mrs. Herb Haines for supper. Helped her hook on her rug awhile. Bus not running for awhile.

Wednesday, March 30 ∽ A man and boy here from Geary, a poor man and boy selling a few notions.

Thursday, April 14 ∽ I'm not feeling well, have this distemper that is going round.

Wednesday, April 20 ∽ Albert has made a new cupboard for the shed. Mrs. Spear has a new carriage for Marie.

Monday, April 26 ∽ Have had all the mattresses out airing, and started to clean the bedrooms.

Friday, May 6 ∽ The children are all in town to some kind of a festival in Normal School.

Monday, May 9 ∽ Had Buddie to Dr. Greow tonite; Morehouse was there too for those lumps. They don't amount to much after all.

Friday, May 27 ∽ Merle finished at the mill. I cleaned the barn.

Sunday, May 29 ∽ Merle gone over Boiestown somewhere to work in a mill for Colter. Don't know for how long.

Thursday, June 2 ∽ Had Institute at Annie Pugh's. The Supervisor there. Had a lovely lunch.

Wednesday, June 8 ∽ Albert been up tonite to a meeting at church, about the roof.

Thursday, June 23 ∽ Mona finished today at Normal School *[where she was training to be a teacher]*.

Friday, June 24 ∽ Bubar's new mill whistled today for the first time. *[It would whistle to start work, to start and finish lunch break, and again at end of day.]*

Sunday, July 3 ∽ Rain all nite and all day today. A terrible rain. Water over road. Bubar's logs ran out *[due to high water]*.

Wednesday, July 6 ∽ Hayward and kiddies down to ball game in Bubar's pasture.

Thursday, July 7 ∽ Had our strawberry tea. About 130 there.

Friday, July 22 ᦆ I got a new davenport *[similar to a chesterfield].*

Thursday, August 4 ᦆ We *[are]* hunting up jacks for to raise the house. *[They may have used wooden or metal jacks. The device usually had some form of spiral thread, and as someone pumped the handle, the top piece of the jack elevated the corner of the house. They placed wooden blocking underneath it to hold it in place; then they raised another corner and placed blocking under that corner as well. This process gradually raised each corner of the home until it was the desired height and as level as they could make it. Then they installed a new foundation wall around the home.]*

Tuesday, August 9 ᦆ We went to the corner for a moonlight walk. The scouts are having a hot dog supper.

Saturday, August 13 ᦆ Merle has the house up as far as he's going to put it *[for the partial foundation wall].*

Tuesday, Aug .16 ᦆTerriblyᏱ hot. Feel sorry for merle working in this heat. Randolph Maybe been hauling gravel for him all day.

Thursday, August 18 ᦆ Not hot. Have the concrete near half done. It's been a busy day for all.

Wednesday, August 24 ᦆ Mrs. Andrew Currie's house burned last nite.

Tuesday, August 30 ᦆ Men fixing concrete form for the well.

Saturday, September 17 ᦆ Merle has cellar finished thanks to goodness. *[This was a root cellar with a dirt floor under part of the house, not a full basement like homes have today.]*

Monday, September 26 ᦆ Lovely day. Been to Willie Brewer's all day; such a lovely walk. Everything so pretty.

Wednesday, September 28 ᦆ Merle making steps today *[for the cellar].*

Friday, September 30 ᦆ Sounds like war is settled for awhile, and hope for ever. *[British Prime Minister Neville Chamberlain gave his famous*

Peace for our time speech after the Munich agreement.]

Tuesday, October 4 ∿ Merle finished the concrete work today. We have put the preserves, potatoes and other things in the cellar today. It's a dear little cellar. *[The dirt floor helped it stay cool, and the moisture kept the vegetables from drying out over winter.]* Mona at girls W.A.

Monday, October 17 ∿ Merle gone to Miramichi to work for Colter.

Tuesday, October 25 ∿ Albert made me a china cabinet from an old cupboard.

Thursday, November 10 ∿ We have all been to a red cross rally in the hall. Very nice. Albert been to Kingsclear scaling some wood for Ellis Dunphy.

Saturday, November 12 ∿ Colder. Had a tramp here for lunch.

Friday, November 25 ∿ A terrible snow storm; so cold and such wind and drifts. And what a time we have had to finish the plaster; what a time had to mix it in shed. Then Merle disconnected the flue and it needed repairs. Oh my, oh my, the mess along with the storm. Have scrubbed all afternoon.

Monday, November 28 ∿ No cars moving. No bus since Thursday,

Saturday, December 3 ∿ The bus finally arrived.

Monday, December 5 ∿ I washed, made hop yeast, and white fruit cake.

Wednesday, December 7 ∿ Mr. Jewett here and put the putty coat on ceiling.

Saturday, December 10 ∿ Merle has the waincoding on. *[Mary referred here to wainscoting; vertical wood strips that were usually tongue and grooved. They were cut in 3 or 4-foot lengths and put on the walls around the room with an added chair rail or finish piece along the top. Originally wainscoting was installed to protect the plastered wall, but it* *became a design option in later homes.]*

Wednesday, December 14 ∿ Merle is now at the shed. Tore paper off ceiling; going to put boards on. Some mess *[but will be a lot warmer]*.

Thursday, December 22 ∿ We Institute ladies met at Mrs. G. Brewers and did up boxes for needy families.

1939

Saturday, January 14 ～ Mona and Lebaron have whooping cough.

Monday, January 23 ～ A terrible wind. I thought it would blow the house over this am before we woke up.

Monday, January 30 ～ Albert been sick and not much better. Dr. was in today.

Sunday, February 5 ～ Albert had another bad spell.

Friday, February 9 ～ Dr. in again and says Albert can sit up for a bit now.

Tuesday, February 14 ～ Mr. McQueen *[Anglican Priest]* here this am and had communion service. Albert doing fine.

Sunday, March 5 ～ Merle gone to Dorn Ridge to see if he can get work in Mill.

Thursday, March 9 ～ Merle at Hayne tallying. The work started on *[a stone]* bridge across the Jones Forks Stream.

Friday, March 10 ⌒ Was to store and got paper for halls. *[Wallpaper was available locally in the community stores.]* Verna is going to help me put it on.

Friday, March 17 ⌒ Finished papering thanks to goodness.

Sunday, April 23 ⌒ Cold, ice ran out of creek today.

Friday, May 5 ⌒ Very nice. Was to hall to W.A. Musical show by the Darkies. *[That term for black people has changed since the 1930s and is considered derogatory or racist in today's society.]*

Wednesday, May 10 ⌒ Merle putting a door in end of shed today.

Friday, May 26 ⌒ A cowboy show in hall tonight.

Thursday, June 8 ⌒ We have been to a play in the hall from Tay Creek.

Friday, June 9 ⌒ Sternie *[?]* Hughson here fixing flue. *[The flue, or chimney, was made of bricks which probably came from the Staples Brick Factory, a short distance west of the station.]*

Saturday, June 10 ⌒ Ruby and all to the city; the city is wonderful for the King and Queen *[to visit].*

Tuesday, June 13 ⌒ King *[George VI]* and Queen visited city today.

Monday, June 26 ⌒ Merle gone to St. Leonard to work for Colter.

Thursday, June 29 ⌒ They're using the new bridge today and tearing down the old *[covered one].*

Monday, July 3 ⌒ Mona gone to F'ton tonite to write normal *[school]* exams.

Monday, July 17 ⌒ Had a little shower about tea time.

Tuesday, July 18 ⌒ Hayward and family down; brought down the lawnmower and mowed our yard.

Monday, July 24 ⌒ Merle working at Dorn Ridge loading lumber.

Albert tallying.

Thursday, July 27 ∾ Merle put down shed floor.

Monday, July 31 ∾ Merle putting side *[siding]* on shed.

Monday, Aug 6 ∾ Merle working the annual road work.

Monday, August 14 ∾ Buddie came tonight. *[In times of need, Mary often helped her neighbours through births and illnesses. Now her family and neighbours have come to support her with Albert.]*

Tuesday, August 15 ∾ Had lots of callers, Avery, Mrs. Inch, Ruby Burtt and Mrs. Madson.

Wednesday, August 16 ∾ Buddie gone home, Mona's here.

Thursday, August 17 ∾ Avery and Horace here to see Ta. *[This must have been a nickname Mary called Albert, but this is the first time she has used it in the diary.]* Mona here tonight; they were all down awhile Mr. McQueen also.

Friday, August 18 ∾ Buddie here tonight.

Sunday, August 20 ∾ Albert worse; right in bed now. Had Dr. in. Ruby and Hayward here all afternoon and evening; Willie Brewer here this evening. Mona's with me.

Monday, August 21 ∾ Dr. here this morning; lots of callers.

Tuesday, August 22 ∾ moved his bed down stairs; easier for all. Lots of callers.

Wednesday, August 23 ∾ Poor Ta, failing fast. Lucy staying tonight.

Thursday August 24 ∾ Ta asked for Merle to be sent for in the night. Rupert has gone after Merle with Hayward's car. He has arrived. Ta has had a talk with him. May Ferguson was here, Mabel Fowler here tonight.

Friday, August 25 ∾ Ta so restless. Merle sits by him most of the time.

Lucy here tonight. *[It appears Lucy Gorman and Mabel Fowler were taking turns staying the night with the Morehouse family. To the author's knowledge, Lucy didn't have formal nursing training but she did help the doctors with baby deliveries and other house calls. Mabel Fowler was trained as a nurse.]*

Saturday, August 26 ∾ Poor Ta failing fast. Mabel fowler here tonight, and Ruby.

Sunday, August 27 ∾ Oh, an awful thing to write. Poor Ta has gone to his long home.

Monday, August 28 ∾ Grace arrived. Ruby came down. Lucy with us and Ethel *[This could be Brewer or MacDonald, Ethel MacDonald was a neighbour.]*

Friday, September 1 ∾ Went to visit Grace in Houlton *[only to hear]* oh dear the war has started. *[Hitler invaded Poland. Poor Mary – just lost her husband and now war is starting. Memories of World War I would still be fresh in the community.]*

Sunday, September 3 ∾ England declared war on Germany.

Tuesday, September 5 ∾ We drove over to line house *[border crossing]* to ask if there would be any trouble *[because of the war]* to cross over and then we went around the stores. *[They stayed few days and went home.]*

Thursday, September 14 ∾ Went up to Ruby's on bus.

Thursday, October 19 ∾ A slight earthquake shock this am.

Monday, November 20 ∾ Election Day. Liberals in again. Conservatives close. McNair defeated. *[This was a provincial election. The Liberals got 29 seats and the Conservatives 19, so she could have been referring to her riding when she said it was a close race. McNair was probably their Conservative candidate.]*

Tuesday, December 12 ∽ H. Clark came and insured the house.

Sunday, December 31 ∽ I can't write good bye old year with its blessing. Many, many blessings I know and am thankful for. But a sad one
for me thinking of the dear one gone to higher service, never to return.
[Her husband, Albert]

Chapter 5

1940-1944

AS THE WAR continued into the 1940s, Red Cross Meetings were initiated to support the war effort and send packages to service men and women in Europe. School children participated by tearing cotton cloth into long narrow strips that were packed into the overseas boxes for use as bandages. Tobacco companies either supplied service men with cigarettes or offered discounts to their family members so they could send some in the packages that were headed to the war zones. The McDonald's Cigarette company ran a *Give them Smokes from Home* campaign. Because of their dedication to veterans, the company retained a large portion of the cigarette market for years after the war was over.

There was increased demand for items to support the war effort. Ships that were normally used to transport food were now needed to move troops and supplies for the war. Things like sugar and tea which came by ship from outside of Canada had no way to get into the country. Canned goods were also scarce because all available metals were used to manufacture war items. In 1942, the Canadian Government set up a rations program, and Canadian food products like butter, produce, maple syrup, molasses, and any canned fruit, evaporated milk, and meat were rationed. This meant that each person or family had an allowance that stated how much of each type of food they could have per week. Any surplus went to military personnel in the belief that the extra food would keep them strong and healthy to fight. Gasoline and kerosene were also rationed.

As the war accelerated, the dreaded telegrams and letters announcing that local people had been injured or killed in action arrived at Burtt's Corner homes. Services were held in the community to mourn their loss and support the families. Although the war was far away, there were a couple of incidents on local soil in which military people were killed.

Several meetings in the hall showed films of the war to encourage people to purchase Victory Bonds, as a way to increase expenditures on military efforts and equipment.

Local residents rushed out to watch as troop trains passed through

Zealand, Burtt's Corner, and Keswick on their way to the Internment Camp near Ripples, NB. The train windows were either boarded up or had the shades nailed down, so it must have been the mere hopes of seeing a prisoner that sent people out to watch the train pass by. The camp originally housed at least 700 Jewish boys sent from Austria through Britain as part of the Kinder transport program, as well as others rounded up from Britain at Churchill's request. Later, prisoners of war, and any Canadians of Jewish, German, or Italian descent who spoke out against the war were imprisoned there until the end of the war. Many of those released became great citizens and business owners in New Brunswick.

Although much of the news and conversations of this period centred upon the war, life in rural communities continued to be as normal as possible. People still attended church functions and entertained themselves. The children went to school, and the adults worked when and where possible.

1940

Friday, January 5 ∾ nice day. Lebaron 14 yrs. Been down home and found out Merle had been home. Then *[he]* went to Boston. Tom Graham died and buried. *[Not sure why Merle went to Boston.]*

Monday, January 8 ∾ lovely afternoon been over to corner to Mrs. Bird. Earle still home. Will be there tonight.

Tuesday, January 9 ∾ lovely day. Over to see Mrs. T. Brewer. Did big wash and got wood in. Stayed for W.A at Mrs. Bird.

Wednesday, January 10 ∾ lovely day. Was up to Corner. Called on Mrs. Haines. She's fine. Stayed at Mrs. B.

Thursday, January 11 ∾ lovely day. Was up to corner and other places. H&R *[Hayward & Ruby]* down this evening. Stayed at Mrs. B's. *[It appears she's staying with others for the night.]*

January 30. ∾ like an April day. Was to Stella's *[Maybe's]*.

Friday, February 2 ∾ lovely day. Mrs. Ambrose Allen and Mrs. Lyman Bubar called. A little cold but wonderfully bright. Mrs. Inch was in for tea. Went to the corner.

Saturday, February 3 ∾ Cold and a little snow. Hayward & Ruby, Buddy and Minot come down tonight.

Sunday, February 4 ∾ wonderful day, cold and windy but so bright. Hayward and Ruby down.

Monday, February 5 ∾ lovely and wonderful. Sent fudge to Merle by Albert Allen.

Tuesday, February 6 ∾ wonderful, wonderful day. Have been at aid at Chapman's, had a nice time.

Sunday, February 11 ∾ storm of the season, snowed all night and all day with sleet mixed. No one on the road all day.

Monday, February 12 ∾ big blow all night and all day. Lebaron came to shovel us out and brought in wood.

Tuesday, February 13 ∾ it's cold, we are all working at our quilts. We had letters from Merle and Earle Burtt.

Saturday, February 17 ∾ wonderful day like April. Merle came home tonight. Hayward and Ruby and all down.

Monday, February 19 ∾ lovely day, washed and done lot of things. Merle gone back *[home for weekend]*.

Tuesday, February 20 ∾ a snowstorm on. Mrs. B. sick and they had the doctor. I let a big stick of wood fall on my foot.

Wednesday, February 21 ∾ a blustery day. My foot better. I'm so glad to say that Buddie came down to help me out. Mrs. B in bed.

Thursday February 22 ∾ lovely day. Quite cold and again tonight. Mrs. B. sat up in the hall. Effie and her mother spent the evening. My foot gaining at last.

Tuesday, February 27 ∿ quite cold bright. Mrs. Bird down stairs today. 6 months since TA *[Albert]* went away. Half a year

Thursday, March 7 ∿ terrible nasty day. Water everywhere. Institute to have been here but none here. *[probably due to nasty weather or high water]*

Monday, March 11 ∿ cold wind. I fell on ice and hurt my knee real bad. Hope it won't lay me up. Merle came home.

Tuesday, March 12 ∿ a little snow. My knee a little bit better. Earle here for supper and Merle to the city tonight.

Wednesday, March 13 ∿ lovely day. Institute here tonight. Mona and Zaida here for the night.

Thursday March 14 ∿ very nice. Merle gone up near Hartland loading for a few days *[maybe spring seed potatoes]* My knee about the same.

Good Friday, March 22 ∿ wonderful morning storm on tonight. Lizzie was here with me tonight.

Saturday, March 23 ∿ terrible storm. Went up on train this am to Ruby's. Knew they couldn't get down.

Easter Sunday, March 24 ∿ terrible cold, wild day and all last night. Couldn't get to church at all.

Wednesday, March 26 ∿ Still cold. Election day. Merle in city tonight.

Thursday, March 27 ∿ Hanson won the election *[but Mary doesn't elaborate with the details like she did for the other elections. Hanson also became the acting Party Leader and acting Leader of the Official Opposition for a couple of years. At this point, the Conservatives were calling themselves the National Government.]* Warmer but colder now. Mona drove home. I washed.

April 9 ᠺ Germany invaded Norway and Denmark

May 10 ᠺ Germany invaded France, Holland and Belgium and Luxemburg

Saturday, May 11 ᠺ Mona got her driving licence.

Wednesday, May 15 ᠺ War terrible *[but she doesn't specify what she reads or hears.]*

Thursday, May 16 ᠺ War news awful.

Monday, June 10 ᠺ Italy declared an ally of Germany.

Thursday, July 25 ᠺ Been to red cross work meeting.

Wednesday, August 14 ᠺ Randolph Maybe had a hog killed by lightning.

Friday, August 16 ᠺ Started a scarf for war. *[Mary participated in the Red Cross Rooms or meetings where the women quilted, sewed, or knit items* for *the boxes that were sent to the men overseas. It was the women's way to support the war effort.]*

Monday, August 19 ᠺ I was up and registered. *[Probably for her National Registration Certificate which everyone had to carry at all times for proof of registration. Canada no longer had an unemployment problem because so many people were needed for the war effort. The National Registration system helped make sure that essential jobs were filled.]*

Saturday, August 24 ᠺ Mr. Cooke died today *[the Methodist Minister].*

Thursday, August 29 ᠺ Been to Red Cross rooms quilting.

Saturday, August 31 ᠺ Merle's been in Colter's office *[working]* a couple of days.

Thursday, September 12 ᠺ Been to Red Cross Rooms working. *[The meetings seem to be held on Thursdays.]*

Monday, December 16 ᠺ Merle gone to Devon to work in the round house *[for the railway]*.

Wednesday, December 18 ∽ Been to corner, sold 85 cents worth of pin cushions.

Friday, December 20 ∽ A slight earthquake.

Monday, December 30 ∽ Mrs. Bubar moved to city.

Tuesday, December 31 ∽ Been a year of war. Hope coming year brings peace.

1941

Monday, January 20 ∽ Bad snow storm; no bus.

Tuesday, January 21 ∽ Still drifting; no bus. Roads bad.

Thursday, January 23 ∽ Another snow storm last night. Main road blowed good.

Thursday, January 30 ∽ At red cross rooms quilting.

Friday, February 14 ∽ Mona came home with measles.

Friday, May 9 ∽ Ben Jones here putting first coat of paint on ceiling.

Monday, June 16 ∽ Washed, cleaned barn, toilet and hen house.

Thursday, June 26 ∽ Been to Mrs. Durwood Jones funeral.

Saturday, June 28 ∽ Germany invades Russia. *[Invasion began on June 22, but Mary probably just heard it announced.]*

Sunday, June 29 ∞ Merle home and has enlisted; oh dear.

Thursday, July 3 ∞ Merle gone to F'ton to get x-rayed.

Saturday, August 3 ∞ Merle quarantined.

Friday, August 15 ∞ All soldiers quarantined again.

Sunday, August 17 ∞ Merle in town. Quarantines lifted.

Wednesday, September 7 ∞ Mrs. Spear and I went to Woodstock and back on train *[passenger train still running.]*

Thursday, September 25 ∞ Merle arrived for 3 days leave before leaving F'ton.

Sunday, October 5 ∞ Merle expects to go to St. John tomorrow.

Saturday, November 22 ∞ Buddie got all the mill wood in *[to use for kindling in the wood stove].*

Friday, November 28 ∞ Buddie down to Stella's for milk.

Sunday, December 7 ∞ Japan bombed US possessions. *[Pearl Harbour].*

Monday, December 8 ∞ The United States in the War *[Britain has been involved from the beginning but now they declared war against Japan as well].*

Tuesday, December 16 ∞ Sold a few fancy things *[could be for the W.A. or the war effort].*

Thursday, December 25 ∞ Merle came this morning on train. Rained so bus was so late last night.

Thursday, December 31 ∞ Grey, a little snow, lovely. Last of year of war and trouble. Oh if the new would dawn on peace.

1942

Saturday, January 3 ∾ A note from Merle tonight saying a bunch of them sent to F'ton last night, to start for Camp Borden this morning. I'm sorry he is leaving near home, but glad it's not England.

Thursday, January 8 ∾ Went to Red Cross Rooms.

Friday, January 9 ∾ Merle left F'ton Sat night, arrived Camp Borden Monday,

Thursday, January 15 ∾ Have made some oven mitts.

Monday, January 19 ∾ Boys loading pulp *[at the station]*.

Tuesday, January 20 ∾ Had a letter from Merle; is kind of expecting to leave this week.

Wednesday, January 21 ∾ Merle arrived just now. Got in F'ton 9 am.

Sunday, January 25 ∾ Merle gone again. Edie Brewer drove him to the *[Fredericton]* Junction *[Railway Station]* and he is now speeding on.

Monday, February 2 ∾ A letter from Merle. Some of the St. John boys that trained with him have been drafted somewhere, maybe overseas.

Monday, March 2 ⌒ Letter from Merle still at C.B. *[Camp Borden]*.

Wednesday, March 4 ⌒ Was out to see the army train but wasn't in. *[She may have meant the troop train that passed through Burtt's Corner, and on through Fredericton to the Ripples Internment Camp where the passengers were held. The reference could also have been for a scheduled train taking troops to Halifax for embarkation to England.]*

Saturday, March 7 ⌒ An awful day; such a cold wind. The wires down and lights out and almost impossible to get around the city.

Tuesday, March 17 ⌒ Quite a nice letter from Merle. They are going somewhere right away; likely to England.

Friday, March 20 ⌒ A letter from Merle. Still at C.B. *[Camp Borden]* expect to move anytime. A big Fire in F'ton tonight. It was broadcasted on radio. The big Ross Drug building meaning Vandine Shoe store, Belmore's also Colwells and Jenning and buildings on York St..

Tuesday, March 31 ⌒ Frank Haines has been killed in England, Elwood Haines son. Oh this terrible war.

Thursday, April 2 ⌒ No word yet from Merle. He must have gone overseas.

Sunday, April 5 ⌒ A memorial service at the corner this afternoon for Frank Haines.

Saturday, April 11 ⌒ Received a cablegram from Merle today from England; sent the 31 March.

Monday, April 30 ⌒ Had a letter from Merle tonight by airmail. Such a nice letter. Was delighted with the trip to England and so glad.

Tuesday, April 21 ⌒ Sent cigarettes to Merle.

Monday, May 4 ⌒ Made fudge for Merle.

Wednesday, May 6 ∽ A telegram from Merle tonight.

Thursday, May 7 ∽ Mrs. Spear's hired woman stays with me at nights.

Friday, May 8 ∽ Two letters from Merle tonight.

Monday, May 11 ∽ Mrs. Brewer *[Spear's maid]* still here nights.

Saturday, May 16 ∽ Grace went home *[to Houlton]* and I went far as Woodstock and back on train. Lovely trip.

Friday, May 22 ∽ Canned a peck of fiddleheads, made bread and painted another cupboard.

Wednesday, May 27 ∽ Had two letters from Merle and part of a Russian paper telling of terrible things the Germans are doing.

Friday, May 29 ∽ Made bread, enamelled sink, and helped Queenie quilt an hour.

Tuesday, June 2 ∽ Doing a box for Merle; only hope he gets it.

Wednesday, June 10 ∽ Been to city to red cross convention.

Thursday, June 11 ∽ Another air mail letter from Merle.

Tuesday, June 30 ∽ Was to Coal Creek. A plane down at the range. Another came looking for it and landed in Bob Weaver's field. All were over to see it.

Tuesday, July 14 ∽ Terrible hot. Waxed my floor. An awful hail storm about 6pm; hail as large as walnuts, broke panes of glass for everyone. Broke 3 panes in our house.

Wednesday, August 5 ∽ War looking terrible.

Tuesday, August 11 ∽ Had a letter and birthday present from Merle.

Saturday, August 29 ∽ Left teeth *[in the city for repair]* and came up on bus. Buddie been x-rayed for stone in kidney.

Tuesday, September 8 ∽ They very busy people packing tomatoes *[at* *railway to ship away].*

Tuesday, September 15 ᘓ Oscar has signed up, going to leave to join army. *[Dr. Oscar Morehouse Jr.]*

Thursday, September 24 ᘓ My Transport picture not came yet. Putting me back in having papers made out.

Monday, September 27 ᘓ To nursing class.

Wednesday, September 30 ᘓ Been to the Keswick Fair went on bus and back.

Thursday, October 1 ᘓ Those horrid pictures; got them at last.

Saturday, October 3 ᘓ Made an uncooked fruitcake for Merle.

Thursday, October 8 ᘓ Expect to go city to get more done about pass card. *[Perhaps similar to a passport so she could cross into Maine.]*

Saturday, October 10 ᘓ Getting ready to go to Houlton and getting Merle xmas box ready.

Saturday, October 17 ᘓ Had a blackout *[in Houlton]* last night.

Sunday, October 18 ᘓ Another blackout *[Houlton]*.

Friday, November 13 ᘓ *[Back at home]* Was to Stanley Pugh's to knitting bee.

Monday, November 23 ᘓ Up to the nursing class tonight. They were bandaging ankle and foot.

Friday, December 11 ᘓ No word from Merle since 18th of November

Saturday, December 12 ᘓ A letter from Merle tonight; 6 weeks on way.

Thursday, December31 ᘓ Our year of 1942 about ended. Hope things will be better; nearer the end of war in the coming year.

1943

Thursday, January 14 ∿ A slight earthquake shock tonight.

Monday, January 18 ∿ War news sounds better tonight.

Wednesday, January 20 ∿ Terrible cold and dreadful wind. No one to school; not Mona *[teacher]* even.

Thursday, January 21 & Friday, January 22 ∿ Still no school even for teacher Mona; too bitter cold and wind. *[There were no school buses so teachers and students walked several miles to school.]*

Wednesday, January 27 ∿ Letter from Merle.

Monday, February 8 ∿ Two letters from Merle, one from Reuben and several others.

Wednesday, February 10 ∿ Sent 300 cigs to Merle.

Friday, February 12 ∿ Hayward was called out. Water over track somewhere at Pugh's Crossing.

Tuesday, February 16 ∿ Very, very cold. Children didn't go to school,

Mona did.

Friday, February 19 ∾ A number coming in for Mona to fix their ration cards.

Saturday, February 20 ∾ Mona been to the school house all day making out the ration cards. *[Ration cards were provided to each family. The cards had coupons that showed how much butter, sugar, gasoline, tea and other items that the family or individual was entitled to. This allowed the government to use the additional goods for the war effort.]*

Thursday, March 11 ∾ Was to corner to Red Cross rooms; was quite a number there.

Friday, March 12 ∾ Icy and water terrible. Got Merle three boxes away; also cigarettes again 1000.

Friday, April 16 ∾ I made some honey today; made it too heavy.

Sunday, April 18 ∾ My cold making me feel mean.

Monday, April 26 ∾ Received a cable of Easter Greeting from Merle.

Saturday, May 1 ∾ Had an airmail from Merle; having his leave in Edinburg *[Scotland]*.

Monday, May 3 ∾ Ben Jones is painting homes around the community.

Tuesday, May 4 ∾ Sent Merle 1000 from MacDonald firm. *[Mary would have gotten the cigarettes from the MacDonald Cigarette company through their "Give them smokes from home" campaign.]*

Wednesday, May 5 ∾ A letter from Merle; wrote 1st day of April. So a long while on way.

Thursday, May 6 ∾ Next letter from Merle received; written month ago.

Saturday, May 8 ∾ Pictures of the war, a band and speeches in the hall tonight for the Victory Loans.

Friday, May 14 〰️ A cable from Merle; Mother's Day greetings sent on that day, and also a letter written after his leave.

Saturday, May 15 〰️ An airgraph *[airmail]* from Merle wrote 30th April

Saturday, May 22 〰️ Another airgraph written May 5th.

Wednesday, May 26 〰️ Made fudge for Merle and frosted his fruit cake.

Monday, May 31 〰️ Mowed lawn, canned fiddleheads and got window boxes fixed.

Friday, June 4 〰️ Sent 300 sweet cap cigs to Merle.

Tuesday, June 15 〰️ The mill started today.

Thursday, June 24 〰️ Sent Merle another 300 sweet caps. *[The sweet caps were also a MacDonald's brand cigarette and were considered superior to the smokes that came in their rations.]*

Thursday, July 1 〰️ Went to red cross rooms.

Thursday, July 8 〰️ Sent to MacDonald's for 1000 cigs.

Friday, July 9 〰️ Ruby and Mona both have mumps.

Monday, July 12 〰️ Big thunder shower tonight. Struck Murray's barn.

Wednesday, July 21 〰️ *[Mary was visiting in Houlton.]* We went in bus to the air base. *[In 1941, the Houlton Air force Base was built adjacent to the Canadian border. Before the States entered WW II, American pilots could not fly planes into Canada because the US was still considered neutral. Instead, they flew their planes to the base in Houlton, and local farmers towed the planes into Canada using their farm tractors. Then the Woodstock Highway was closed off so the planes could use the highway as a runway and officially take off from Canadian soil because Canada was already in the war. This may have been part of Roosevelt's Lend Lease Program, in which the United States made arrangements with Allied* *countries to lend/lease equipment for the war effort. No info was found to confirm this statement.]*

Saturday, July 24 ∽ Letter from Merle. He's in Whales *[Wales]*, or was when he wrote.

Sunday, August 8 ∽ Buddie very sick with mumps. Had Dr. Jewett early this am. *[Dr. Jewett was replacing Dr. Morehouse who had enlisted. Hugh is 19 and of age to enlist. With a high school education, and because there was a shortage of teachers during the war, Hugh was given special permission to teach. His health may have prevented him participating in active war anyway.]*

Thursday, August 12 ∽ Harold brought my wood today; stopped in and payed *[paid]* him 55 dollars for 5 cord *[$11.00 per cord in 1943; $200-250 per cord in today's dollars].*

Saturday, August 21 ∽ Such a nice letter from Merle. He's got a stripe L/Cpl. He was already for his leave. It was Aug 8th.

Friday, August 27 ∽ 2 letters from Merle — back letters. The Disciple Church having a picnic on Mrs. Bubar's flat this afternoon. I'm doing bean salad and rhubarb juice.

Thursday, September 16 ∽ My new bed and spring arrived today. *[The new bed was a mattress, not a tick. The spring was a series of springs and thin, narrow metal slats hooked together. The mattress laid on top of this.]*

Friday, September 17 ∽ Busy, enamelled bedstead, canned plums. Made crab-apple jellie, and lots of odds and ends. A letter from Merle today.

Tuesday, September 21 ∽ Lovely day. Canned apples, made fudge and cookies for Merle's Box. Mona lost her watch tonight; all corner out looking.

Wednesday, September 22 ∽ Lovely day. Been to Maud's to W.A.

Mona's watch found unharmed by Cloie Pugh on Forks Road; great rejoicing and thankfulness.

Friday, September 24 ∾ Mailed Merle's box (20th).

Tuesday, October 5 ∾ Sent 300 cigs.

Thursday, October 7 ∾ Sent 300 cigs. *[Shows how often she's sending parcels overseas.]*

Friday, October 8 ∾ Cold. Collected some for the solders boxes.

Tuesday, October 12 ∾ Quilted an hour or two on quilt at Ashley's store. Quilt for United Church.

Thursday, October 14 ∾ Wonderful. Was to red cross. Also collected for the soldiers boxes. Sent 300 cigs.

Monday, October 18 ∾ Mona got the car down waiting for Ed Brewer to fix it. *[Edison bought the hotel property and tore the hotel down. He used the lumber from the hotel and built a garage in 1939.]*

Tuesday, October 19 ∾ Word came that Reggie Brewer wounded in Italy; don't know how bad.

Friday, October 22 ∾ Getting Merle's box ready and send 300 cigs. Eldon *[Bird]* home on leave.

Tuesday, October 26 ∾ There are pictures in the hall for the school this am. Also tonight for the Victory Loan entertainment *[These were moving pictures to encourage people to buy the victory bonds that supported the war effort.]*

Monday, November 1 ∾ Time changes for winter months.

Friday, November 5 ∾ Sent 1000 sweet caps *[cigarettes].*

Sunday, November 14 ∾ Church tonight had honour roll for our soldier boys *[closest Sunday to Remembrance Day].*

Tuesday, November 16 ∾ Got a bag of flour today; want to see how long it lasts.

Monday, November 29 ◌ Been to town; did get mantles for the lamp.

Thursday, December 2 ◌ Sent Merle 1000 cigs from MacDonald's.

Tuesday, December 7 ◌ Got a box of holly *[plant]* from Merle. Also an air mail.

Thursday, December 9 ◌ Ronald Yerxa fixed snap on the well.

Saturday, December 11 ◌ Minot *[Ruby's son]* came down and got more nubbins *[wood ends from the mill]*. A cute card from Merle and view of Isle of Man where he's been on leave.

Monday, December 13 ◌ Had a cable xmas greeting from Merle. Received his xmas boxes. Also got my present from him, a money bracelet. Just sweet and two nice cards and two letters.

Tuesday, December 28 ◌ Made cookies and fudge for Merle's boxes.

Friday, December 31 ◌ Last of the old year. Hope the new *[year]* brings peace and our boys back.

1944

Tuesday, January 4 ⌇ Letter from Merle. Sent Merle 300 sweet caps.

Sunday, January 9 ⌇ LeBaron sent 1000 cigs to Merle.

Friday, January 14 & Saturday, January 15 ⌇ Letters from Merle *[both days]*.

Thursday, January 20 ⌇ Wonderful all day. Been down home and to Mrs. Fowler's for dinner, then to Red Cross Rooms in pm. *[She stayed at Ruby's for the winter.]*

Friday, January 21 ⌇ 2 yrs. since Merle came home for last leave.

Sunday, January 23 ⌇ Lovely like April. Been to church twice.

Monday, January 24 ⌇ Very nice; just like spring. Sent 300 cigarettes to Merle from McDonalds.

Tuesday, February 1 ⌇ I'm doing a new pattern doily.

Thursday, February 3 ⌇ Staying at Kate Hagerman's. Water frozen here *[at home]*; in a mess.

Monday, February 7 ∿ Got the water started yesterday; 3 days without water.

Wednesday, February 9 ∿ Been to W.A. at Mrs. Crouse's. Sent for 1000 cigs.

Tuesday, February 15 ∿ An airmail from Merle. Has had lead in his eyes.

Wednesday, February 23 ∿ Reuben *[was there for a visit]*; sharpened all the knives.

Friday, February 25 ∿ Mailed two Easter Boxes to Merle.

Monday, March 6 ∿ A letter from Merle; taking another course.

Wednesday, March 8 ∿ An air mail from Merle. Lovely day. Down to Maybe's for milk.

Wednesday, March 15 ∿ A letter and picture from Merle.

Thursday, March 16 ∿ Another letter from Merle, Perley Gilby

Monday, March 20 ∿ A plane crashed and burned two men at Scotch Settlement. *[The plane crashed on March 19th, but Mary had just heard about it. The lightweight bomber was on a training mission. It took off from Pennfield in southern NB and crashed in Scotch Settlement. Two crew members were killed, but two others survived.]*

Friday, March 24 ∿ Sending another box to Merle (30th). *[She kept track of how many boxes she sent.]*

Monday, March 27 ∿ Bus stops *[running]* tonight for awhile *[gas rationing maybe?]*. Down to have papers fixed to go to Houlton.

Tuesday, April 4 ∿ Been to Mrs. Herb Haines to United Aid.

Thursday, April 6 ∿ Mrs. Morehouse to Houlton to visit relatives. *[Canadians were still able to go back and forth to the United States.]*

Monday, April 17 ∿ Sent 1000 cigs.

Tuesday, April 18 ∾ Quite nice. I cleaned the clothes room. *[She kept up with her routine even though there was a war on.]*

Monday, April 21 ∾ Lovely. I came home *[from Ruby's]*. Burned the yard. Clouded; cold. Mr. Spear's mother died this am.

Thursday, April 27 ∾ Nice a Victory load *[Victory Loan]* lecture in Hall tonight and pictures.

Friday, April 28 ∾ Cold; awful cold. Done no cleaning. I stayed at Fowler's tonight. *[The women were taking turns staying with the widows and those with men away at war to keep one another company.]*

Monday, May 1 ∾ Cleaned Merle's room. *[What thoughts she must have had doing that with him away at war.]*

Thursday, May 4 ∾ Ralph Bubar spading my garden. Institute tonight.

Tuesday, May 9 ∾ Sent a big box to Merle and 300 cigs.

Friday, May 12 ∾ Worked in my yard awhile. Went to see Billie Brewer about some wood.

Saturday, May 13 ∾ Had Mother's Day Greetings from Merle. Stayed at Mrs. Birds last night. Going to Ruby's tonight.

Sunday, May 15 ∾ Mrs. Spear and I got lawn chairs *[home-made wooden ones]* down from over shed.

Tuesday, May 16 ∾ A letter from Merle

Saturday, May 20 ∾ To city; got my glasses.

Monday, May 22 ∾ Very nice day. Came home from Ben Jones. Clifton Burtt was killed by truck this am.

Wednesday, May 24 ∾ Wonderful day. Mona and Elsie and I to Dolass *[Douglas]* on a hike. Rhoda Miller and Mrs. Phil arrived in my upset house. Was to clean living room; all upset *[A mess]*.

Thursday, May 25 ∾ Mary Bird died. Little Clifton buried yesterday.

Tuesday, May 30 ∿ Sent 300 cigs to Merle.

Tuesday, June 6 ∿ Nice morning. Just heard that the dreaded invasion has started. Only God knows what's ahead of us.

Wednesday, June 7 ∿ Nice; a little shower tonite. To a play in hall for Keswick. Finished enamelling kitchen yesterday.

Wednesday, June 14 ∿ Lovely still painting. Mona to a party at Bart Brewer's. Sent 1000 cigs.

Thursday, June 15 ∿ Nice painted all morning. To Red Cross this pm. A letter from Merle; not since invasion.

Monday, June 19 ∿ Sent Merle two boxes.

Sunday, July 2 ∿ Lovely day. Grace and I had a pleasant day. They are starting the band tonight. I don't want to hear it *[because Merle played in it before he went overseas]*.

Monday, July 3 ∿ Lovely went to Woodstock. Two letters from Merle; he's still in England. Was I ever pleased to hear.

Friday, July 7 ∿ Lovely; quite hot. Have washed quilts and blankets. Stay*[ed]* at Lucy's last night. Mrs. Bird Away.

Friday, July 21 ∿ Rain; hope for all day. Am starting Merle's 38th box; sending 600 cigs.

Tuesday, July 25 ∿ Hot. Byard here at last putting shingles on roof.

Saturday, July 29 ∿ Roof finished tonight. Staying at Mrs. Birds.

Saturday, August 12 ∿ Terrible, terrible hot. Arrived home this am. I suppose Buddie operated on. A letter from Merle. He's in France.

Monday, August 14 ∿ Terrible hot fires at Minto; awful.

Tuesday, August 22 ∿ Quite hot. LeBaron passed army test *[and must have planned to enlist]*. Another Harley Burtt passed and also Miss Manda Gorman.

❧ *1944* ❧

Saturday, August 26 ᵔᵕ Nice two letters from Merle.

Sunday, August 27 ᵔᵕ 5 yrs since Albert passed.

Tuesday, August 29 ᵔᵕ Nice. Made a little cherry jellie. A letter from Merle; Ellis Dunphy missing. *[Ellis never returned from the war and left a wife and family of small children.]*

Monday, September 11 ᵔᵕ Lovely morning. Came home canned pears. Sent 600 cigs to Merle.

Wednesday, September 13 ᵔᵕ To Mabel Jones to W.A. Sent a box to Merle.

Monday, September 25 ᵔᵕ Cold; another big frost. Came home. Sent 300 cigs. Quilted at the Red Cross Rooms awhile.

Tuesday, September 26 ᵔᵕ Cold; feels like snow. Lucy and I over Trip Settlement. Made lots of calls.

Friday, October 6 ᵔᵕ Raining. Been up and mailed Merle's 41st box; also 3 dollars worth of cigs. *[One dollar bought 300 cigarettes or one pound of tobacco from the Macdonald's company. She would have ordered through their overseas department in Montreal.]*

Monday, October 9 ᵔᵕ Rained at times all day. Came home and made 6 small fruit cakes and fudge for overseas. Thanksgiving Day.

Friday, October 13 ᵔᵕ Lovely; worked all day at the boxes. Four of them ready for Merle.

Monday, October 16 ᵔᵕ Cold am. Came home. Merle in Belgium now.

Friday, October 20 ᵔᵕ Victory Loan in hall tonite.

Thursday, October 26 ᵔᵕ Another letter from Merle.

Wednesday, November 1 ᵔᵕ Been to a shower at Murray Spencer's. They lost near everything in the fire.

Saturday, November 4 ᵔᵕ Sent for 900 cigs to send to Merle.

Thursday, November 9 ∾ Been to chicken sandwich supper at Charlie Burtt's.

Saturday, November 11 ∾ Rained all night and all day today. Quite a number at the monument for Remembrance Day and has it ever poured.

Wednesday, December 6 ∾ A letter from Merle and a picture of him.

Friday, December 15 ∾ A letter from Merle and he received our boxes.

Tuesday, December 26 ∾ A telegram from Merle of greetings. So pleased to get it.

Thursday, December 28 ∾ An awful snow storm. Everything blocked. No bus. Letter from Merle.

Sunday, December 31 ∾ Last of old year. Hope for victory and peace in the New Year.

Chapter 6

1945-1949

THE HIGHLIGHt for nearly every Canadian in this period was the end of the war. Friends and family members were headed home. There were victory celebrations around the world and at home for the end of the war. When the servicemen returned home, there were celebrations in major cities like Fredericton as well as in small communities like Burtt's Corner. A special turkey dinner at the IOF Hall welcomed the returning men and women. There were numerous speeches by dignitaries, and the band played. Some rationing continued into 1946, but it soon disappeared.

Instead of people walking to local farms to get milk, farmers started offering regular milk delivery to their homes. They dropped off fresh milk and picked up the empty glass milk bottles to refill and return another day. Mary had another improvement introduced to her home — the addition of electricity. With that came the option for new appliances.

Radios had improved over the last decade, and many home owners had one. The daily programs continued to entertain listeners, and those unable to attend church could listen to Sunday services on the radio. When people passed away, their death announcement was also relayed over the radio so anyone who knew the person would get the details of the funeral service.

1945

Wednesday, January 3 ⟨⟩ quite nice. Everything a glade of ice. Rueben *[Mary's brother]* went back *[to Houlton where he lived]*. Went to devon tonight; came home on bus. Fell by the front door and broke my wrist.

Thursday Jan 4. ⟨⟩ Mabel got me to hospital today. I'll be here awhile.

[Date missing] ⟨⟩ broken wrist.

Saturday, January 20 ⟨⟩ Been in hospital 17 days. Came out this morning. Learned to take insulin myself. *[Mary went to Ruby's for the winter.]*

Thursday, January 25 ⟨⟩ cold, 3 years since Merle went to Camp Borden to go over.

Monday, January 29 ⟨⟩ Another storm brewing. No *[public]* bus; children not at school.

Monday, Feb 5 ⟨⟩ snowing a bit. Expect to go to town to have cast off.

Tuesday, February 6 ⟨⟩ Lovely day. Letter from Merle he's 37 today.

Friday, February 9 ᨀ Snowed and blowed all day. Mona didn't get home from school.

Saturday, February 10 ᨀ Quite nice but no plow or bus. Mona came by train.

Friday, February 16 ᨀ World's Day of Prayer.

Thursday, February 22 ᨀ Mailed Merle's Easter Box.

Saturday, March 31 ᨀ Lovely been to city. The ice ran out *[of the Saint John or Keswick River]*.

Thursday, April 12 ᨀ Wonderful day. Was to pictures. Pre Rosevelt *[President Theodore Roosevelt]* died. Teddy Jewett been killed.

Monday, April 17 ᨀ Wood pile getting smaller. Cook cars put in today *[for railway repair. She must have moved back home for the summer.]*

Tuesday, April 18 ᨀ Cook cars and carpenter's cars *[are here]*; shingling roof *[on the railway station]*.

Friday, May 5 ᨀ Raining and so cold. Going up on bus tonight. War about over.

Sunday, May 6 ᨀ Quite nice a little rain about church time. Wonderful news.

Monday, May 7 ᨀ Nice. War over, thank the Lord. Minot doing some wood.

Tuesday, May 8 ᨀ Nice but such a wind. This is V.E. Day *[Victory in Europe]*. Lots in town. Church tonite.

Wednesday, May 9 ᨀ Had a parcel from Merle.

Saturday, May 12 ᨀ Merle sent me lovely flowers for Mother's Day.

Saturday, May 19 ᨀ A terrible rain; water over the flats. My cellar a dose *[has water in it]* again.

Tuesday, May 22 ∽ Merle's letters from England.

Friday, August 3 ∽ Got one overseas box ready.

Saturday, August 4 ∽ Got two boxes ready for overseas.

Tuesday, September 4 ∽ Tilly Bird elected Conler *[councillor]*.

Sunday, September 30 ∽ All of them gone to city to see Carleton and York Regiment coming home.

Tuesday, October 16 ∽ Mona has scarlet rash.

Tuesday, October 23 ∽ Made an Eaton order. Merle not out of Holland yet.

Sunday, November 4 ∽ Buddie took rash; second treatment face.

Thursday, November 29 ∽ Had great word from Merle; started from Holland.

Tuesday, December 4 ∽ A letter from Merle; he's in England.

Friday, December 21 ∽ Merle's name in *[news]* paper. Coming on Duchess of Bedford *[ship]*.

Monday, December 31 ∽ We were all down to meet Merle. All so glad to see Merle.

[The comment below was written on the inside of the back cover of Mary's journal for 1945.]

Sailed from Liverpool England Saturday December 22, 1945. Arrived *[Fredericton]* New Year's Eve.

1946

Thursday, January 3 ～ Went to soldiers dinner tonight. It was very nice. *[The dinner was put on by the Women's Institute and held in the IOF Foresters hall. The hall had no running water or appliances, so residents carted pails of water and vegetables to the hall and cooked on Coleman stoves. They cooked the turkeys at their homes and carried them to the hall. There was a large crowd in attendance for the dinner, and dignitaries gave speeches to honour the men who had fought in the war.]*

Thursday, January 24 ～ Ronnie *[Brewer]* here tonight to see about wiring the house *[for electricity]*.

Friday, January 25 ～ Ronnie and Merle wiring house.

Friday, February 1 ～ Merle making a box for the meter.

Monday, February 4 ～ Taken the floor up upstairs for the wiring.

Tuesday, February 5 ∼ Ronnie came today. Also the man with the meter and two other men to put post up. Lights on tonight.

Wednesday, February 6 ∼ Ronnie here all day. They finished. All but putting the floor down. Lovely to have the lights; hardly seems possible.

Friday, February 15 ∼ Lovely like April. Water everywhere.

Wednesday, February 20 ∼ A terrible snow storm and so cold. It's surely wild tonight; the wind raging.

Thursday, February 21 ∼ No better today; drifted and snowed all day. Only two at school. Mona closed it at eleven and came home.

Friday, February 22 ∼ Still blocked up. No school. Milk Man didn't arrive; real cold.

Monday, February 25 ∼ A terrible snow storm. Worst in years. *[33 cm recorded on the 24th, with another 17 cm on the 25th.]* Everything blocked; no one to be seen.

Tuesday, February 26 ∼ Still no bus or road plow; teams *[the horse-pulled plows]* are out. Milk delivered by team this am.

Saturday, March 9 ∼ Poured all night; water everywhere. Merle came tonight and brought me an electric iron. *[Irons were one of the first electrical appliances the women wanted, because they did away with the need to keep putting the irons back in the fire.]*

Sunday, March 17 ∼ They been blasting the ice in front of the house to get a drain through the ice to get water off the road. The water gone down a lot.

Tuesday, June 11 ∼ Went to Vella's about the dinner that the Institute served for the music club. To be in hall tonight.

Tuesday, June 18 ∼ Called on Mrs. Inch. She's sick and I'm on the sick committee in Institute.

Saturday, June 22 ∾ Got the barn cleaned out at last. First since it was built 34 years ago.

Saturday, June 29 ∾ Was to band concert tonight.

Saturday, August 17 ∾ A letter from Grace with a dollar, a pretty card and lovely hankie for my birthday.

Saturday, August 24 ∾ Merle got a new radio. *[Another electric appliance.]*

Saturday, September 21 ∾ Merle came on bus and did he ever surprise me with a lovely new washing machine. *[This would have been a wringer-washer, and not an automatic washing machine like we have today. Mary would have had to manoeuvre the clothes through the machine by hand. Wringer-washers were still used in many Canadian homes in the 1960s.]*

Monday, September 23 ∾ Tried the new washing machine. It's great.

Saturday, November 16 ∾ Merle came on noon bus. He put tar paper on the toilet *[outhouse]* roof this pm. *[Indoor plumbing was not yet common in rural areas. That would arrive in the late-1950s to mid-1960s.]*

1947

Monday, January 13 ∾ Chapman's house was burned this morning. Lost all their clothes and nearly everything, but got Mrs. C. out. *[She was in a wheelchair.]*

Tuesday, January 14 - Chapman's are at Mabie's for the present. A Mr. Firth in collecting money today.

Monday, March 3 ∾ Sure some storm; the worst in years. Hydro poles and telephone poles down. *[This was probably Mary's first power outage.]* All 58 down between Bill Brewer's and Keswick. Train stuck at Barton all day. Never got down until about one this morning.

Tuesday, March 4 ∾ Snowed at times all day. No prospects of light; gone back to the old *[kerosene]* lamps. *[Wonder what she thought about the new electricity and all its so-called benefits then.]*

Saturday, April 19 ∾ A pie social in the hall tonight for the ball games.

I was up. Made over hundred dollars.

Sunday, May 11 ᨒ Mother's Day. Got a toaster. *[Another electric appliance. It was probably the model where the two sides folded down to put the bread in, then the sides were flipped back up to toast.]*

Monday, June 23 ᨒ Painted the sink and enamelled stove pipes and other jobs.

Thursday, June 26 ᨒ Varnished hall, cleaned under winter sink and greased the winter stove for the summer.

Saturday, August 9 ᨒ Merle got a lovely new light for the living room.

Thursday, October 23 ᨒ A terrible wind. Started in the midst of it, Alfred Curries House burned. So awful dry and such a wind. I don't see how they ever got it controlled for it caught all over the woods. We were all scared people for some time.

Monday, October 27 ᨒ Was up to see Mrs. Bubar before she left. She and Ralph have now gone to F'ton. Makes me lonesome for she may never be back again as her home and furniture is sold and she lived beside us 37 or 38 years.

Wednesday, November 5 ᨒ Been to town to W.A. at Mrs. Eldrick Staples this evening. *[They had moved to Fredericton.]*

Monday, November 9 ᨒ Were to Neo's *[Neno's]* helping get the Institute boxes ready for Holland and Belgium. *[Canada was still sending relief boxes to Europe.]*

Thursday, November 20 ᨒ We heard the Royal Wedding. *[Princess Elizabeth, now Queen Elizabeth II, and Duke of Edinburgh]* It was lovely, so plain as if it was right here.

Sunday, December 21 ᨒ We are listening to xmas stories on the radio.

❧ 1947 ☙

1948

Saturday, January 3 ᔆ The new *[outdoor]* rink lighted up tonight for the first. Looks very pleasant. *[Mary saw this from her home. The rink sat on a flat space near the railway west of the station.]*

Saturday, February 7 ᔆ Bill Brewer was killed by the bus at noon. Eldon and Mona were on the bus. A wonder that all on the bus weren't killed as it went over the bank.

Wednesday, February 11 ᔆ An inquest was held in the *[IOF]* hall for the bus driver. They passed him not guilty. *[Today inquests are held in a court room.]*

Tuesday, February 24 ᔆ Ruby was here. Came on Bus *[from Zealand]* to do some shopping. *[The village still offered a large selection of goods and supplies.]*

Sunday, August 29 ᔆ The Orangemen Marched; band played for it.

Sunday, September 19 ᔆ Mr. and Mrs. Durant were here to supper. Hadn't seen them in twenty-two years.

Wednesday, October 13 ∽ Delless Brewer has started the milk route.

Thursday, October 28 ∽ The Institute put on an entertainment to raise money for the rink. It was very enjoyable so many dressed in Halloween costumes. Sold lunches, played Bingo and so forth.

Tuesday, November 23 ∽ Was to corner to get my Simpson order; didn't get all of it. They're testing for TB at hall today *[a new round of Tuberculosis]*.

1949

Wednesday, June 29 ᗡ They have started to pave the *[Keswick]* road *[through the main village]*.

Tuesday, July 12 ᗡ Orangemen parade with band playing.

Thursday, July 28 ᗡ Fuller Brush man here this am. *[This was not a new company, but it's the first it is mentioned in Mary's journals, so this may have been new to Burtt's Corner.]*

Thursday, November 17 ᗡ Cecil Burtt died tonight. Just came over radio *[new method of announcing deaths]*.

Chapter 7

1950-1958

MARY'S JOURNAL is sparsely filled in the 1950s, with most of her entries about daily visitors, days they attended church, and friends and neighbours in the community who had passed away.

With electricity in many homes, electric water pumps were installed to bring water from the well to a tap above the sink. This replaced the steel hand pump or eliminated the winter trek to the outside well where they would have to struggle with a crank and bucket to retrieve water if the line to the house had frozen up. The new inside water also allowed people to install comfortable washrooms and say goodbye to the bum-numbing wooden seat of the outhouse. Many homes were not built with space for washrooms, so the first washrooms only contained a flush toilet and sink. Bathtubs and showers arrived in the 1960s.

The railway service that so many New Brunswickers depended upon shut down on August 22, 1950 for a nine-day national strike. No mail or other goods arrived at the Burtt's Corner station during the strike and the only way to travel was by automobile. Luckily, the government had made road improvements in 1949 when the old Keswick Road that ran through the community of Burtt's Corner was renamed Route 104 and converted from a dirt road to one with a chip-sealed surface.

Railway costs began to rise, but the Burtt's Corner station stayed operational, and diesel train engines replaced the steam engine. Eventually, the passenger service between Woodstock and Fredericton was eliminated in 1957. Freight service continued along that route for nearly 40 years before the railway was eliminated altogether.

Farming and lumbering continued to be the main sources of employment in the area, but the smaller mills began to disappear, and larger regional mills were constructed. A new school that accommodated many classrooms and children from grades 1-12 was built in the community in 1952. A real high school in the community gave all children the opportunity to receive a high-school education. In the past, students like Merle,

Mona, and Hugh, who wanted a high-school education had to travel or board in the nearest city and attend school there. A school bussing system that transported children to school every day was initiated with the new school. No more walking several miles on the coldest days of winter. Tuberculosis and infantile paralysis (polio or poliomyelitis) reappeared and all school children were tested for tuberculosis into the 1960s. They are still inoculating against polio, diphtheria, whooping cough, measles and mumps today.

1950

Friday, April 21 ～ An awful rain and another flood in the making. Coming fast as possible. *[23 mm on the 20th and another 57 mm on the 21st recorded at UNB Fredericton.]* Pulping *[at the mill next door]* flattened everywhere. It's *[water]* in cellar nearly to the *[main]* floor. Do hope it won't come in that far.

Saturday, April 22 ～ Water gone down quite a lot. Washouts all over. There's no train since Friday, morning and no mail. Merle had an appointment in Montreal to see about his back. No train out of F'ton.

Sunday, April 23 ～ Water away down but it's been a terrible time everywhere. Hayward has thirty men on railroad; worked all day today. Also don't know how long before a train or mail.

Thursday, April 27 ～ Train and mail today. *[Four days before the rail line repairs were finished.]*

Friday, June 23 ∾ The old bridge at upper Keswick went down when one of Colter's trucks was crossing. Using the new bridge now

Wednesday, July 12 ∾ Marlene Estey has TB and will be going to Sanatorium.

Sunday, August 13 ∾ Down to see Basil's *[Fowler]* new house. *[It was located in front of the community cemetery.]*

Tuesday, Aug 22 ∾ The strike is on. No train this morning anywhere. *[The railway workers staged a nine day strike across Canada to protest working conditions and hours.]*

1951

Wednesday, May 30 ◞ Bev Lawrence died this morning. *[Mr. Lawrence was the local undertaker and owned the grocery store on the corner of Jones Forks Road and the Keswick Road.]*

1952

Wednesday, February 6 ∼ King George 6 passed on this morning. Now we have a new queen and a young one *[Queen Elizabeth II]*.

Thursday, February 21 ∼ Still snowing. All day plows still at work on roads and railroad. Snow piled above your heads everywhere.

Monday, May 5 ∼ Howard Burtt passed on suddenly *[Former hotel owner]*.

Monday, June 16 ∼ Mrs. Elmer Brewer had six young cows killed by lightning in yesterday's storm.

Sunday, July 20 ∼ Will Hagerman passed on. *[Owner of Hagerman's store.]*

1953 ∼ All entries consisted of daily chores and visiting.

1954

Tuesday, March 4 ᕦ Nice evening at *[Women's]* Institute. Merle was up for the lunch. *[The men came for lunch.]* Quite the entertainment. *[The Federated Women's Institutes of Canada has a chapter in each Province. The organizations fosters the development of leadership and the involvement of women in building stronger communities, families, and countries. The New Brunswick Woman's Institute (NBWI) is dedicated to informing and educating women about issues that concern them and their communities. It also has a strong homemaking and craft heritage.]*

Monday, April 26 ᕦ I aired all the coats and put them in the garment vault *[closet or trunk]* and de-mothed them. *[They used moth balls made from chemicals and pesticides to keep moths from eating holes in their clothes.]*

Saturday, June 5 ᕦ Murray Bird was here putting in an electric pump. *[for her water. This gave her running water in the kitchen and eventually a washroom in the house.]*

On January 28, 1958 Mary fell and broke her hip. She never recovered.

CONCLUSION

THERE ARE MANY STORIES written about celebrities in the news, government, or sports. Mary was not popular for any one of these reasons. Due to her exceptional faith, Mary devoted her life to her family and community. Her life began with a tragic childhood, and she was lucky to survive a diphtheria epidemic to become an ordinary women in a small piece of New Brunswick, Canada.

Unfortunately she will never know the importance of her daily journal as a tool that teaches people of the 21st century how people of the early 20th century lived and survived, the small and interesting details not found in any history book

Those who lived from the early 1900s to the 1950s saw many changes in their daily lives. Running water, electricity, and the small and large appliances that were invented to work with both certainly made home life much easier for everyone.

New schools and school bus routes eliminated children walking miles to school in bitter winter weather. Children who lived in remote areas couldn't possibly walk the required distance to get to school, so they lived their lifetime unable to read or write. Today, every child has that opportunity to learn and become a productive member of society.

Travel changed as well from horse and wagons and walking to cars and trucks. Train travel evolved from smokey steam trains that required frequent stops for fuel and water to diesel engines that travelled faster and farther. After World War II, commercial airplanes provided another means of travel to long-distance destinations and took people to places they could only have imagined before.

Improvements to motorized equipment gave farmers new tools to work with that increased their production while allowing them to work fewer hours.

Horrible diseases like the diphtheria that killed most of Mary and Reuben's family in 1884 reappeared, but the consequences weren't as severe because of the new vaccines that had been developed. Pharmacies existed in early New Brunswick, but only in major centres, so rural doctors prescribed and supplied medications to their patients. Today doctors living in rural communities often travel to larger centers to practice, and patients filling prescriptions may or may not be able to do so in their home community.

There have been many lifestyle changes since Mary and her neighbours visited each other on a daily basis. Although the improvements were welcomed, there were negative spin offs as well. With modernized equipment, machines have replaced the people who previously performed the tasks in the fields, woods, factories and at home. This has to a degree meant people have had to travel farther away to find work as Merle did during the post-war recession. Some families are fortunate to have all their relatives remain in their community to live and work, but many others have family members that have had to travel farther away in order to earn a living.

Somewhere along the line, families became busier with work, then filled their evenings with organized activities for themselves and their children several nights of the week. With the current lifestyle, few remember the importance of being connected with their neighbours or community. It might be interesting to walk up to the house next door and introduce oneself to a neighbour, have a cup of tea, and sit on their front porch for a few hours. Who knows? That neighbour you don't know may be your best comfort in a time of need.

GLOSSARY

A, B

Alabaster ✦ a course gypsum-like material that was used to cover walls and ceilings. It could also provide a textured surface.

Abdicate ✦ to give up a right or responsibility to fulfill a duty; as in giving up the right to sit on the throne of England or the United Kingdom as King.

Armistice ✦ an agreement between parties at war to cease fighting.

Bartering ✦ the practice of trading work for other work or goods. For example someone who could do carpentry work might trade a few hours for a side of beef from a farmer. No money changed hands.

Burtt's Corner ✦ a rural community about 17-20 miles northwest of the capital city of Fredericton, New Brunswick. During the 1900s employment was mostly from farming, lumbering, the railway, and small businesses. At some point, the apostrophe was dropped, and the community name became Burtts Corner.

Bloomers ✦ frilly underpants worn by small children over their diaper. For small girls, they are worn over their underpants and have a bit longer legs for wearing under their dresses.

C, D

Chard, Swiss ✦ a leafy vegetable similar to spinach.

Chivaree ✦ a noisy celebration at the home of newlyweds typically after they would have gone to bed. Neighbours and friends gather banging on pots, pans and any other noisy apparatus to disturb the sleeping couple.

Clothespress ✦ a storage space for clothes such as a wardrobe or closet.

C.O.D ✦ or Cash on Delivery, a way to pay for a purchase. The customer paid for the order when it arrived, not when it was ordered.

Darkies ✦ was the newest term given to black people when it was realized that "coon" was not appropriate. It is considered rude and racist today.

Davenport ✦ an earlier name for a chesterfield. Some could be pulled out into a makeshift bed.

Drawers ✦ a term used for men's long underwear.

Dresser Scarf ✦ a piece of linen on top of a dresser that was used to protect the wood. Usually hand sewn with multi-coloured embroidery designs.

Dress chickens ✦To prepare them for cooking which at Mary's home meant to kill, remove or pluck the feathers and any other body parts not included with the bird for cooking.

E, F

Erysipelas ✦ a streptococcus bacterial infection that affects the upper layer of skin. Causes red patches, fever, and a general overall illness.

Felon ✦ an abscess on the underside of the finger tip that can become infected. Usually caused by a puncture by something such as a huge splinter.

Fahrenheit ✦ used to measure temerpature degrees before Canada switched to the metric system on April 1, 1975 and began measuring temperature in degrees Celsius.

Fiddleheads ✦ the young furled frond of the Ostrich Fern that grows along brooks and streams. They are considered a delicacy among Maritime people. The young fronds are boiled and eaten as a spring vegetable with butter and a small amount of vinegar or lemon juice to taste.

Fire Motor ✦ a term used for fire truck.

Forward Movement ✦ Forward Movement was a ministry of the Episcopal Church. Its mission was to energize the life of the church.

F'ton ✦ a shortened (written only) form for Fredericton, the capital of New Brunswick

G, H, I

Gal. ✦ an abreviation of the measure Gallon.

Gleaner ✦ was the Fredericton area newspaper. It is still in publication today.

Grippe ✦ the flu

Holy Rollers ✦ a nickname given to the Pentecost Church people for their lively singing and dancing.

Ice House ✦ a small shed-like building. Ice blocks were cut from the rivers and lakes in the winter and covered with sawdust from local mills to keep them from thawing. The blocks of ice were then used in the icebox which was used to store meat and other food products typically kept in a modern day fridge. Some years, the ice in the ice house lasted until the next winter.

Imperial measurements ✦ the system of measurement that was used before the Metric System was introduced in Canada in 1970. A cup is approximately 250 ml. There are two cups in a pint, two pints in a quart, and four quarts in a gallon. Dry measures also include eight quarts in a peck and four pecks in a bushel.

Infantile paralysis ✦ also known as poliomyelitis or polio. It is a contagious disease that can cause paralysis or death.

J, K, L

Jaundice ✦ a disease that gives the skin a yellowish tinge. Often caused by an elevated level of bilirubin in the blood.

Lard ✦ When people slaughtered their pig, they removed the pig fat and melted it down to make the lard used for cooking and baking. Some farmers used to forecast how cold the coming winter would be by the thickness of the pig's fat.

Lath ✦ narrow strips of wood about one inch wide and 1/8 inch thick used to cover walls in homes. The narrow strips were nailed across from one stud to another to cover the open space.

Log drive ✦ a spring event in which the woods workers slid all the logs that had been cut over the winter into the river. As the river current moved the logs to local mills, men stood on the logs to keep them from jamming along the river bank.

Log boom ✦ a series of logs chained together across a river to keep the logs together as they approached the mill which was built on the river. The angle of the boom could steer the logs directly towards the mill. In some cases where the river was very wide, a boom would be enclosed and a boat used to haul the logs to a specific area.

M, N

Mackinaw ✦ a heavy coat made from a woolen plaid material. Most common is red and black.

May Poles ✦ the phenomena of ice spikes that are formed when a container or small body of water, such as a puddle, freezes quickly around the edge and forces water in the middle upward to form a frozen spike of water.

Milliner ✦ is someone who designs, makes and trims hats.

Mixed sponge ✦ the process of mixing flour, water, and some yeast and letting it ferment so the yeast works better. They made their own yeast so it wasn't fast acting like the processed yeasts used today. They would save a little dough from their baking so they could start the next batch of good yeast.

Moth balls ✦ small round balls made from pesticides and chemicals to keep moths in the larvae stage from eating clothing. Any clothing stored for a long period had a few moth balls added to the closet, trunk or where they were stored.

Motor car ✦ was the small motorized cart that ran on the railway. Men used it to travel along sections of the track so they could see where repairs were needed.

Muresco ✦ a powder mixed with water and acted as an early form of paint before oil, wax or milk paints existed.

National Registration Certificate ✦ In 1940, the Canadian Parliament mandated that every Canadian citizen register in a directory. Then they received a small card that was to be with them at all times for proof of identification. The government also used it to identify where citizens worked and to address any shortages of trained workers.

Neuralgia ✦ a burning and severe pain that occurs along a damaged nerve. It is most common in the face and neck, but can occur anywhere in the body.

O, P

Oil cloth ✦ originally a canvas based type of flooring cured with oil to keep it from becoming brittle. Linoleum and later cushion flooring replaced oil cloth for high traffic areas such as kitchens.

Orangemen ✦ supporters of King William III of Orange during the Battle of the Boyne. Members of the Orangemen were Protestant in faith and at one time discouraged any association with Catholics. For example, a Protestant who married a Catholic could not become a member of the Orange Order.

Outhouse ✦ see Toilet.

Page wire fence ✦ came in rolls and looked like pages of a book or squares. This type of fencing was about four feet high and was used before electric fencing allowed a single strand of wire to contain farm animals.

Patched ✦ refers to covering holes in something. Mary often sewed small pieces of cloth over holes in clothing where they wore out, such as at the elbow or knee. When clothing wore out, they took the last bit of cloth that was good and kept it for patching other pieces of clothing.

Petticoat ✦ is a fine piece of clothing similar to a slip and worn under lady's or baby's clothing to add fullness to the garment.

Princess Pine ✦ is a low feathery club moss that looks similar to pine. It was used for ornamental wreaths and other Christmas decorations.

Pts. ✦ an abbreviation for the measure Pints.

Q, R, S

Qts. ✦ an abbreviation for the measure Quarts.

Ration Cards ✦ were small booklets or cards provided to each family. They contained coupons that could be exchanged for the family or individual's allowance of rationed goods such as butter, sugar, gasoline, tea and other items. This provided the government with a surplus to send to the men in the war zones.

Remnants ✦ left over pieces of material from a roll of cloth. They are sold as pieces for quilting or small sewing tasks.

Roller towel ✦ is a large piece of fabric sewn like a tube and hung on a wooden rod. As one section of the towel became wet from use, the towel was turned to a dry section.

Sad iron ✦ A solid iron base and combination iron/wood handle. They sat on top of the wood stove to heat before they were used to iron out wrinkled clothing. They came in different sizes. Smaller ones were used for lacy or fine clothing so that they didn't get too much heat at a time.

Scaling ✦ When logs were sold, they were measured and identified by species to determine the sale price based on the current market price.

Shoepack ✦ A thick warm lace up boot usually made of animal hide.

Stitch in his back ✦ refers to a kink or ache, not an actual sewn stitch.

Swamping ✦ the action of clearing underbrush and trees in order to make a trail through the woods.

T, W

Tack ✦ Two pieces of cloth of equal size are laid upon each other with a layer of quilt batting between them. Then small strips of yarn are pulled through the entire three layers with a darning needle and tied in knots every so many inches to ensure the blanket holds together.

Tat ✦ the art of making lace from thread.

Temperance Movement ✦ was founded to eliminate the consumption of alcohol. Members favoured Prohibition or the ban on selling alcohol.

Ticks ✦ the earliest form of mattresses. People filled a cloth casing with feathers, straw or any other soft materials available. There were no box springs in this time period, so often the tick was laid on either a metal spring or on a series of ropes stretched across the bed frame.

Toilet ✦ a small outside building commonly called the *outhouse* with a wooden bench-like seat. The seat had a hole to sit on and carry out the bodily functions typically done today in a bathroom. Designs ranged from the 'one-holer' to the 'three-seater' with two regular height holes and a lower one for children.

Tongue clip ✦ a procedure to clip the membrane that attaches the tongue to the bottom of the mouth to aid in suckling. The procedure was not necessary for most children.

Truss ✦ a belt-like piece of cloth made specifically to hold a rupture in place for better healing.

Wainscoting ✦ is 3 to 4-foot long wood strips, usually tongue and grooved, attached vertically on the bottom section of a wall around a room. Another piece of tapered or designed wood around the top created a finished edge. Originally wainscoting was for protection of the plastered wall, but became a design option in later homes.

Wash boiler ✦ a copper or metal tub that was filled with water and heated on top of the kitchen stove . Clothes were stirred with a wooden ladle or fork until they were as clean as possible. Then the clothes were wrung out by hand and hung on the clothesline.

W.A. ✦ an abbreviation for the Anglican Women's Aid group.

Waist ✦ A shorter kind of corset that covers the waist area. If worn low on the ribs to just above the hips, it was called a waist cincher.

Water closet ✦ a small room or compartment that held a toilet. In the 1920s, it would be an inside outhouse in one corner of the shed. Later, when water was pumped into the homes, it would have had running water for flushing and washing.

Wheel ✦ bicycle

Wringer washer ✦ a portable washing machine with a large tub for the water and an agitator that swirled the clothing. After an allotted time, women fed their clothes through two rollers on the top piece and squeezed out any excess water. The clothing dried on an outside clothesline.

SELECTED BIBLIOGRAPHY

Albers, John. n.d. "How does a driven point well work?" eHow. http://www.ehow.com/how-does_4795489_driven-point-well-work.html.

n.d. "Armistice Day becomes Remembrance Day." Canadian War Museum. http://www.warmuseum.ca/cwm/exhibitions/remember/1931remembrance_e.shtml.

Boudreau, Michael. 2010. "Bennie Swim." UNB Saint John Faculty of Arts. http://www.unb.ca/saintjohn/arts/projects/crimepunishment/cases/bennieswim.html.

Canada, Chief Electoral Officer of. 2007. A History of the Vote in Canada. http://www.elections.ca/content.aspx?section=res&dir=his&document=index&lang=e.

Canada, Government of. n.d. Historical Data-Climate-Environment Canada. http://climate.weather.gc.ca/historical_data/search_historic_data_e.html.

CBC. n.d. "1936: Moose River mine disaster." CBC Digital Archives. http://www.cbc.ca/archives/entry/1936-moose-river-mine-disaster.

n.d. "Chloroform." Discoveries in Medicine. http://www.discoveriesinmedicine.com/Bar-Cod/Chloroform.html.

Cumming, L.M., R.F. Miller, and D.N. Buhay. 2013,2015. "Abraham Gesner." The Canadian Encylopedia. http://www.thecanadianencyclopedia.ca/en/article/abraham-gesner/.

n.d. "Dream." Kingston Pennisula Heritage. https://sites.google.com/site/kingstonpeninsulaheritage/dream.

n.d. "Fredericton Business College." Archives CANB. http://search.canbarchives.ca/fredericton-business-college-ltd.

Hallowell, Gerald, and Richard Foot. 2013,2015. "Prohibition." The Canadian Encyclopedia. http://www.thecanadianencyclopedia.ca/en/article/prohibition/#h3_jump_0.

Institute, New Brunswick Women's. 2014. New Brunswick Women's Institute. http://www.nbwi.ca/.

Jones, Ted. 1988-1989. Both sides of the wire : the Fredericton internment camp (v1-2). Fredericton: New Ireland Press.

Lennon, M.J. 1981. On the homefront : a scrapbook of Canadian World War II memorabilia. Erin, ON: Boston Mills Press.

LeRoyShield1930. n.d. "King George V - Silver Jubilee Message to The Empire - May 6, 1935." You Tube. https://www.youtube.com/watch?v=qA602awwMb4.

MacPherson, Ian. 2006. "United Farmers of Canada." The Canadian Encyclopedia. http://www.thecanadianencyclopedia.ca/en/article/united-farmers-of-canada/ .

Manuel, Dave. 2016. Inflation Calculator. http://www.davemanuel.com/inflation-calculator.php.

1895. "Montgomery Ward Catalogue." Google Books. https://books.google.ca/books?id=AjqYCgAAQBAJ&pg=PA270&lpg=PA270&dq=were+makinaw+-coats+waterproof&.

Morehouse, Mary. 1920-1958. The Mary Morehouse Journals. Burtt's Corner, NB: unpublished.

Olver, Lynn. 2004. "FAQs: baby food." Food Timeline. http://www.foodtimeline.org/foodbaby.html.

Parliament, Library of. n.d. History of Federal Ridings since 1867. http://www.lop.parl.gc.ca/About/Parliament/FederalRidingsHistory/HFER.asp.

n.d. The History of Vaccines. http://www.historyofvaccines.org/content/articles/diphtheria.

Timeanddate.com. n.d. "Thanksgiving Day in Canada." Timeanddate.com. http://www.timeanddate.com/holidays/canada/thanksgiving-day.

About the Author

Like Mary Morehouse, Sharon Bird is a former resident of Burtt's Corner and has previously published two books on the history of the village —*A Peek Around the Corner* and *From the Shoebox*. Sharon Bird is a member of the Professional Writers Association of Canada and has written for *Saltscapes* and *Celtic Heritage* and has over 40 newspaper and magazine articles to her credit. She currently resides in Alberta, but plans to eventually return to her native province of New Brunswick.

Other Books

A Peek around the Corner, Burtt's Corner — the Early Years, 2011

From the Shoebox, 2014

My Canada, Flying Frog Publishing. Maryland, USA. 2014